D1038501

Women Want More

ALSO BY MICHAEL J. SILVERSTEIN

Trading Up: The New American Luxury (with Neil J. Fiske)

Treasure Hunt: Inside the Mind of the New Consumer
(with John Butman)

WOMEN
Want
MORE

How to Capture Your Share
of the World's Largest,
Fastest-Growing Market

MICHAEL J. SILVERSTEIN

and KATE SAYRE

with *John Butman*

HARPER
BUSINESS

An Imprint of HarperCollinsPublishers
www.harpercollins.com

WOMEN WANT MORE. Copyright © 2009 by The Boston Consulting Group. All rights reserved. Printed in the United States of America. No part of this book may be used or reproduced in any manner whatsoever without written permission except in the case of brief quotations embodied in critical articles and reviews. For information, address HarperCollins Publishers, 10 East 53rd Street, New York, NY 10022.

HarperCollins books may be purchased for educational, business, or sales promotional use. For information, please write: Special Markets Department, HarperCollins Publishers, 10 East 53rd Street, New York, NY 10022.

FIRST EDITION

Designed by Ellen Cipriano

Library of Congress Cataloging-in-Publication Data

Silverstein, Michael J.
    Women want more : how to capture your share of the world's largest, fastest-growing market / Michael J. Silverstein and Kate Sayre; with John Butman.—1st ed.
        p. cm.
    Includes bibliographical references and index.
    ISBN 978-0-06-177641-0
    1. Women consumers. 2. New products. I. Sayre, Kate. II. Butman, John. III. Title.
    HF5415.332.W66S55 2009
    658.8'343082—dc22   2009013607

09 10 11 12 13 WBC/RRD 10 9 8 7 6 5 4 3 2 1

*To women worldwide for
their courage and ambition*

Contents

Women Want More

Preface

⌒

Women want more.

More what? Above all, more time. More understanding would be good, too, especially of the complexities that come with playing multiple roles. More value and satisfaction from the products and services they buy. More love, of course. (We could all use a little more of that.) More money? Not really. For most women, money is not the point.

From whom do women want more?

You. The businesspeople who develop products, run companies, shepherd brands, manage retail operations, and provide services. You, the husbands and partners who may actually earn less than the women in your lives and who also do less work around the house. You, the policy makers who don't do enough to help women with the particular challenges that come with being working mothers and heads of families.

It's not difficult to find out what more women want. Just ask them. As we did.

In 1831, Alexis de Tocqueville journeyed from France, his home country, to travel through the United States. His observations of everyday life here, his talks with citizens, his collections of data, and his analysis served as the basis for his landmark book, *Democracy in America*, a classic work of social commentary. We do not claim to be modern-day Tocquevilles, but we have approached our subject—women and the consumer economy—in a similar fashion. We have devoted more than two years to research, discussion, and study in search of answers to a deceptively simple question: what do women want?

Very early on, a more relevant question emerged: what *more* do women want?

What more do they want from the revolution in earning power, commercial influence, and political clout they are already so successfully waging?

What more do they want for themselves and for their friends and families?

And (of most interest to us, as management consultants) what more do women want from the products and services they buy and from the companies that provide them?

We asked a final question—what more do women want for their societies and the world at large?—because, as we'll see, that want plays a large role in the other questions.

The summary answer to all these questions is that, even with the remarkable increases in market power and social position women have accomplished and enjoyed in the last century in the United States and elsewhere, they still find themselves undervalued in the marketplace, underestimated in the workplace, and underappreciated in the social arena. Today, women are as well educated as men. They control half the wealth in this country. The majority of women work. The majority of those women play multiple roles, as spouse, mother, caregiver, and household manager. Women are sophisticated buyers and consumers and make or influence the majority of consumer purchases.

Yet it's still tough for women to find a pair of pants that fits, buy a family meal that's both healthy and delicious, make the time to keep fit, or work with a financial services adviser who isn't patronizing.

Something's got to give. And that's what this book is about: how companies can develop and market their products and services—and how they can make their companies better places for women to work—to serve the wants and needs of the world's demanding consumers.

Over the next decade, the rewards for those companies that serve women well will be enormous. We believe that the 1 billion working women across the globe will continue to gain economically, will drive fundamental changes in markets, and, worldwide, will spend an incremental $5 trillion or more on goods and services of all kinds.

To arrive at these conclusions, we have pursued many avenues of research. In 2008, we fielded a large and comprehensive study of women, The Boston Consulting Group (BCG) Global Inquiry into Women and Consumerism. It was administered both across a network of thousands of friends and through a variety of purchased samples to ensure that it provided a rigorous statistical sample as well as richness of response. More than 12,000 women, in more than forty geographic areas and from every income level and many walks of life, responded.

The survey consists of 120 questions—both multiple-choice and open-ended—that enable women to deliver their opinions and respond with great candor (and often disarming intimacy) about many aspects of their lives, including their education, incomes and finances, homes and possessions, jobs and careers, activities and interests, career goals, relationships with family and friends, shopping behaviors, hopes and dreams for the future, fears, and anxieties, as well as spending patterns in some three dozen categories of goods and services. (You can learn more about the survey, the questions, our methodology, the respondents, and their responses, and take a short version of the survey, at our Web site, www.womenspeakworldwide.com.)

We also conducted interviews with hundreds of women—some of them well-known and influential, but many of them with no special claim to fame—in ten countries. We tell many of their stories in this book as a way for the reader to better understand what more women *do* want.

During the course of our research, we studied fifty organizations, in thirteen different fields of endeavor, to better understand how they serve women. And we drew on our forty collective years spent working with companies and organizations in every category of goods and services to help us synthesize and analyze the findings of our research. These companies provide models and practices for others to follow and to adapt for their own product categories, markets, and customers.

This book is not intended to provide The Answer to the question of what a company must do in order to produce goods and services that women want. It does provide, however, a framework that can be used to arrive at an answer for a specific company, industry, and set of female consumers.

As we write this, the number of working women in the United States exceeds the number of working men. In the current economic cycle, three-quarters of the rise in unemployment has involved men. Education, ambition, and career choices have helped, in part, to insulate women from the crisis—although lower average wages for women and more part-time female employees have also been factors. When this downturn abates, we believe that women will not only represent one of the largest market opportunities in our lifetime but will also be an important force in creating recovery and new prosperity.

Introduction

A Revolutionary Opportunity

A quiet economic and social revolution is taking place. Worldwide, 1 billion women work. More than half of university students worldwide are women. Women control half the wealth in the United States. The female economy will have a global economic impact greater than the BRIC countries (Brazil, Russia, India, and China). This economy represents the most important commercial opportunity in our lifetime.

A quiet economic and social revolution is taking place as we write this book.

There may not be violence in the streets, but there is upheaval in the workplace, turmoil in the home, radical change in the marketplace, and a struggle for influence in government and society as a whole. It is a revolution of, by, and for women—driven by a desire for more: for ongoing education, better ways to nurture themselves and their families, increased success as executives and entrepreneurs, higher earnings, and better ways to manage and leverage their accumulated wealth.

It is a revolution of dissatisfaction in which women are using their checkbooks to vote no on large sectors of the economy, including financial services, consumer electronics, consumer durables, and healthcare. They are saying: "You don't understand me," "There are too many demands on my time," "I have an overwhelming share of household chores and a full-time job," "Help me or I'll find another provider."

Some observers say that the most important economic and social changes of the early twenty-first century are taking place in China and India. We believe that the emergence of a whole new social and economic order, which can accurately be labeled a *female economy*—in every country and every arena—is an even more significant upheaval. The data we have gathered during the course of research for this book are clear and startling:

- Worldwide, 1 billion women participate in the workforce.
- The number of working women in the United States has increased by 50 percent in the past twenty years, to 75 million.
- Working women in the United States generate $4.3 trillion in earned income annually.
- Women account for 57 percent of the students of higher education in this country and 47 percent worldwide.
- Women worldwide make or influence at least 64 percent of all purchases in a wide variety of categories, and a much higher percentage in many of them.

On the basis of our quantitative research and our interviews with women around the world, we believe that these indicators will continue to move upward. And, as we've said, over the next several years, women will drive an incremental increase of up to $5 trillion in global earnings—bigger than any bailout package.

WITH GAINS COME DISSATISFACTIONS

However, the women we have come to know during our research for this book tell us that the revolution is far from over. As encouraging as the data may be, the stories these women tell us reveal that ascendancy has come at a price.

In the responses we gathered in our survey and in the interviews we conducted, women told us that the gains they have achieved have not brought them the happiness and satisfaction one might have expected. Even very successful women still experience significant stress, tension, and dissatisfaction. Very few women say they have enough time, money, help, or love in their lives. And almost all women experience simple, chronic frustration with particular products and services (as well as some whole categories of goods), which seem to have been created and marketed by companies that have little to no understanding of who women today are and what they want.

Ironically, much of women's dissatisfaction comes about as a direct result of their achievements.

Women find themselves caught in an upward spiral. If they and their families are to continue to achieve higher levels of prosperity, health, education, and accumulated wealth, they have virtually no choice but to work full-time. Particularly in the developed world, a cycle has been created in which families—in order to increase their income—have become dependent on each new generation of women to improve their education and to progress higher in the workforce. In the United States, women contributed nearly 100 percent of the change in family income in the past decade.

To work or not to work is no longer a question for the majority of adult women.

And, although the status of women has changed, much of the world seems not to have noticed or adjusted to the new reality. For example, the great majority of women participate in the workforce, but these women still do most of the household chores—the cooking, cleaning, laundry, grocery shopping, bill-paying, and childcare—that women have always done. As a result, working women feel there are too many demands on their time. Married women with children experience the most pressure of all.

What's more, although women control the spending in most categories of consumer goods—including food, clothing, personal care, household goods and services, travel, healthcare, financial services, and education—too many companies continue to make poorly conceived products, offer services that take up way too much of women's precious time, and serve up outdated marketing narratives that portray women as stereotypes.

WOMEN'S MULTIPLE AND CONFLICTING ROLES CREATE A NEED FOR LEVERAGE

Our research confirms that women continue to play many roles in their lives and that, because these roles often overlap and conflict with each other, women want and expect the things they buy to provide multiple solutions as well. Women are the major consumer spenders in the economy and also the primary savers, so they seek value. They are usually the nurturer of the family but also seek independence and personal fulfillment, so they want goods that help the family and also give the woman herself a lift or a touch of pleasure. They are hardheaded household purchasing agents but also tenderhearted dreamers, so they want quality and effectiveness as well as attention to design and a marketing narrative.

Above all, women want agents of leverage—ways to find time, save time, free up time. They want to do business with companies that care, listen, and respond to their needs and desires. They want to associate with brands that respect and honor a privileged relationship with the female consumer; they want to align with companies that act as enablers, enhancers, protectors. And when women find a product or service that truly meets these needs, they can become apostles for that brand. They will compliment brands that deliver and will complain about brands that don't. They will share their opinions within their social networks, which can be far-reaching.

They can help a company increase its profits quickly and help a brand take root in the society.

THE OPPORTUNITY WITHIN THE REVOLUTION: A CALL TO ACTION

The emergence of the female economy holds the potential for the creation of vast wealth—the $20 trillion of consumer spending now controlled by women could climb to as high as $28 trillion in the next several years. Women's $12 trillion in total earnings could grow to as much as $18 trillion in the same period.

The phenomenon is worldwide. Although we found differences between women in the countries we studied, similarities are more significant. A woman living in Guangzhou, a second-rank city in China, has expectations very different from those of a woman who lives on the East Side of Manhattan. But the Chinese woman influences the purchases in her household just as women do in New York and around the world, and the wealth of her household is steadily increasing. The Chinese woman—even if her absolute spending power is lower than that of consumers in other countries—is a highly profitable customer.

The rise of the worldwide female economy will challenge assumptions about how companies do research, how they develop products, how they sell and merchandise, and how they add services to their value proposition. Companies must rethink how they segment their audiences, how they react to changes in consumers' behavior, and how they capture the imagination.

Further, the female economy will challenge corporate leaders and managers to reexamine their human resources practices—how they recruit, select, develop, integrate, retain, and provide support to their people and how they help nurture and facilitate a healthy work-life balance.

The bad news is that only a small percentage of the companies we studied understand the significance of the female economy to their business. If they respond to this economy at all, they do so by fiddling with segmentation or by making small adjustments to their product line or to their organizations, as if these powerful trends were nothing more than incremental shifts in existing patterns. These companies do not look at the world and how it is changing through a woman's eyes. They do not prioritize the way their female consumers prioritize. They fail to recognize that time is scarce for women or that easy access to information is essential; and as a result, few companies achieve the position of trusted adviser.

The good news is that some companies do recognize the opportunity and respond to it brilliantly, with skill, nuance, and genuine engagement. They occupy a privileged position in the market. They enjoy breakout growth, unprecedented consumer loyalty, and category dominance. Companies like Gerber, Banana Republic, Ecute, Haier, Harpo, and others really *get* women and serve them well.

We have found that these companies follow a set of practices that we call the four R's.

Recognize. They understand the size of the opportunity in women's goods and services and commit themselves to researching where, how, and what the opportunity is for them.

Research. They study how their product or service is consumed, from the beginning to the end of the process of consumption, paying careful attention to frequency of use, habituation, the process by which dissatisfaction occurs, and the total time each consumer segment requires to buy, use, and finish with a product or service.

Respond. They identify, with brutal honesty, the good points and the unsatisfying points of their offering and then aggressively respond to each source of dissatisfaction.

Refine. Finally, they take their ideas to market in a way that creates lasting relationships with their female consumers, they build connections and bridges, and they continually improve their products to strengthen those relationships.

Our hope is that as more and more companies adopt the business practices described in this book to better serve women, they will not only succeed for themselves but will also enable more women to succeed and prosper.

In the chapters that follow, we will first examine forces that drive the female economy, what more women want from their lives, and some archetypes that can help companies better understand their customers. Then we'll look carefully at the categories in which women report their deepest levels of interest—and corresponding dissatisfactions. These are the areas that offer companies opportunities to develop products and services that serve women better than ever before:

Food. Women love food, just after love itself, but find that food shopping and preparation are chores that never end and take up far too much of their precious time, and that healthy options often are hard to find, cost too much, or take too long to prepare.

Fitness. Most women want to be healthy and fit but are not interested in bodybuilding or working out for its own sake. They rank fitness activities low on the list of priorities and try to squeeze fitness in during spare pockets of time.

Beauty. Women are constantly in search of new and better ways to achieve a holistic kind of beauty that includes appearance, especially of the face and hair, and also wellness of skin and body. They expect the most advanced technologies, constantly improved efficacy, and also the latest in colors, forms, and styles.

Apparel. Women want apparel to do a lot of work for them—make them look and feel good, minimize what they consider their physical shortcomings, make the right statement at work, be comfortable, and let them express their personal style.

Financial services. In most households women handle the finances, and the majority of women say they dislike the job. Financial products are confusing and complicated. Financial advisers are predominantly male. Women typically pay more for insurance than men do and have compensation and retirement packages that are not as good as men's.

Healthcare. Women generally like their doctors and the care they receive from them but are not pleased with the delivery systems in which their doctors must work. Too little access. Too much waiting. Not enough contact. Billing and management processes that are far too complex.

In this book, we examine these areas and describe companies that are leading the way in each area—and how they are doing so. Perhaps even more important, we provide you with firsthand observations and insights from a number of women we met in the course of our research whose engagement and intelligence speak more clearly than we ever could about what women truly want and how they are exercising their buying power as never before.

PART I

The Female Economy

The World's Most Demanding Consumers
The Archetypes and Life Stages
Brands That Understand

1.

The World's Most Demanding Consumers

Women have achieved a great deal but still have important dissatisfactions. The triple time challenge: "Too many demands on my time. Do not have enough time for me. I have conflicting priorities." They have the double duty of working at the job and working at home, and they wage a battle for balance. Despite the complexity of their lives, women are generally optimistic. Women want products and services that help leverage time, facilitate connection, and contribute to happiness for themselves and their families.

Although Nicole Green has a great deal to be thankful for, she still wants more.

At 43, she is slim, youthful, and fit. She is in a stable marriage to a nice guy. They both have good jobs, she as a healthcare administrator; her husband, Peter, as an executive in a nonprofit organization that does poverty research. They have three healthy kids—Zack, age 8; and two girls, Megan, and Holly, 7 and 4. They have lived for a decade in a Victorian house in an affluent Boston suburb with good schools and neighborhood services. Their household income is $160,000. As in many households where both spouses work, Nicole earns more than Peter does. She makes about $87,000; he makes about $73,000.

But a stable marriage, happy kids, and a high income—seemingly the ingredients of an ideal life—do not seem to guarantee happiness or even a modest degree of contentment for Nicole. In fact, quite the opposite. She is seriously time-deprived, is almost absurdly overbooked, and has to employ every scrap of her time, energy, brainpower, and emotional strength to keep it all together.

This is a woman who—to save both time and money—cuts her wavy, light brown hair only twice a year, in a style that will grow out nicely. Who can't remember the last time she bought clothes for herself. Who, as desperately as she craves sleep, misses books so badly that she will prop her eyes open for twenty minutes of reading rather than crash instantly at 1 or 1:30 A.M. or whenever she finally gets to bed. Whose days are so crammed with work, tasks, and appointments that it took three weeks to find a time when she could sit down with us for a one-hour interview.

Nicole, who speaks with intensity and animates her thoughts with quick gestures, starts by describing a typical weekday. "The alarm goes off in our bedroom at 6:30 in the morning. Peter and I have a half hour to get ourselves showered and dressed, so we can wake Zack and Meg at 7 in order to get them downstairs by 7:25. Zack pops out of bed right away, picks out his own clothes, and is downstairs sitting on the sofa reading in ten minutes flat. But Megan pulls the covers over her head and stays there until I come in and literally poke her, and it can take fifteen minutes to get her organized. Then those two have to eat breakfast, brush their teeth, fill their backpacks, put on their shoes, and get out the door in twenty minutes so they don't miss the school bus at 7:50. There's always a tremendous amount of yelling. 'The bus is coming! You need to find your shoes! Where's your recorder?' The school bus is the driving factor that really kick-starts the day. Then I get Holly, the 4-year-old, ready and drive her to preschool. It runs from 9 to noon, although there's daycare available from 8 to 9 and 12 to 6. You get billed at $8 per hour for the time you use, though, so I try to drop her right at 9. It's painful to drop her at 8:45 and have to pay for the full hour."

Notice that Nicole does not have a lot of time to linger over personal grooming, wardrobe choices, or preparation of elaborate meals for the children or herself. She is in a race against the clock.

Nicole hurries on to work, a twenty-minute drive, and plunges into her daily round of meetings, calls, and paperwork. Her office workday ends around 4 because she picks up the kids between 4:30 and 5. "The pick-ups can be challenging. Sometimes the kids don't want to leave. Or they have a meltdown. So I have a lot of upbeat music that I play in my car to get myself revved for dealing with it."

Nicole and the kids get back to the house about 5:30, and then things get even crazier. "Peter usually gets home around 6:30, so from 5:30 to 6:30 is the 'witching hour,' the time when I am trying to get the kids to do their schoolwork. Zack is just horrible with homework. He's supposed to spend forty-five minutes in the after-school program working on it, but he'll come home and will have finished maybe three out of twenty-five math problems. So he sits at the kitchen counter and works. Meanwhile, the two girls have spent the entire day being good, following all the rules, and they just kind of want to go insane. I start dinner so we can eat by 6:30. I know it will take me the entire hour to do it, because I have to stop every forty-five seconds to get somebody gum or water or resolve a fight or help Zack with a math problem. It's a pretty crazy hour."

Notice that although Nicole allots a full hour to preparing dinner, the actual time she can spend on it is probably half that.

The Green family's bedtime routine begins around 7:30 and—depending on whether this is bath night, how long the reading goes on, and how many times which kids call out or come downstairs after being tucked in—it's usually 8:45 before all is quiet. "And that's when my next shift begins. I need to finish cleaning up the kitchen from dinner, empty all the lunch boxes, get the dishwasher loaded and going, and pick up whatever messes there might be around the house. I always do at least one load of laundry every day, because if I don't, it would be insane. I make all the lunches for the next day. Then I have to sort through the seventeen inches of paper that I seem to bring home every night. I technically spend only five or six hours doing work in the course of a day, so I always have some to catch up on at night. That's the only way that I'm going to make it work. We usually don't get upstairs until midnight."

Nicole has three hours to wash the dishes, clean up the kitchen, wash and dry a load of laundry, make five lunches, and do the equivalent of about three hours of office work. Notice that she did not mention watching television, surfing the Web, chatting on the phone with friends, luxuriating in a warm bath, exfoliating or moisturizing, sipping wine, or nibbling chocolates. These would be luxuries for Nicole.

Weekend days are filled up, too. Ice skating, swimming lessons, ballet, gymnastics, flute, and karate. "There's so many things that kids need to do, and it's so hard to find the time to fit it in. Last year, I crammed it all in on the weekends, which was tough because my husband was working a lot on

Saturday and Sunday. So I spent all weekend shuttling people around from one lesson to another lesson. But I felt it was my fault that the kids had to do the stuff on the weekend, so I needed to make the sacrifice. It gets down to, well, if I didn't work, the kids could do these things more easily and it wouldn't impact our life on the weekend so much."

Nicole feels guilty for working, but if she didn't work, the Greens probably wouldn't be living in their Victorian home in their leafy suburb and their kids wouldn't be involved in so many special activities. Nicole makes more money than her husband does, after all. Lately, however, she has also been feeling guilty for doing *too* much. "I sometimes feel their lives aren't as good for them as they would have been if I didn't work. Maybe they needed more time to just hang around the house?"

Even with all she does, Nicole worries that it's not enough, or is too much, or is not right in some way. Like most women we spoke with— especially married women with children—Nicole puts herself and her own needs last on the list of priorities.

It's unlikely that the Greens' routine will change much until the kids get a little older, and Nicole is already looking forward to those days. "With one kid already in middle childhood, I'm starting to see that I'm going to love the middle childhood years. There's going to be about four or five years when all three of my kids will be much more self-sufficient, but I will always know where they are. I think of that as the 'golden window.' That's going to be a lot nicer, because I think so much of my daily stress now is just because so many people need so much from me. I just do and do and do and do and do and do for others. There's a fixed number of things that absolutely have to happen and they already fill eighteen hours every day. I am always robbing Peter to pay Paul with my time."

THE STRESSES AND DISSATISFACTIONS OF WOMEN TODAY

Nicole Green is no anomaly. Our research shows that women around the world—especially working mothers, but not only working mothers—feel incredibly stressed, overburdened, out of balance, and dissatisfied. Work, ambition, and education have inarguably produced wealth, power, and

Overall a woman is stressed, time-pressured, and money-tight

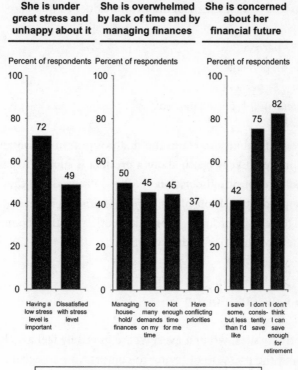

She is under great stress and unhappy about it	She is overwhelmed by lack of time and by managing finances	She is concerned about her financial future

Looking for agents of leverage and savings
to help her mitigate these challenges

Source: Online survey, questions Q24 / Q28 (Absence of stress is very important or important / absence of stress is below or far below expectations), Q30 (What type of challenges do you face in your daily life); Q77 (How would you describe your household's current financial situation?); N = 11,747.

influence for women. But they have also created stress, disequilibrium, frustration, unhappiness, and a host of difficult decisions, trade-offs, and compromises.

We spoke with many women for this book, in countries around the world, and found that, for the most part, *women don't really care about goods and services as such.* Yes, they pay very careful attention to what they buy. They know in detail the good points and bad points of all the products they purchase. There are certain brands they love and respect. But products, services, companies, and brands take a very distant backseat to the things that truly demand women's attention, care, and love: family, health, security, lovers, friends; learning and education; work and career; helping others and giving back.

Women told us that the most important values to them are:

- *Love*, 77 percent
- *Health*, 58 percent
- *Honesty*, 51 percent
- *Emotional well-being*, 48 percent

So a product's ability to claim the first position in a woman's mind or life is very limited. Every claim about a product is subject to scrutiny, discussion, and often amused derision ("Who do they think they're talking to?"). Every product relationship is subject to instant revision, should the product fail to keep its promise, or should another product come along that can better help women live as they want.

The Triple Challenge of Time

Above all other issues, women everywhere intensely feel a lack of time in their lives and the pressure of trying to contort time to accommodate everything they want to achieve. The time pressure is very real, and nearly all our survey respondents mentioned it. "I'm afraid of being overworked and having life pass me by," one woman wrote.

And it's not just a simple shortage of time. Women find themselves caught in an almost inescapable *lack* of time. Typically, a woman says she must deal with:

- *Too many demands on my time.* There are just too many things to do in a day. Nicole Green says that every second of every eighteen-hour day is accounted for. *Demands on time* were cited as the number one challenge by 47 percent of our survey respondents.
- *Too many conflicting priorities.* Not only are there too many things on the to-do list, but many of them seem to conflict with others.

Triple challenge of time

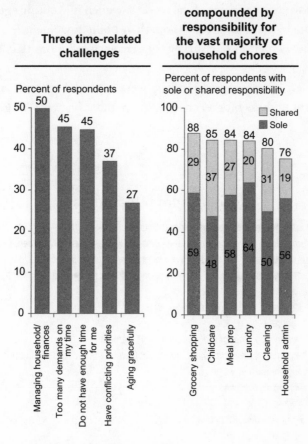

Three time-related challenges

compounded by responsibility for the vast majority of household chores

Percent of respondents

Percent of respondents with sole or shared responsibility

Source: Questions Q30 and Q17 of survey, N=11,747.

- *Not enough time for me.* When do I get a moment to close the door to the bedroom, take a walk by myself, read a book, sit and gaze out the window? Never. *Not enough time for me* was at the top of the list for 45 percent of our respondents.

The fundamental cause of the triple time challenge is that most women now spend many of their hours in the workplace:

- In the United States, hardworking nation that we are, 75 million women go to work—about 46 percent of the U.S. labor force and about 70 percent of the female population of working age. This is a huge rise from the 18.4 million women who worked in 1950.

- Worldwide, 58 percent of the world's women of working age participate in the labor force—more than 1 billion women.
- Of the women in our survey, 39 percent work more than forty hours per week.
- In 2006, 70.9 percent of mothers were in the labor force, and 56 percent of those mothers had children under one year of age.

Headlines from the Survey

Here are just a few of the headlines from the survey:

- *Demands on time* were cited as the number one challenge by 47 percent of our respondents. We call this the triple challenge of time, and it includes too many demands on "my" time, not enough time for "me," and conflicting priorities.

  Managing household finances was the top challenge for 48 percent.

  Not enough time for me was cited by 45 percent.

- The predominant *sources of arguments* between the respondent and her spouse or partner were:

  Money, 19 percent

  Chores, 15 percent

  Work schedule, 12 percent

  Children, 10 percent

  Sex, 10 percent

- About 68 percent of the respondents believe they are significantly or slightly higher than their *ideal body weight.*

- Only 25 percent of the women surveyed believe they are *extremely or very attractive.*

  26 percent say they rarely or never feel beautiful.

  44 percent say they rarely or never feel powerful.

  Women who are always or often frustrated—32 percent.

- The great majority—66 percent—believe that their *own hard work* will help drive their success.

- 72 percent of women say that their *mother is the dominant parental influence* in their lives; 56 percent say their father is.

- Women say there are *three things their partner could do* to help them deal with their time stress:
  Arrange dates, 27 percent
  Do more *household chores*, 23 percent
  Listen better and more, 22 percent
- The values that are most important to them are:
  Love, 77 percent
  Health, 58 percent
  Honesty, 51 percent
  Emotional well-being, 48 percent
- Women are concerned about their financial future:
  82 percent don't think they can save enough for retirement.
  75 percent don't consistently save.
  42 percent save some money, but less than they would like.
- What makes women extremely happy?
  Pets, 42 percent
  Sex, 27 percent
  Food, 19 percent
  Shopping, 5 percent
  The economy, 2 percent
- Are women optimistic? Yes, the majority of our respondents (66 percent) believe *my daily life will be better* in five years

The Double Duty of Job and Housework

You would think that, with women in the workplace so many hours, something would have to give at home—working women would hire help, get their husbands to do more chores, or simply let a few things slide.

But no.

Most women are not able to afford cleaning and household help. Even the Greens, with a household income of about $160,000, have had to make trade-offs when it comes to help. Before their second child was born, Nicole had cleaners who came in once a week. But their second child, Megan, was born three and a half months early and was then in and out of the hospital. In order to look after Zack, go to the office for a few hours in the morning, spend time with Megan in the hospital in the afternoons, and continue doing work at home, Nicole hired a live-in nanny, but she could not afford the cleaners, too, so they had to go. Still, she prides herself on having nursed her kids. "They never took a bottle. I got very good at nursing and typing at the same time."

When the third child came along, there was no room for the live-in nanny, so they hired a full-time "live-out" nanny. "That took almost every last penny of my take-home salary. Between the nanny and preschool tuition we were paying out almost $50,000 a year in childcare expenses. But I kept working just to maintain my standing in my field so that I would be able to keep working after we didn't need a nanny anymore. So I went without cleaners. It was absolutely insane. It was awful."

Most women, however, cannot afford to hire live-in nannies, or live-out nannies, or enough help to do all the household tasks that need to be done.

As a result, women spend, on average, sixteen hours a week on household chores. Married women with kids feel the most pressure, largely because their husbands do not help out as much as they might.

- *Of the women in our survey, 38 percent say their husbands or live-in partners do virtually no household chores.*

Peter Green, Nicole's husband, does a fair amount of what Nicole calls "hands-on" work with the kids—like getting them dressed and taking them to the bus stop. "But I'm the big picture. They would never have boots or clothes that fit or doctors' appointments or anything like that without me. I do all the shopping, all the cooking, all the laundry." Over the years, the Greens have settled on a fairly traditional division of labor. "I get the inside of the house and he gets the outside of the house. He does the shoveling and raking and mowing the lawn and dealing with the garbage."

On average, women are committed 113 hours a week—including hours spent at work, purchasing household supplies, cleaning, preparing meals, doing laundry, caring for children, and helping with homework. About 13 percent of our respondents say that as a result of all their commitments, they have to get by on five hours or less of sleep a night. Nicole Green supports that finding—her head hits the pillow at 1 or 1:30 A.M. and the alarm goes off at 6:30 A.M.

This middle-life intensity leads to a V curve of satisfaction. Women are happiest between the ages of 18 and 25, when single, and again after the age

At least one-third of men never help their wives with chores

How often does your spouse/partner
help with household chores?

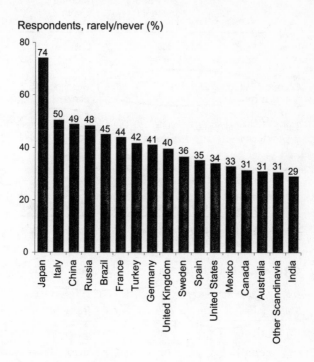

Respondents, rarely/never (%)

Note: Question not asked in Middle East.
Source: Question Q87 of survey.

of 50. In between, the demands of children and marriage cause a remarkable increase in stress and a decrease in happiness.

The Battle for Balance

In addition to their work and family obligations, women have an appetite for excelling and experiencing and taking on "extracurricular" activities. They want to socialize, watch their favorite shows on television, spend

She ranks herself second or last: family comes first

What is your first priority?

	Single	(%)	Married without kids	(%)	Married with kids	(%)
First	Your parents	27.4	Husband/ partner	46.7	Children	61.2
Second	Self	25.1	Self	20.8	Husband/ partner	15.2
Third	Husband/ partner	12.1	Your parents	13.2	Self	7.3

	Empty nest	(%)	Divorced	(%)	Widowed	(%)
First	Husband/ partner	43.2	Children	46.2	Children	44.7
Second	Children	23.7	Self	17.8	Self	16.2
Third	Self	15.2	Your parents	7.1	Religion/ religious groups	7.9

Source: Question Q25 of survey; single N = 3,496; married w/o kids N = 1,918; married w/ kids N = 3,289; empty nest N = 1,565; divorced N = 1,099; widowed N = 228.

time on the Internet, look after themselves, read, exercise, travel, learn, and engage in community and charitable activities.

Nicole Green laughs about such things. "Before I had kids, I was incredibly organized. My office at work was very tidy. I would finish everything up. I would put everything away." She and Peter had plenty of time to spend together. "My husband and I used to like to just go out and about. We lived in the city. We liked to stroll around, go places, window-shop, sit in a public garden, read the Sunday *Times*, go antiquing."

Now she rarely spends time alone with Peter. "Ideally, we would touch base after the kids are in bed. But it just doesn't happen. It should. And it's an issue. It is a real issue."

Nicole has only a few social commitments that she faithfully keeps. "One is my group I call 'my ladies.' We're all moms of young kids. We all work. Every three weeks, we go out. It's really critical for me that we have that time together."

Nearly all women, whether single, married, divorced, or widowed, when asked who is the priority in their lives—themselves or their spouses, children, or parents—rank themselves second or third. Only one group of women we surveyed—Mexican women—put themselves at the top of the list.

Qin Liu: The Triple Time Challenge in China

If Nicole Green strikes you as a quintessentially American woman, a type that would not be found anywhere else in the world, think again. There are Nicole Greens in every country.

Qin Liu, for example, is a 31-year-old woman who, in many respects, is Nicole Green's Chinese equivalent—a working mother dealing with the problem of too much to do and too little time to do it in. Like Nicole, Qin holds a full-time job; she is head of project planning for a commercial real estate company. Unlike Nicole, who has three children, Qin has one daughter, Yanyu, age 7. (One child per family is a rule still in effect in China, although many parents get around or disregard it.) But Qin's mother lives with Qin and her husband, Jian; and Qin also looks after her parents-in-law, often cooking meals for all of them several days a week.

Qin was born in 1978 not far from Shanghai, in a small city, population 200,000. She is the only child of employees of the local state-owned utilities facility. They lived in a cottage in which the sole appliance, a fourteen-inch black-and-white television, was given to Qin as a gift on her eleventh birthday. Qin's parents emphasized the importance of education, as is the Chinese tradition, and she took it to heart. She was the top student in her high school and was guaranteed admission to two of the best universities in China: Peking University in Beijing and Fudan University in Shanghai. She chose the latter because of its proximity to her hometown, and she eagerly took the leap toward the big city.

Qin was not sure what subject to choose as a major. "Everyone said that international trade and finance were the hot topics. I thought these would guarantee me a promising career future, so I chose them." They were the most competitive majors at Fudan, with the most stringent requirements for admission, but she was accepted.

After graduation, Qin joined the real estate firm where she still works, and she married Jian, whom she met at Fudan, soon after starting work. "My marriage was as simple as my job. My first love was also the man I ended up marrying!" The first two years after marriage were tough going. The young couple moved to Shanghai, and Jian started his own company. Though at first it was a struggle to make ends meet, Jian's business began to take off, Qin's salary rose, and they began to feel settled and stable in their new lives.

Then came two dramatic pieces of news. Jian received a promising job offer from a company in Singapore. A day later, Qin learned she was pregnant. What to do? Qin did not want to leave her job and move to Singapore, but she thought that the job was too good an opportunity to pass up and encouraged her husband to go without her. "He did it for the future of our family." Although her mother often came to visit during Qin's pregnancy, she had times of overwhelming sadness. "The hardest times were when I went to the hospital for a checkup. I remember one time I was all alone, while all the others were accompanied by their husbands or families. There was a huge crowd of people at the hospital. I waited the whole morning and it still wasn't my turn. When I was eating alone and saw the other women's husbands caring for them and bringing them food, I felt so lonely that I couldn't help crying."

But, rather than dwell on her loneliness, Qin turned her attention once again to education. "There is no use in complaining. You have to look for a practical solution." As she prepared for her daughter's birth, and while still working full-time at the real estate company, Qin studied for and successfully received her certification as a professional accountant. She gave birth to Yanyu and was soon back at work; this is the default approach in China. Communist principles of gender equality have given rise to one of the most well-defined attitudes in the world when it comes to the "working mother." Not only are girls expected to excel in school and find stable full-time jobs, they are expected to continue working after having their child. However, the government and employers in China provide little direct support or legal framework for young parents in the form of subsidies or paid maternal-paternal leave.

The enforced separation did not last long. Jian received a promotion after a year in Singapore and returned to Shanghai. Even so, he was busier than ever and—as in most Chinese families—Qin continued to shoulder most of the child rearing and housework on top of her daily work routine.

Gradually, things got better and a little easier for the Liu family. The Chinese economy boomed, Qin's firm grew into the biggest real estate conglomerate in the region, and her career progressed along with her company's success. The family bought a 120-square-meter (1,300-square-foot) four-bedroom apartment in Shanghai for RMB 1.6 million ($250,000), bought a car, and live comfortably on their combined household income of RMB 600,000 ($90,000). The girl who grew up with a single black-and-white TV and no other appliances is now a woman with three flat-screen LCD television sets, a computer-controlled refrigerator, and a state-of-the-art washing machine.

Now that she has some disposable income, Qin loves to shop, especially for clothes. "A woman can never have enough clothes, right? I was going to turn one of our bedrooms into a library, but now it has become a big closet instead." Since she does not have much time to go shopping, she visits neighborhood shops and takes advantage of online malls like Taobao, the Chinese equivalent of eBay.

Qin takes great pride in her job, which to her is not only a source of income but also a platform that enables her to reach her individual potential. As one of the most experienced employees of her firm, she has been instrumental in helping it grow from a small firm to a large conglomerate now preparing to go public. As head of project financing, she is in charge of billions of RMB and aspires to become CFO of an even larger firm one day.

But the foundation of Qin's happiness—as it is for most women around the world—is her family. She puts her own interests last, after ensuring the comfort of her child, husband, and parents, with the familiar result: Qin admits that she is plagued by a shortage of time and that she must sacrifice her personal freedom and interests for the sake of her family. Free time is a rare luxury. She loved to write poetry in college, but she has not written anything in years. Her hobbies, including gourmet cooking, have been put on hold until retirement.

Even so, Qin, like most Chinese women, remains optimistic. "We are very happy now. We have a harmonious family, a lovely daughter, healthy

Overwhelming demands on her time

The married woman with children has the least time for
leisure pursuits; she is squeezed by kids, work, home.

Time spent per week (hours)

Activity	Single	Married without kids	Married with kids	Empty nest	Divorced	Widowed
Work outside home	41	43	37	36	38	32
Work at home [1]	13	14	21	20	18	19
Caring for family [2]	9	7	33	10	15	11
Total commitments	63	65	91	65	71	62
Personal pursuits [3]	55	44	40	48	50	51

She sacrifices sleep to meet the demands
of her hectic, time-squeezed schedule

	Single	Married without kids	Married with kids	Empty nest	Divorced	Widowed
Sleep 5 hours or less per night (%)	10	5	12	13	15	16

> Multitasking is a necessary skill that adds
> to the time crunch and stress in her life.

1. Includes cooking, cleaning, laundry, grocery shopping, household maintenance. 2. Includes caring
for children, shopping for others, family activities. 3. Includes TV, Internet, reading, personal hygiene,
exercising, socializing, hobbies, shopping for self, volunteering.
Note: Averages do not include women who do not work outside the home.
Source: Questions Q15 and Q16 of survey, N = 11,747.

parents, stable jobs and incomes. We don't have many worries in our life.
We are really very happy."

And so it is in every country. Although women are much the same
around the world, there are endless and significant individual and cultural
differences—some subtle, some pronounced. Companies that want to serve
women—within a distinct geography or across many regions—must understand and respond to both the cultural nuances and the big societal issues that pertain to women.

Talk About Multitasking!

Here's how one woman described the demands on her time and goals she has for her life.

I would like to:

Have more children and raise them all to be happy and well-adjusted individuals

Be a good wife to my husband and maintain a happy and constructive marriage

Do more volunteer work

Access my full earning potential in order to buy a second property with my husband, so that we can build our portfolio of assets for our children and our enjoyment

Achieve a healthy work-life balance

Travel and see more of the world

Help my parents and parents-in-law in their old age

Maintain a large number of friendships and keep up a healthy social life

Stay attractive and well-groomed throughout my life

Maintain a healthy lifestyle

Women Have Plenty of Money to Spend

Not only do women hold the purse strings of the economy; there's a lot of money in those purses, and much of it women have earned themselves. Together, working women around the world earn the equivalent of $12 trillion in salaries and wages annually. American working women earn about $4.3 trillion of that. Three in ten working women (29 percent) make all or almost all of their family's income, and six in ten (62 percent) earn about half of it. In developed economies, 40 percent of women control 91 to 100 percent of household spending. Women in the United States have the greatest influence over purchase and consumption—more than 72 percent of total spending is controlled by women.

Women Billionaires on the Rise

Forbes magazine said there were 99 female billionaires worldwide in 2008, sixteen more than in 2007. Still, women accounted for only about 9 percent of the world's 1,125 billionaires.

Ten of the female billionaires on the list were self-made, and they included these:

Oprah Winfrey. The queen of daytime television and the founder of her own media enterprise, Harpo Productions. Estimated wealth: $2.5 billion.

J. K. Rowling. Author of the Harry Potter series of books and recipient of much wealth from them and the movies based on them. She was a single mom, living on welfare, before her books took off. Estimated wealth: $1 billion.

Meg Whitman. Former president of eBay, she helped eBay become a business and social phenomenon. She stepped down to take over as national cochair of John McCain's presidential campaign. Estimated wealth: $1.3 billion.

Zhang Xin. A Chinese property developer, Zhang Xin runs SOHO China with her husband. Like Oprah and Rowling, Zhang Xin is a rags-to-riches story—she started out working as a laborer in the factories of Hong Kong at the age of 14. Estimated wealth: $3 billion.[1]

Women Are Highly Educated, Love Learning, and Apply Their Skills to Consuming

The most important driver of women's increased earning power and influence has been education. At every stage of the educational process, women are not only increasing in numbers but also excelling in performance. Women take education very seriously and continue their focus on learning throughout their lives.

More women than men—of all cultural backgrounds—take the SAT in preparation for their college applications. In the United States in 2008, 53 percent of white test takers were female; 51 percent of Asians; 57 percent of Hispanics; and 57 percent of African-Americans. In 2007, 70 percent of female high school graduates enrolled in college, up from 40 percent prior to 1972. Women make up the majority of the college population. Before 1972, 44 percent of all undergraduates in the United States were women; by

2005, 60 percent were women. At many of the country's most prestigious institutions of higher education—including Harvard, Yale, and Princeton—women make up about half of the undergraduate population.[2]

A higher percentage of women than men stick with the college program and receive their undergraduate degrees, with the result that the percentage of American women who hold a bachelor's degree has surpassed the percentage of men who do—30 percent of women to 28 percent of men. And more women than ever before are pursuing advanced degrees. In 1972, 11 percent of the students enrolled in first-professional degree programs were women; in 2005 the percentage of women reached 49.[3] (First-professional degrees are for fields that require a license to practice, including architecture, law, medicine, engineering, accounting, education and social work, and many of the healthcare professions.)

Women have applied their knowledge and penchant for learning to the practice of consumption. They are much more likely than men to do extensive research into companies, products, services, and brands. What's more, they will gather, evaluate, and share information long after a purchase has been made. In short, they will continue to behave just as they did in their educational careers—as dedicated, persistent, and relentless learners.

Women Take the Honors

Women take more advanced placement (AP) and honors classes in high school than men do:

ON THE ENGLISH SAT

40 percent of test takers had taken AP or honors English.
39 percent of those were male; 61 percent were female.

ON THE MATH SAT

33 percent of test takers had taken AP or honors math.
46 percent of those were male; 54 percent were female.

Girls also have higher overall numbers in years of study and variety of subjects studied, often by a wide margin:

continued

IN ENGLISH

57 percent of girls studied English for more than four years, compared
with 43 percent of boys.

Between 10 and 11 percent more girls than boys took American literature,
composition, British literature, world literature, and English as a second
language.

IN MATH

54 percent of girls took four years of math, compared with 46 percent of
boys.

55 percent of girls took algebra and geometry, compared with 45 percent
of boys.

56 percent of girls took math courses other than algebra, geometry,
calculus, or trigonometry, compared with 44 percent of boys.[4]

Women Wield Great Commercial and Social Clout

The combination of hard work and education has brought women to a position of power and influence in business, politics, and social endeavors.

The rise in professional and graduate education has caused a dramatic
swing in participation, by gender, in many well-paid professions. As of
2007, 30 percent of the lawyers in the United States were women, up from
25 percent in 1997; 29 percent of the physicians, up from 22 percent in 1997;
39 percent of the faculty members, up from 32 percent; and 14 percent of
the military, up from 12 percent ten years ago.[5]

The number of women executives in business has also grown over the
past decade. Of the highest-earning officers in the Fortune 500 companies in
1997, 61 were women; in 2007 the number had climbed to 142. The numbers of
women serving as all officers, as board members, and in management have all
grown. There were two female CEOs running Fortune 500 companies in
1997; ten years later there were thirteen. And we predict that once another decade has passed, there will be at least eighty female CEOs in the Fortune 500.[6]

Women's presence in the established corporate world, although increasing, is modest in comparison with women's success as business owners and
entrepreneurs. In 2007, women accounted for ownership of 40 percent of

firms based in the United States—which employ about 13 million people and generate $1.7 trillion in sales. Businesses owned by women are growing at twice the rate of all U.S. firms and faster than businesses owned by men.[7]

Women have also been making remarkable gains in the political sphere. In global politics, there has been a steady increase in the number of women leaders. In the United States, although Hillary Clinton did not become the presidential nominee for the Democratic Party, she did become secretary of state. Sarah Palin, the Republican vice-presidential nominee, was one of nine women governors.

According to a study conducted by the United Nations Development Fund for Women (Unifem), women around the world have entered politics in greater numbers than ever in the past decade, accounting for 18.4 percent of members of parliament worldwide. That's an increase of 7 percent since 1995. "Much of the increase was driven by women realizing that they needed to attain power rather than just lobby for change," said a UN spokeswoman. If the rate continues, the report concludes, women will reach parity in parliaments by the year 2045.[8]

And there is an intriguing cohort of women who influence and often dictate traditions and trends in women's consumer culture and in society as a whole. Although their clout rarely extends beyond their own country, these women, through vast personal discretionary income, high-profile celebrity status, and a concerted awareness of and interest in women's issues (health, equal rights, fashion, etc.), occupy a kind of super-terrestrial authority whose opinions sometimes matter more to many women than do those of their own friends and colleagues. Think of Oprah and Martha Stewart in the United States; Angela Merkel in Germany; Wu Yi in China; Sonia Gandhi in India; Lorena Ochoa in Mexico; Michelle Bachelet in Chile; and Aung San Suu Kyi in Burma.

Annalie Lindstrand: Even Those Who Have Everything Will Soon Want Something Different

It is easy to see why women like Nicole Green and Qin Liu, with their frenetic lives, are looking for as much help as they can get from products and services. But even women who do not feel the pinch of time or the burden of too many responsibilities are still careful shoppers who are always looking for the next improvement and the better value. Even these women may be dissatisfied with goods and services they buy and may want more from them.

Annalie Lindstrand, for example, ranks as one of the happiest young women we met during the course of our research—or the course of our lives, for that matter. She was born in a small town just north of Stockholm, Sweden, the only child of two successful parents, a doctor and a business executive.

Annalie had a happy childhood. Both of her parents paid attention to her, helped her, looked after her, and loved her deeply. The family was prosperous, and her parents owned a home from before Annalie can remember. They traveled abroad both winter and summer. She grew up into a beautiful young woman with classic Swedish looks: she stands five feet ten inches and has long blond hair and Mediterranean blue eyes. She mastered English early in school and is highly articulate in her second language.

Annalie did well in school and went on to one of Europe's oldest educational institutions, a world-class research university in central Sweden, and there she found both her future profession—science—and her husband. "It was love at first sight," she told us. She continued her education, as did he, got her advanced degree, and immediately landed a good job. She progressed quickly there, then moved to a company she liked even better, where she hopes to spend a long career. She spent several happy years with her husband as a young couple. They learned about each other, traveled, worked, cooked, made friends, hiked, read, and enjoyed life. When they were ready—both financially and emotionally—they decided to have a baby.

Today Annalie and Tobias, an assistant college professor, share an airy apartment of 100 square meters (a little more than 1,000 square feet) in Stockholm. He bikes to work. She drives their only car, a Seat Ibiza. Tobias cooks many of their dinners at home. He specializes in wild mushroom omelets but occasionally serves reindeer fillet with a sauce he invented himself.

The Lindstrands make good money by any standard. Annalie earns about 63,000 Swedish kronor (SEK) per month and Tobias 32,000, for a combined monthly income of 95,000 SEK, or about $13,350—an annual income of $160,200.

Annalie, at age 32, is still paying off her student loans. Although the state pays full college tuition for every student in Sweden, it does not pay for books and living expenses, but it will provide loans for those things. So

Annalie still owes 280,000 SEK, a little over $40,000. She has no trouble paying off about $7,000 a year. She and Tobias also save about 25,000 SEK a month ($3,500), a phenomenal rate compared with that of Americans.

When we met Annalie she was expecting twins—a first-time mother at age 32, which she considers the perfect age to bear a child. Although her pregnancy was considered high risk, she had plenty of support from her family, her friends, and Tobias. "He wants me to rest a lot," she told us. "So it's fantastic. I come home from work around 6:30 or 7. I lie down on the sofa and read a book or a paper while he prepares dinner."

When Annalie learned she was pregnant, she had only recently landed a new job at a large healthcare company, one of the world's leading firms. But she had no worries about her coming pregnancy leave. She would take off at least eighteen months, probably two years, and her job would be waiting for her, guaranteed. Money would not be a problem, either. She would receive nearly full pay throughout her leave, a large portion of it coming from the state.

Annalie would seem to have it all. A good education and a career she enjoys. A strong marriage and a circle of close friends. Children (planned) on the way. More than enough money. A nice home. And, last but far from least, a female-friendly political and social environment.

"It's easy to live here in Sweden, because you have a good quality of life," she said. "Everyone accepts that women have careers. When you have children, everyone understands that, of course, you are going to keep working. Fathers these days are taking much more paternity leave and it's very equal in that respect. Also, the whole employer market—they appreciate that this is the fact. So it's not so much different to employ a woman or a man today because both will be home with children if they are at that age." Annalie and Tobias's children will even be guaranteed a place in childcare and, later, in kindergarten.

What more could any woman (any person) want?

Actually, even Annalie—with all she has and the happiness she feels—has many things on her wish list. She would like a larger home with a garden. She wants to improve her professional skills and take on more responsibility at work. She hopes to have a third child, preferably of the opposite gender to her identical twins. Tobias would like to become a full professor at one of Europe's major universities. Annalie needs a better bike. They both want a dog.

Above all, Annalie says she wants what virtually every woman we spoke with wants, "A good balance between work and time for meeting with friends and family. Everyone healthy. And also enough time for things that are important just to me."

WOMEN ARE (STILL) OPTIMISTIC, HOPEFUL, AND FULL OF DREAMS

As a result of their successes—and despite the stresses, gaps, and lacks—we have found that women, if not quite as content as Annalie Lindstrand, are fundamentally upbeat and optimistic, especially about their personal situations. They believe that their sacrifices, especially for their children, are worth making and will pay off in the long run.

The majority of women we polled believe that they will be better off personally five years from now—their financial situation will have improved, their daily lives will be better, they'll be happier, their families will be in better shape, and they will have found a way into what Nicole Green calls a "golden window." "There will be much more of a harmony in our home. My kids will want to be here, to feel like part of a family, part of a team. And everyone's giving to what is needed to make our family go."

Our respondents also tell us they believe that women will continue to make gains. They will increase their presence in the professions, hold more political positions of importance, wield greater influence, continue their educational rise, and enjoy greater economic power. And the respondents strongly believe that they will achieve their future success through their own hard work, rather than through their partner's success, or through luck.

- The majority of our respondents (66 percent) believe *my daily life will be better* in five years.
- The great majority of women—66 percent—believe that their *own hard work* will help drive their success.

Women do not seek greater incomes or influence simply because they wish to make more money. They are not, in general, avid accumulators of wealth; nor do they measure themselves or others simply by how much

What women want:
Time, value, a better life

Love and Connection

- A lasting romantic relationship and love
- Trust, support, honesty, and commitment in a partner
- A happy, healthy family
- Connections with family, friends, colleagues, and neighbors
- A sense of community

Fulfillment

- Freedom to pursue happiness and satisfaction however they choose
- Empowerment and flexibility
- Absence of suppression
- Unlimited boundaries
- Encouragement to achieve

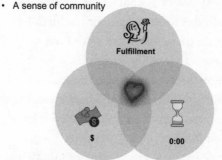

Money as a Marker

- Women earning and controlling more; balancing inflow and outflow
- Careful, hungry for insight on how to spend money wisely
- Expectations about value for money increasing; skeptical about claims
- Seeking security, higher savings, a better future; willing to sacrifice

Work-Life Balance

- Time-stressed and strained, looking for agents of leverage and convenience
- Worried about how to make it all happen, making trade-offs and tough decisions
- Women taking on more – juggling work, family, and home; looking for ways to "source time" or share the burden

money they earn or how impressive their assets are. However, money is still important to women, primarily as a marker of status and influence within the household. When women increase their earnings, make a contribution to the household finances, and control their own assets, they become more powerful. All women work hard to balance the inflow of money into the household with the outflow, and the more money they earn, the more successful they can be at this task.

Money also creates flexibility for women. It enables them to buy back time—by outsourcing low-value activities. As Kathy, a 51-year-old Empty Nester, said, "Money is important in letting me do the things I like."

At all income levels and at all stages of life, however, women are careful, even cautious, with their money. They look for advice and insight about how to spend it wisely, and they constantly seek value for money. In addition to buying power, money means security and a better future for their families.

Brea, 36, is constantly worried about having enough money set aside. She and her husband are saving for a house or large apartment in Chicago, so she has cut off all other indulgences in order to save. She would like to get LASIK surgery, she says, buy designer jeans, and get a weekly massage or pedicure, but she can't justify spending the money. Her husband and friends get her gift certificates for massages for her birthdays, but, she says, "It takes me months to use them. I feel that once I use it, it's gone. As long as I don't use it, I still have it to look forward to."

Although women don't particularly care about money in and of itself, they highly value its ability to bring love and happiness. In our survey, the higher the income, the more women said that they felt loved, satisfied, appreciated, successful, and fulfilled.

A majority of women in the lower and lower middle ranks of income said that they do feel loved (54 percent), but they also said they feel frustrated, disappointed, sad, and lonely. For women in the middle ranks and above, none of those negative feelings appeared in the top five. And the flip side is also true: women in the lower income ranks said that they *least* often felt powerful, successful, beautiful, and important.

- Very few high-earning women say they feel *unsuccessful, depressed, lonely, sad, or angry.*

The great majority of women in our survey tell us that love—including love between friends and family members, as well as romantic love—and connection are highly important to them, and they seek products and services that help them find love, keep it, and strengthen it.

They look for trust, support, honesty, and commitment in their partners. They look for ways to build connections and create a sense of community with extended family members, friends, colleagues, and neighbors.

These feelings hold true for women of all ages in all parts of the world.

WHAT WOMEN WANT IN PRODUCTS AND SERVICES

Now, to this picture of education, affluence, influence, spending power, ultra-full days, family complexity, work pressure, and time-starvation, and the search for love, let us add the commercial element: the interface between women and the goods and services they rely on to keep their families running and their lives intact.

This relationship has changed dramatically over the years. Women rarely are able to devote hours to deep-cleaning their homes, doing once-a-week major shopping at the supermarket, or spending an afternoon at the mall buying clothes.

As Nicole Green puts it, "I have to spread everything out into tiny little chunks."

Shopping for food? "I do power shops. Twenty minutes on my way to pick up the kids. Or a half hour while my son is at karate. I end up shopping four times a week for fifteen or twenty minutes." Nicole will pay more money for groceries that are healthy but also fairly quick to prepare. "It costs me a lot more to get those cans of black beans that already have chilies and garlic in them than to just buy a bag of dried black beans. We could eat a lot more cheaply if I could do go the completely homemade route. But I can't."

Laundry? "Same thing. I don't have time to do seven loads of laundry in one day on the weekend. That's why I do one load every day."

Cleaning? That gets tucked into the children's post-bedtime hour. One bathroom at a time. The kitchen countertops. Maybe the front hall.

Shopping for clothes? "The jeans I'm wearing are at least five years old. I have them in four different colors. I found a pair that fit and were on sale, and bought them in blue, brown, green, and black."

Notice that the women we spoke with did *not* say they wanted many more material goods. They didn't say, "I would like a lot more clothes." Or kitchen appliances. Or cars. Nor did they talk much with us about brands or specific companies, until we directly asked about these—and even then, although the women demonstrated expert product knowledge, they didn't show any particular enthusiasm. Women care about products and services—and, by inference, about the companies that provide them—only insofar as those products and services can help them save time, connect with others, and live their lives better.

Women have serious dissatisfactions in many categories

Greatest opportunities to better serve them: financial services, healthcare, consumer durables

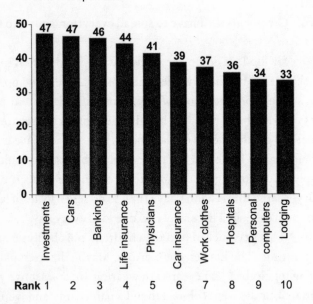

Which categories should focus more on
understanding and meeting women's needs?
(10 worst of 58 categories tested)

Percent of respondents

Source: Question Q97 of survey, N = 11,747.

Agents of Time Leverage

Companies that *do* understand women and their time pressures respond by offering simple, straightforward solutions that deliver the time savings women want along with the emotional benefits they seek.

Time and convenience are most important to Nicole Green and to women around the world. The triple challenge of time—and the stress and anxiety it can create—colors virtually everything women do. Products and

She is willing to pay top dollar for better products and services

Top ten products and services where she will trade up

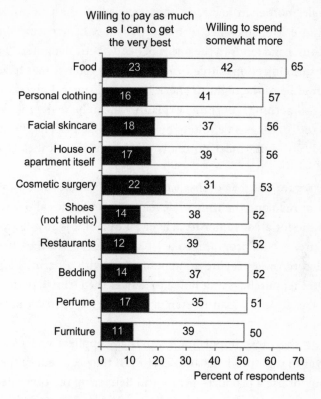

Willing to pay as much as I can to get the very best | Willing to spend somewhat more

Food	23	42	65
Personal clothing	16	41	57
Facial skincare	18	37	56
House or apartment itself	17	39	56
Cosmetic surgery	22	31	53
Shoes (not athletic)	14	38	52
Restaurants	12	39	52
Bedding	14	37	52
Perfume	17	35	51
Furniture	11	39	50

0 10 20 30 40 50 60 70
Percent of respondents

Note: Figures do not necessarily sum due to rounding.
Source: Question Q98–Q100 of survey; N = 11,747.

services that can "give time back to them" are seen positively. Good products act as agents that enable women to make the most of time, regain more of it, and spend it as they want to, rather than as they have to. Products that require them to spend time in ways they don't want, or see as unnecessary, are villains. Goods that squeeze the most out of time—by making it more engaging for them personally or by enabling them to connect with others more deeply—are especially valued.

For example, Nicole Green told us she likes Trader Joe's. "It's a time-related thing. I pay a lot of attention to nutrition for myself and for my kids. But it's also hard to find the time to make great things from scratch. At Trader Joe's, though it costs a little more, I can get at least the very quick beginnings of a good meal, and I feel I've done something that was decent for my kids."

Similarly, when asked what brand or service she loves, Lorraine Menzies, a single mother in her early thirties, praised the Curves workout center because it enables her to make the most of her time. Lorraine works full-time and tends to the needs of her diabetic daughter. "I need to give her insulin injections three times a day and I sometimes have to get up in the middle of the night to check her blood sugar. I always seem to be cooking something," Lorraine explains. "It can be really tough going, but going to Curves has definitely helped me cope better. The workout is only half an hour, and I normally just go in the clothes that I am wearing."9

In this regard, the idea of *time-based competition* takes a new meaning: it's not about reducing the time to develop a product; it's about reducing the total time for a consumer to deliver an outcome—buy clothing; enroll in an after-school program; bake a birthday cake; learn to program a digital video recorder; secure an appointment with a dermatologist; return an Internet purchase that failed to deliver the claimed performance, color, or size; secure a loan to start a business; or open an investment account.

Time is the most important lever that suppliers can use to win women over to their products and services. If they can reduce the time it takes to buy or use a product—while still delivering the other necessary benefits—they can change from being an inflicter of pain and frustration to being a provider of leverage and convenience. This advantage in time is one of the main reasons that people shop and buy online. For married women with children especially, shopping at traditional stores is far too inconvenient and time-consuming, and often impossible with children in tow.

Any meaningful reduction in the time required of the consumer can translate into an increase in profits for the supplier. If a food company can reduce by half the time needed to cook one of its prepared meals, it can double its profit. Frozen peas sold in a traditional bag sell for about $1.50 for twelve ounces; peas sold in a microwavable bag sell at $2.19 for ten ounces.

The difference? It can take up to three minutes to get the traditional bag out of the freezer, cut it open, put the peas in a microwavable bowl, and add the two tablespoons of water required. It takes 15 seconds to place the microwavable bag on the oven turnstile.

Decrease time, increase profits. How can you save your consumers a few precious minutes?

Promoters of Holistic Health, Beauty, and Well-Being

Women want to be attractive (although most women say they don't feel beautiful very often), but today they put beauty into a larger context of general good health, wellness, and fitness. Beauty is no longer painted on; it must radiate both from within and without.

As we'll see, Olay, a $1 billion global brand, has succeeded over decades by connecting beauty with health. Today's Olay is very different from the product, costing 15 cents an ounce, that our mothers used in the 1970s. Olay is one brand that deeply understands how women feel about skin and skincare and has morphed from being a low-end product with a simple purpose (moisturizing) that about 2 percent of the population used into a high-end product with a wide variety of applications that has 40 percent household penetration.

Facilitators of Comfort and Pampering

As a result of the unrelenting pressures of job, housework, juggling multiple roles, caring for family, and finding time for oneself, women place a high value on achieving comfort—and even moments of indulgence and personal pampering—whenever they can.

The one thing that Nicole Green has promised herself—"once Holly is in first grade and all of our childcare expenses have gone way down"—is a weekly massage.

Ecute, a Japanese company, recognized that as the population of working women in Japan increased, more of them traveled to their workplaces by train. But Japanese railway stations had been generally dismal, unwelcoming, even uncomfortable places for women. Ecute developed a whole new kind of station mall, with shops and eating places designed for women, and it is enjoying high profits and rapid growth as a result.

Contributors to the Environment and Promoters of a Greater Social Good

Women care that goods and the companies creating them use environmentally friendly materials and sustainable processes, and develop organizations to promote women and give back to their societies.

For example, the personal care company Origins, launched in 1990, chose to focus on a specific need in the women's beauty market: natural, holistic health. Its mission is to provide women with a line of skincare and beauty products derived from healthful, natural ingredients. From its inception, Origins has placed great emphasis on environmentally sustainable practices: the company uses recycled paper and soy ink for its printed materials, strives to minimize its carbon footprint by using alternative energy sources, and selects only renewable ingredients for its product lines. This company also led the movement to eliminate animal testing, becoming the first cosmetics manufacturer that chose not to test on animals and not to rely on animal-derived ingredients. Origins has became a major competitor in the beauty industry: it ranks among Estée Lauder's top five brands, and today has 125 freestanding stores and 450 counters at department and specialty stores in more than twenty-six countries.

Women's Influence in Nontraditional Categories

In certain categories, including some that have traditionally been considered "male" products, women make almost all the spending decisions. Women control the following percentages of purchases in the following categories:

- 94 percent of *home furnishings*
- 92 percent of *vacations*
- 91 percent of *homes*
- 60 percent of *automobiles*
- 51 percent of *consumer electronics*

WHAT WOMEN WANT CAN, IN FACT, BE DELIVERED

Women want a lot.

They want equality, parity, opportunity, and fairness in the workplace and in society.

They want empathy, understanding, connection, health, love, security, and happiness.

From products and services, they're even more demanding—and less willing to overlook shortcomings.

They want you, the provider of goods, to listen to them.

They want you to understand how they really consume your product or service.

They want you to register their dissatisfactions.

They want your new product development to be oriented toward their current and emerging needs.

They want you to know that they are members of powerful social networks and that they are *communication machines.* This means that they will tell many, *many* others about the wonderful attributes, or the distressing shortcomings, of your product or service—immediately, consistently, and repeatedly.

They want you to understand that women control 72 percent of the dollars spent in this country. And that they view the money they spend as *their* money, not their husbands' money. They view themselves as independent, highly educated purchasing agents with a lot of economic power.

They want you to know they have money available to spend on the goods that offer value and meaning and time savings, but not on products that are cynical, are aimed at stereotypes, are self-absorbed, or fail to understand women's needs.

They want you to take seriously the issue of time and its lack—to do much more with the enormous commercial opportunity involved in taking this scarce resource, time, and substituting leverage and providing women with ways to accomplish tasks in different ways. The task could be anything—meal preparation, cleanup, helping the kids with homework, you name it.

They want you to ask about their daily lives, their wants and needs, their hopes and dreams. They want you to ask, as we did, "What do women want?"

And then they want you to deliver an answer—products and services that meet their individual needs and deliver meaning and love.

QUESTIONS THAT LEAD TO UNDERSTANDING

Each company must seek to understand the wants and needs of women in the context of its own industry and its particular constituencies. To help themselves do so, they can ask a series of questions:

- Are *listening and responding* second nature at our company? Do we, in fact, have a profile—constantly updated and refined—of what's happening in the marketplace?
- What are the *dissatisfactions* in the category? How do they rank in importance to consumers? Which ones can we address most successfully? Which can we address fastest?
- How can we *define our market* as broadly as possible? What minute-by-minute time savings are needed or could be developed? Are there emerging market segments that are underserved? What are the dissatisfactions and needs in each of them?
- How do women make the *purchase decisions* for this category? What do they want? What do they need? How do they buy? When do they buy? What is the life cycle of the product for the consumer?
- Is the *product design* appropriate for women? Is it pleasing to the eye? Does it accommodate women's needs in use? Is the design based on the needs of the particular consumer segment? Will women respond to the ingredients and raw materials used?
- Does the *merchandising* communicate the special way that the product or service responds to women's specific needs for time savings, connection, love, and beauty?
- How does the product deliver advantage at three important *moments of truth*—purchase, consumption, and referral (or lack of referral)?
- Does the *sales force clearly understand* why the product or service is better for women and more responsive to their needs?

- Does the *marketing deliver fireworks imagery* in the marketplace? Does it speak the truth? Does it tell a story? Will it turn skeptics into believers? Or will it show up on YouTube as yet another example of clueless marketing?
- Do we think of the product or service as just a step in a neverending *process of continuous improvement, experimentation,* and *learning?*
- Are we thinking about this opportunity as a source of major *big, new business,* rather than as a small, ancillary segment?

2.

The Archetypes and Life Stages

The female economy is not a homogeneous market. You need to apply rules of segmentation. Our research identified six main archetypes, each with different wants and needs. Each represents a market opportunity. Women in all segments suffer time stress and are overburdened with tasks. The V curve of happiness means women are happiest in their early and later years. Companies must remember that they compete for scarce disposable income across categories. Consumption is elastic. Most women make difficult trade-offs between themselves and family members, and few women rank themselves first.

Every woman's life tells a unique story. Yet, from the results of our survey, we find that women worldwide cluster into six basic segments—primarily defined by income, age, and lifestage—each of which we think of as an archetype.

They are:

- *Fast Tracker*
- *Pressure Cooker*
- *Relationship-Focused*
- *Fulfilled Empty Nesters*
- *Managing on Her Own*
- *Making Ends Meet*

Two of the archetypes—Fast Tracker and Pressure Cooker—have two subsegments, which we'll discuss in a moment.

The power of segmentation is that it allows a company to consider an

Six key segments of female consumers: tailor offerings to needs of each; focus on Fast Trackers, worth 34% of total

U.S. consumer segments and sizing

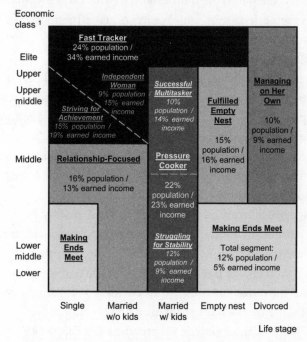

Economic class [1]

Elite		
Upper		
Upper middle		
Middle		
Lower middle		
Lower		

Fast Tracker
24% population /
34% earned income

Independent Woman
9% population /
15% earned income

Striving for Achievement
15% population /
19% earned income

Successful Multitasker
10% population /
14% earned income

Fulfilled Empty Nest
15% population /
16% earned income

Managing on Her Own
10% population /
9% earned income

Relationship-Focused
16% population /
13% earned income

Pressure Cooker
22% population /
23% earned income

Making Ends Meet
Total segment:
12% population /
5% earned income

Making Ends Meet

Struggling for Stability
12% population /
9% earned income

Single Married w/o kids Married w/ kids Empty nest Divorced

Life stage

1. Economic class defined by annual household income as follows: upper middle and above: at least $100K; middle: $35K - $99.9K; lower and lower middle: below $35K.
Note: Percentages based on U.S. women 18 years of age and above. Population percentages do not add to 100 percent, owing to rounding.
Source: 2006 U.S. census data: http://www.census.gov/hhes/www/cpstc/cps_table_creator.html and http://pubdb3.census.gov/macro/032007/hhinc/new06_000.htm, BCG online survey.

archetype and say, "How would Nicole Green or Annalie Lindstrand or Qin Liu react to this product? Would she try it? Would she buy it again? Would she tell her friends about it? Would she say, 'Wow'?"

THE FAST TRACKER

The archetype that offers the greatest opportunity—largely because these women control the greatest percentage of wealth and are the most sophisticated consumers—is the *Fast Tracker*: the educated female economic elite.

Mary Ellen Iskenderian: On the Fast Track Since Fifth Grade

Mary Ellen Iskenderian is the quintessential Fast Tracker woman, a driven, high-achieving perfectionist who wants to make the most of everything she does.

Mary Ellen got started on the fast track early.

When she was in fifth grade, her teacher encouraged her to do a community service project. She did some research and discovered that the Peace Corps could build, for $2,500, a school in any village in the world where it had a volunteer. Mary Ellen organized kids in the four elementary schools in her hometown, Glen Rock, New Jersey, to solicit parents in the PTA, hold bake sales, and run car washes. They exceeded their goal, and the Peace Corps, as promised, built a school in Peru.

The experience made a profound impression on Mary Ellen. "I had the sense that I could stand up in front of people and speak about something that I believed in and convince them to follow me." In many of our profiles of individual women, we'll see how important the desire to do good for the world is and how women want to do business with companies and buy brands that share their values of altruism and philanthropy.

Today, Mary Ellen Iskenderian is president and CEO of Women's World Banking (WWB), the world's largest network of microfinance institutions and banks. She leads the WWB global team, based in New York, in providing technical services and strategic support to more than fifty top-performing microfinance institutions and banks in thirty countries in Africa, Asia, eastern Europe, Latin America, and the Middle East. WWB's network members consistently rank among the top three microfinance institutions in their countries. More than 75 percent of their clients are poor female entrepreneurs.

Iskenderian followed a fairly straight line from her fifth-grade success to her current position. She majored in international economics at Georgetown University, earned her MBA at the Yale School of Management, and then worked in a succession of positions in financial services institutions, including Lehman Brothers and the International Finance Corporation (IFC), the private sector unit of the World Bank. Her work took her to countries around the world, including Pakistan, Sri Lanka, Bangladesh, and Zimbabwe, and throughout Latin America, particularly Colombia. All told, she estimates that she placed $200 million of loans in her years with the World Bank and that the investments have had a tremendous multiplier effect. "The equity funds that we invested in are worth billions of dollars today. I am proud of having seen some of these businesses really take off."

In 2006, Iskenderian left the World Bank to become president and CEO of Women's World Banking (WWB), based in New York. "I was up for a change. I loved the idea of running something. I had seen how successful microfinance could be in helping to alleviate poverty and was eager to learn more. I knew that women were the backbone of microfinance, I knew that they were very important to how the industry had come about. But it wasn't until after coming to WWB that I learned how absolutely crucial women are, not only to the development of microfinance, but in the role that they play in moving their families out of poverty."

Even while she is consumed with her current responsibilities, Iskenderian keeps her eye on the future. She wants to educate banks and other traditional lenders about the need for microfinancing. "Women around the world need access to capital, to education, to healthcare. I suppose it could be summed up by access to respect for their human dignity. There are still far too many places in the world where women aren't even allowed out of their home."

Subsegments of Fast Trackers: Striving for Achievement and the Independent Woman

There are two subsegments in the Fast Tracker archetype that are worth keeping in mind: *Striving for Achievement* and the *Independent Woman*.

Women Striving for Achievement are driven by achievement at work and want to get recognition for it. Their job and career are top priorities. They put in lots of hours at work and are often overwhelmed by the demands on their time. This group represents 15 percent of the population of the United States and about 19 percent of the earned income.

Key characteristics of women Striving for Achievement include these:

• Job is a top priority.
• Achievement is a core value.

- Recognition is very important.
- They have a positive financial outlook and are regular savers.
- Forty-one percent hold graduate degrees.
- Hours worked per week: 45.

The *Independent Woman* is highly educated and works the most hours of any of the archetypes. She has a strong motivation to be successful and independent. She is better able to prioritize the demands of her job relative to her obligations to people in her life outside work. She has established sufficient professional success that she puts a little less value on achievement than do the strivers. These Independent Women represent 9 percent of the population and 15 percent of the earned income.

Key characteristics of Independent Women include these:

- They have no children at home.
- They are the most educated group: 46 percent hold a graduate degree.
- They work the most hours per week (48).
- They spend the least time working at home (11).
- Their job is a top priority.
- Love is a core value; friends and family have high priority.
- Autonomy is a core value (an important distinction from women Striving for Achievement).

A Force in Every Society

Fast Trackers are a well-known segment in the United States, and you will also find them in other countries around the world.

Banu Balaban, for example, lives in Istanbul, Turkey. She is a professional woman who earns $213,000 a year in a household with total income of $240,000. She has been married six years, has one child, and works an average of sixty hours a week. She influences as much as 70 percent of household expenditures. Like many Fast Trackers, as successful and influential as she is both in the world and in the household, she wishes her husband would do more chores around the house, would save more money, and would develop a long-term financial plan. Despite her differences with him, however, she says that one of the things that gives her greatest happiness, in addition to her own success, is "being with my husband."

Iskenderian, Balaban, and almost half of all Fast Tracker respondents say their number one challenge is dealing with the many demands placed on their time, including managing household finances and trying to find time "for me"—but never getting enough.

Unlike Iskenderian, whose father was an early influence in her life, most of these women (80 percent) see their mother as the main influence and have often followed the mother's example to do well in school, get a good job, and succeed in every endeavor they undertake. Much like Iskenderian, they tend to identify themselves as achievers and strivers very early in their lives—often in grade school—and then set to work creating the perfect life by progressing through a number of well-defined life stages and acing every one of them.

They begin by doing everything they can in school to build their academic portfolio: taking advanced placement courses, studying hard, achieving top grades, engaging in as many extracurricular activities as time allows, and getting involved in community and "enrichment" pursuits as well. By building the superb résumé—which they may start compiling in junior high, the better to land internships and summer jobs—they seek to get the "first big position" that will put them on the path to advancement and financial success. Once they have settled in enough to feel reasonably secure, they set out to meet a man who can match their credentials and with whom they can create the perfect family.

Fast Trackers, obviously, have very high standards and place intense demands on themselves and those around them, including colleagues, family, friends, and eventually partners and children.

Fast Trackers drive themselves relentlessly. They love taking on new responsibilities and challenges and try to fill every minute of their days with activity and accomplishment. Not surprisingly, then, they feel that time is their enemy. And despite their high energy, they say they feel stressed and tired much of the time.

Many Fast Trackers say they are still looking for the fulfillment they thought would arrive, almost automatically, if they traversed the stages correctly. These women still find themselves wrestling with two concerns that plague many of the archetypes: physical appearance and personal power. Forty-eight percent of the Fast Trackers said they consider themselves extremely or very attractive. Eleven percent said they rarely or never feel beautiful. Twenty-eight percent said they rarely or never feel powerful. Fast Trackers know that society still places a high value on looking good, especially for women.

Not only do Fast Trackers set high standards for themselves; they expect the same of those around them, especially their partners or potential partners. As a result, many Fast Trackers claim that they can't find a mate who measures up and simply stop trying.

An example is Bao Bao Wan, 26, a jewelry designer who divides her time between Hong Kong and Beijing. "I don't need a man to buy me anything," she says. Wan's parents grew up on a farm in rural China, and her father steadily worked his way up to become a government minister. He was successful enough to send Wan to be educated in France and the United States. Now she works for herself as a jewelry designer. "Every piece of my jewelry represents myself and a generation of Chinese women who are fragile yet very bold and crazy," she says. Wan says she wants to get married eventually. At 26, however, she does not feel any great pressure to do so. Besides, Wan says, most of the men she meets don't come up to her standards. "He'll probably have to be Western," she says. "Chinese men just don't *get* women from the new generation."[1]

Fast Trackers believe that they make their own success, and as a result most (76 percent) say that their lives will be better in five years. And they tend to have ambitious dreams for themselves. Banu Balaban, for example, hopes to start her own business one day, as did a remarkable number of the women we surveyed. Other Fast Trackers told us that they want to:

- Own a restaurant
- Learn more languages
- Adopt a child from Africa
- Achieve an ideal weight
- Live abroad
- Write a book
- Live an active life into their eighties
- Travel for months at a time

- Become a motivational speaker
- Find a man who fully understands them and who is absolutely loyal, without a lot of jealousy
- Be ridiculously in love

Fast Trackers don't ask for much!

The Lines Often Blur Between Archetypes

Women often move from one archetype to another as their circumstances and life stages change. Women also may have characteristics of two or more archetypes.

FAST TRACKERS

- Fast Trackers who are married women with children are almost invariably also identified as Successful Multitaskers.
- Single Fast Trackers are often pulled into the Relationship-Focused archetype.

MANAGING ON HER OWN

- High- and mid-income divorced or widowed women are spread across the archetype clusters.

RELATIONSHIP-FOCUSED

- At the middle income level, these women tend also to be Striving for Achievement.

PRESSURE COOKER

- This group splits into two segments, roughly by income: Successful Multitaskers and Struggling for Stability.

FULFILLED EMPTY NESTERS

- There are some high-income Empty Nesters who are also Fast Trackers.

MAKING ENDS MEET

- Low-income divorcees often move into Struggling for Stability.

The Commercial Opportunity with Fast Trackers

Fast Trackers, despite their busy schedules, have or make time to shop. They think of themselves as sophisticated and worldly, and most, in fact, are. They seek adventure and learning, and will spend a lot of time researching products, scouring the Web for news, and paying close attention to goods they see in the workplace, on the street, and in their friends' homes.

Fast Trackers truly like and appreciate goods, especially those with an emotional calling. They are particularly attracted to products and services that give them conversational value, that are innovative, and that have news they can share with others. They adopt such products and services earlier than others but will drop them just as quickly when something better or more emotionally satisfying comes along.

Fast Trackers are highly desirable consumers, because they have money to spend, are not especially price sensitive, and will continue to buy even in difficult economic times. This is the main trading-up segment—above all others, they will pay a premium for those goods and services that really deliver for them. When they adopt a product, they tell many others in their segment. As a result, a lot of companies think of Fast Trackers as their main archetype.

Both of the Fast Tracker subsegments have rich pools of disposable income and are in the market to buy. The difference is that the woman Striving for Achievement identifies herself a little more by her possessions and is more driven by the need to be seen by those around her, especially at work but also on the social scene, as current and knowledgeable. So she spends more time shopping and more money on items that send signals of strength and accomplishment.

The Independent Woman has reached a position where she is secure and does not feel the need to augment herself through a display of financial strength. Nevertheless, she takes advantage of the finer things in life. She enjoys high-quality restaurants and treats herself to expensive beauty products, apparel, and, of course, shoes. She cares about possessions and tends to have a distinct personal style, so she will spend without reservation on goods and services that she deems important and valuable. She also trades down in a number of categories, including household supplies (where women in most archetypes will trade down), mobile phones, pay television services, car rentals, and car insurance.

The Independent Woman is a heavy user of consumer electronics—not so much the home variety, such as televisions and sound systems, but PDAs and computers. These women travel regularly, both for work and for pleasure, and feel that these electronics products can better meet their needs. The Independent Woman is particularly dissatisfied with financial services. She represents a particularly large opportunity for providers of financial services because she has a high income and significant net worth. She wants control over her finances and would like to work with a trusted adviser who will treat her like the successful woman she is.

Key categories of interest for Fast Trackers: Premium-quality meats and produce, electronics, travel. Fast Trackers want goods and services that make them look good and providers who can free up significant amounts of time for them. They are running a race every day, and they seek agents of convenience.

Favorite brands of Fast Trackers: Apple, Nike, Zara, Banana Republic, Sony, Ann Taylor, Gap, Chanel, Coke, Starbucks.

PRESSURE COOKER: SUCCESSFUL MULTITASKER AND STRUGGLING FOR STABILITY

Of all the archetypes, *Pressure Cooker* women feel the stress of too little time and too many responsibilities most acutely. There are also two important subsegments in this archetype: *Successful Multitasker* and *Struggling for Stability.*

The women in the Successful Multitasker subsegment are married with children and often have a career as well. They are fairly comfortable financially and have a supportive spouse, and these factors help alleviate some of their stress. They are generally happy and have a very positive self-image. They represent 15 percent of our sample. (About half of these women are also Fast Trackers.)

Key characteristics of the Successful Multitasker include these:

- She is the most satisfied with work-life balance and stress levels.
- She feels that the support of her partner is critical to her success.
- She is happy with how her partner contributes to taking care of the household and children.

- She works fewer hours at work (36) and more hours at home (23) relative to most other segments.
- She feels in control of her life.
- She reports satisfaction above expectations (53 percent).

The woman in the Struggling for Stability subsegment has a tough time managing her heavy household burden; she feels stressed and often out of control. Managing the finances is an additional challenge, and, together, chores and finances overwhelm her life. She has little time for herself and has a negative self-image overall.

Key characteristics of women Struggling for Stability include:

- Fewer working hours (33) and heavier household burden than the Successful Multitasker (26).
- Low frequency of exercise; 64 percent exercise once a week or less.
- Love is a core value for most.
- They are highly dissatisfied with their stress level, work-life balance, level of stability, and control.
- The spouse is much less supportive and helpful than that of the Successful Multitasker
- Greatest challenge: managing household and finances.

Rebecca Montague: Take It or Leave It?

Rebecca Montague feels she is living in a pressure cooker. She has too little time for her children, her work, her husband, and herself. The list of tasks is never completed. And she doesn't have enough money to buy much leverage or assistance.

Rebecca lives in Rockville, Maryland, with her husband of three years, her 2-year-old daughter, and two cats. Rebecca, a 38-year-old, earned an undergraduate degree from a liberal arts college and generally works thirty-two hours a week as a manager in a midsize company near her home. She earns $53,000 a year, and her husband, who is in sales, earns $44,000. Rebecca characterizes the family as middle-class.

Rebecca says that the demands on her time create stress, strain her marriage, and make her feel she is always running on empty. She is in a leadership position at her job that requires her to make trade-offs with her responsibilities at home, but she has no intention of quitting: $53,000 and future opportunities at the company are at stake. Besides, she and her husband are able to save about 15 percent of their earnings each month, and having money in the bank is one of her few stress relievers. Her dreams include "traveling the world with my family" and "retiring comfortably." Her biggest fear: "not having enough money."

But not all women Struggling for Stability are willing to make the compromises that Rebecca does; nor do they place such a high value on the safety and security of a steady job.

For example, Karyn Couvillion, at 34, returned to her job as a brand manager at a large technology company after taking maternity leave and found that the responsibilities in her department had doubled in her absence, but a hiring freeze prevented any new help from coming aboard. Karyn had a lot on her plate. "Does this sound familiar?" she wrote on her blog. "350 e-mails a day in my inbox. BlackBerry, cell phone, and laptop constantly in tow. Check my Outlook calendar and see that I'm double- or triple-booked in meetings every hour, plus a 7 A.M. global conference call." Her boss was less than understanding about her new status as a mom. And on top of everything else, her father was fighting a losing battle against leukemia, but all her sick days and vacation days had been swapped for maternity leave, so she could not make the out-of-state trip to visit him.

Karyn decided to quit her job. Her husband, who was facing a similar situation at his advertising agency, left his job as well, and the two decided to go into business together. "We decided that life was too short and we had had enough. What was our worst-case scenario if we quit? Having to sell our home and look for jobs elsewhere? Better than losing our marriage and our sanity," she explains. Using the savings they had been building for years, they launched a marketing consulting business they called reboot strategy, so called because "We needed to hit Control+Alt+Delete on our lives and start over." Their friends and colleagues thought they were crazy. "Rumors were flying that we had come into some family money. Nope. Just several years of saving for a rainy day." A year later, the business was booming, Karyn was able to spend more time with her child and at home, and when her father died she was by his side.[2]

The Commercial Opportunity for Pressure Cooker Women

Pressure Cooker women may be satisfied with many of the goods and services they buy, but they are constantly on the lookout for anything that will give them additional leverage over time and help them to de-stress. They feel that they are largely ignored by providers and see only stereotypes of themselves when they look at advertising claims and marketing materials.

The woman in the Struggling subsegment is particularly dissatisfied with cars. She needs a vehicle that meets the demands of her lifestyle as a busy mom who is often shuttling children—her own and those of others— to and from school, as well as to after-school and weekend events. Because her household income is stretched, she also wants a vehicle that gets good gas mileage, has low maintenance costs, and is in all ways as kind to the environment as possible. But she is not ready to completely abandon her aesthetic sense and wants a car that looks nice, suits her style, and offers attractive features.

Because taking care of the children is their top priority, all Pressure Cooker women want investment and life insurance products that will help make their future secure. And they become much heavier users of health-care services than they were when they were single.

Key categories of interest to Pressure Cooker women: Value-added food for serving at home. Household services.

Favorite brands of Pressure Cooker women: Nike, Sony, Gap, Apple, Adidas, Target, Nokia, Samsung, Dove, Kraft, Zara.

RELATIONSHIP-FOCUSED

Women in this archetype are well educated but are more motivated by having a happy family and household than by achieving a successful career. (Some Fast Trackers who focus more on family than on their job overlap with this archetype.) Relationship-Focused women are generally contented with their lives and highly optimistic. Whether single or married, they are in a serious and committed relationship. They don't have kids and aren't particularly worried about when they will, or whether they will, have children—either because they are young enough that they have plenty of time or because they are secure enough in their relationship that they are confident about having children when the time is right. They earn steady middle incomes (at least $35,000 per year and up to $80,000), but they don't care overly for goods and money. These women are focused on their partners, friends, jobs, and life experiences—travel, dining, learning.

Key characteristics of the Relationship-Focused woman include these:

- She ranks family members and friends high on her list of priorities.
- Of all segments, she spends the most time per week socializing.
- She is typically college-educated or holds a graduate degree.
- Love is a core value.
- She does not have children.
- She has a positive self-image, although she is less likely to see herself as successful.
- Of all segments, she is most optimistic about how her life will improve in the next five years.

Relationship-Focused women are typically in their mid- to late twenties and early thirties. Most are successful, enjoy their work, and have ample discretionary spending power, primarily because they have their own incomes and because their expenses are relatively low.

Unlike the other segments, these women have time. They get plenty of sleep. They exercise. They can linger over a meal. They are fit and young, so they don't need a lot in the way of personal care and adornment. Their responsibilities at work are manageable within a reasonable number of hours per day. Living is enough for them.

This happy group makes up about 16 percent of the population.

Michelle Lam Chi-san: Content with Life as It Is

There are many different ways of being relationship-focused.

For example, Michelle Lam Chi-san, 35, is a surgeon in Hong Kong. She lives with her boyfriend of eight years—also a doctor—but the two have no plans to marry. They enjoy their lifestyle as it is, she says. Their dual income allows them to live comfortably (though Michelle is quick to point out that they are by no means rich); their debts from college and medical school are paid. Michelle is now focused on her work and on enjoying her comparatively free schedule.

Medical training took up most of her twenties and early thirties. She spent six years on surgery specialty training after she graduated from medical school at age 25. "The workload in the hospital was so heavy and the training was so tight that I did not have time to think of getting married at all, let alone having a baby," she said. "In my late twenties, my parents did urge me to get married. But now they have realized that generally people are getting married later, so they are not worried about me anymore."[3]

The Commercial Opportunity for Relationship-Focused Women

These young women may be enthusiastic about goods and services, but they are not particularly materialistic. Their real loves are family and friends.

The single and younger women in this segment want to spend money on things that will create memories of this time in their lives: travel, experiences, entertainment and dining out, special goods and collectibles.

Married women, older members of the segment, and those who are planning to be married are entering the most capital-intense period of their lives. They look forward to having a beautiful home and want to be able to furnish and equip it so it looks like the home of an adult couple—not the students or young lovers they were a short time ago. They want furniture, bath fixtures, and up-to-date consumer electronics.

All Relationship-Focused women want to have one big vacation a year that they can gush about to friends and remember fondly for themselves, and that will help create lasting bonds with their husbands or boyfriends.

These women have a willingness to buy on credit and assume debt because they believe they are making very important, long-term, onetime investments for their families. They expect that their high-income years are just ahead. Even so, they are careful about buying, and they comparison-shop. They have substantially less money to spend than their older friends, and they often shop in pairs. They look for and rely on recommendations and referrals from friends, colleagues, and others they consider expert in certain categories.

Key categories of interest to Relationship-Focused women: Food, house or apartment, personal clothing, skincare and other cosmetics, restaurants.

Dream Days

As part of our survey, we asked women to describe what a "dream day" would be like: a day when they could do anything they wanted, with anybody they chose, and when any amount of money and time would be available to them.

The dream days they described, although very different, included a number of common elements such as enjoying a good meal, spending time with family, relaxing and taking time "for me," and traveling.

TYPICAL COMMENTS ABOUT ENJOYING A GOOD MEAL:

> "I'd have a beautiful dinner somewhere with a view—just my husband and me. We'd drink a cocktail or a glass of fine champagne before dinner, then have an elegant meal with stimulating conversation."

> "I'd have breakfast with my partner, daughter, father, and stepmother at their place in the country. Croissants or pancakes or French toast."

> "The day would end with my partner and me having an intimate dinner together in a lovely restaurant with fine food and wine in a romantic setting."

ABOUT SPENDING TIME WITH FAMILY:

> "We'd go to a beach with our entire family—kids and grandchildren—and have somebody fix all our meals so that we could just enjoy being together and playing at the beach."

> "We'd take time to hang out with the kids in bed, read, and tell stories. Then we'd go outdoors to see something they might be interested in. I'd have my husband home all day."

> "We'd have a great adventure as a family—drive somewhere exciting, see something we haven't seen before, do something educational."

ABOUT TAKING TIME FOR ME:

> "I'd sleep in, go for a run, take a long bath. I'd go shopping for me, have lunch in a restaurant, go to the movies, have afternoon tea, grab another movie, then have a pedicure and manicure. All on my *own*."

> "I'd have a private yoga lesson, then go to the spa and get a massage, manicure, and pedicure, and have my hair and makeup done."

> "I would sleep in and not have to get up at 5.30 A.M. when my toddler wakes up. I'd read the paper in bed with a cup of tea."

continued

ABOUT TRAVELING:

"I would invite friends and fly to a big city in Europe, like Paris or Madrid, and have a great day seeing all the new things, shopping, and eating."

"I'd travel with my husband and little girl in a culture very different from our own, complete with interactions with local people, eating native foods, and enjoying cultural experiences."

"I'd go for a yacht ride, drink champagne, and eat fantastic food in the south of France."

Favorite brands of Relationship-Focused women: Apple, Nike, Gap, Sony, Zara, Banana Republic, Target, Coke, Nokia, Dove.

FULFILLED EMPTY NESTERS

Fulfilled Empty Nesters are usually in their fifties or older. Some are still working; many are not. They are married, and for the most part their children no longer live with them. They have the opportunity to focus more on themselves and their husbands. They are concerned about health and aging gracefully, but in general they have a positive self-image.

Many Empty Nesters, even those who have left long-held jobs, are thinking about or actively engaging in some new enterprise. They want to start a business, take a part-time job, get involved with philanthropy, or seriously take up a new hobby or activity. They may want to move to a new location. Get extremely fit. Travel around the world. And some of them may find that their nest is not so empty as they might have expected: an adult child or grown grandchild may end up living with them for some period of time.

Key characteristics of Empty Nester women include these:

- Job is not a priority.
- They spend the least time at work (27 hours) of all segments.
- They spend the second-highest number of hours on household chores (25 hours).

- They have the most leisure time of all segments (62 hours a week).
- They spend the most time volunteering.
- They exercise the most of all segments; 65 percent exercise several times per week.
- Their greatest challenge is aging gracefully.
- They are not very optimistic about their financial future.

Linda Welby: A Traditional Empty Nester

This is not to say that all older women are budding entrepreneurs or are taking up skydiving. Linda Welby is 56 years old, has been married to the same man for thirty-two years, and lives with him in their home near Upminster, England, a village about twenty miles east of London. Their eldest child, a son, lives with his family in California. One daughter, the middle child, is single and lives and works in Germany as an engineer. And the youngest child, their daughter Clarey, lives with her husband and two children in the village of Hornchurch, not five minutes away from the family home in Upminster.

Linda earned her undergraduate degree at age 22, worked for a time before marriage, then left her job to raise her family and has not returned to the workplace. For Linda, life is still about family, children, and tending to others. Her greatest wish for her life is to "move away from Upminster and live closer to our children, but not on top of them." But with her family so scattered, that will be tough to do. Her dream day involves traveling with her daughter Clarey and Clarey's family to California, where they would all meet up with her son and her engineer daughter, just in from Germany.

Although the Welbys are financially secure, Linda still worries about money and is a particularly uninterested consumer of goods and services. "I dislike brands per se," she says. "I have no absolute favorite in any category. I would never be tied to any one brand."

Ashanti Vree: The Restless Retiree

Other Empty Nesters are not so settled and take some time to figure out how to fulfill themselves after they leave the workforce.

Ashanti Vree, for example, thought that when she retired she would be satisfied spending her time finally enjoying the relaxation she had earned. She rented an apartment in New York and divided her time between the city and the beach, filling her life with volunteering in her community, socializing, attending cultural events, and traveling. But after just a few years, she became restless and started thinking about another career. At the same time, the market's steady decline convinced her that working again not only would be stimulating and fulfilling but would also help her ensure that her hard-earned savings would last what might be another several decades of an active life.

She and all her female friends were consumed with the subject when they gathered for their biweekly mah-jongg game. Not one was ready to slow down, and many thought they would not have to work in these years but now still needed to earn a living. Still, they had certain demands. They wanted to work autonomously, during hours they choose, with the flexibility to travel or take time off to spend with grandchildren or aging parents. "It's just too hard to work for someone at our age," Ashanti explained, though she said that she would consider working part-time for someone if she could find a job that worked on her terms.

One friend of hers is creating a dog-walking service. Several are real estate agents, working hard, but relishing the freedom to make their own hours. One, with a background in retail, talks about seeking a way to earn money without standing on her feet all day. Others want to find outlets for their talents and experience or to turn their hobbies into careers but don't know where to start. Ashanti herself wants to turn her talent for shopping and her good taste into a personal shopping business and will probably take that part-time job until she gets the business off the ground—as long as her boss knows she can't work Wednesdays, since that is the day she visits her mother.[4]

The Commercial Opportunity with Fulfilled Empty Nesters

Most marketers ignore Empty Nesters or take them for granted. As one executive of a packaged goods company told us, "Why should we advertise to these women? They don't offer an additional meaningful subsegment for us."

Why innovate for and market to this archetype? Because they are loyal and inspirational to women in other segments. They look for meaning and quality in everything they buy. They are the core group of women who care about better food, better wine, good travel, and simple ideas for home improvements and renovations. These women dine out often, usually with their husbands but often with friends, and justify the expense by saying that it is actually cheaper than cooking for two and also more fun and stimulating than dining at home.

Empty Nesters tend to be financially stable, with pensions, Social Security payments, investments, savings, insurance, and equity in their homes and other possessions. Their expenses are usually quite low, because they have most of the things they need and are no longer acquisitive. Expenditures tend to be for things that connect them with family and friends.

Empty Nesters plan family trips and outings. They need suppliers that understand them instead of taking them for granted. They are open to new habits and they entertain regularly, talk with one another, and share good ideas when they find them.

Key categories of interest to Empty Nester women: Food away from home, wine, and travel, especially with grandchildren.

Favorite brands of Empty Nesters: Sony, Nike, Panasonic, Liz Claiborne, Kraft, Apple, Coke, Dell, Ralph Lauren.

MANAGING ON HER OWN

Widowed or divorced, young or not so young, these women are single again and having to manage their own finances and often pay their own way. They are career-driven women who value their autonomy more than love. Managing the household and finances is a challenge for them. The financial odds are often against this group, because their pensions and Social Security benefits may be lower than those of men, or their parachutes not quite as golden as they might have hoped. These women make up 10 percent of the population, and represent 9 percent of earned income.

For these women, the pursuit or protection of wealth can take precedence over the search for renewed love. They live in conditions that are usually less comfortable than they experienced before they found themselves alone. They may be disconnected from people who once formed their circle, and they may feel regret, even anger, about their change of situation.

Key characteristics of the woman Managing on Her Own include these:

- Her job is a top priority.
- She does not rank love among her core values.
- Average hours worked at job: 41. Average hours worked at home: 15.
- More than half (52 percent) rank autonomy as a core value; this is a key distinction from other segments.
- She has an average self-image—less positive than that of Fast Trackers.
- She values knowledge and wisdom.

Laura Meyer: Sudden Shift of Archetype

Laura Meyer, 36 and newly divorced, lives alone for the first time in nine years. She is a professional, earning $85,000 annually, with a good package of benefits and a healthy savings account, thanks to her habit of saving at least 20 percent of her take-home pay each month. With her ex-husband she bought a home eight years ago, and despite the housing downturn of 2008, the property has appreciated by about 20 percent and has been appraised at $280,000. She is the sole owner of it now. Laura has no debt apart from her mortgage.

Laura talks about herself as a Fast Tracker when she was younger, and she also had a period when she was Relationship-Focused—young, married, working at a good job, and furnishing a new home. But for now, she accepts that she is Managing on Her Own and takes the challenges head-on. (One of them: a nonexistent sex life.)

Laura thinks of herself as a healthy person, physically and emotionally. She is satisfied with her appearance and keeps fit through daily exercise. She has many good friends and sees them regularly, sometimes cooking for them in her home, but more often going out for a glass of wine or a meal. Among her favorite things: "Chocolate, working out and being active, lying in the sun, laughing, taking in the view of the city, good wine, and good company."

Although Laura is not happy that her marriage ended in divorce, she has no lasting regrets. "I felt trapped in the relationship," she told us. "Ten years from now, I would like to be married again. In a happy, healthy relationship. I'd like to be living in a bigger place, but still in the city. I'd like to travel more, hopefully to a few more exotic places. Other than that, though, I would say that I'm pretty much happy with where my life is."

The most important person in Laura's life right now is Laura.

The Commercial Opportunity with Women Managing on Their Own

Women who are Managing on Their Own are eagerly, sometimes desperately, looking for ways to make connections, keep themselves happily occupied, and meet like-minded people.

Many are just like Laura, who considers herself a conservative spender but likes nice things—classy and of good quality, but not extravagant. They will spend money on a special outfit for an important date. They care about their appearance and their sense of style and want to be up-to-date. They seek products that provide comfort in all ways. They are big buyers of books, both fiction and nonfiction. They watch more than their share of television. And they control 100 percent of their expenditures. They have complete freedom to spend their resources any way they want, with no complicated decision-making process involved.

Key categories of interest to women Managing on Their Own: Books and entertainment. Personal safety. Communication devices. Financial services.

Favorite brands of women Managing on Their Own: Nike, Apple, Sony, Adidas, Zara, Coke, Samsung, Target, Nokia, Gap.

MAKING ENDS MEET

The woman Making Ends Meet has a hard time in one or more ways. She is overwhelmed by managing her finances, which become a burden that drives every aspect of her life. She is truly unhappy and doesn't spend time or money on beauty or exercise. Often, a woman Managing on Her Own is also a member of the Making Ends Meet segment, as the result of a negative self-image and financial strains that often in turn are the result of a divorce or the death of a spouse.

Women Making Ends Meet may have low-paying jobs or be unable to find work. They may have trouble making ends meet on the amount they bring home or, worse, may have gotten into debt they can't handle. They may have difficult family relationships. They may have health problems or may be struggling with their weight and with a lack of fitness. This group is large enough to be disturbing: 9 percent of the population. Its members make a disproportionately small amount, 5 percent, of income.

These women come into a situation of struggling through one of many lacks, missteps, or mishaps. Perhaps the most important of these is a lack of education; we know there is a direct correlation between level of education and level of income. They may not have had the family means to attain an education or may not have found the right path to or through school. Women Making Ends Meet may also be thrown into hard times as the result of a layoff, an accident, divorce, sudden widowhood, a debilitating illness of their own or their spouse, or the illness or special needs of a child.

When such catastrophes happen, families that are already financially strapped or living on the margin can be quickly thrown into a downward spiral. If they don't have their own personal network to help them, or if their social network is inadequate, matters can become desperate. Understandably, women who are struggling have a difficult time retaining optimism and a positive attitude and become less and less able to improve their situation on their own. Their relationships with their spouse, children, extended family, and friends frequently become strained.

We may think that such women are to be found only in developing countries, but the sad fact is that plenty of them live in the United States and other developed countries.

Key characteristics of women Making Ends Meet include these:

- Few working hours (31 per week) and heavy household burden (21 hours).
- Least likely of all clusters to exercise; 59 percent exercise only once a week or less.
- Low levels of satisfaction, and high levels of dissatisfaction regarding control of their life.
- Negative feelings about themselves.

- Negative financial outlook.
- Do not save money.

Karen Dunrack: Getting By on $9,000 a Year

Karen Dunrack is a single woman who lives alone in a tiny house near the town of Bull Shoals, Arkansas, population 2,000. It's not so much a town as it is a retirement and vacation center, situated on the edge of a man-made body of water, Bull Shoals Lake. From her front porch Karen can see vacationers zipping by in their powerboats or suiting up for scuba diving, but she has no such expensive pleasures in her life.

Karen has a technical degree and works part-time, about twenty hours a week, at a small manufacturing company nearby and earns, on average, $9,000 a year. "There's never enough money," she says. "I roll extra change as my savings and then have to use it to pay bills." Her money troubles frequently cause her to feel sad.

Karen is 45 years old and, at 215 pounds, is constantly struggling with her weight. "I wish I had enough money to pay for a gym membership," she says. What's more, she smokes and wishes she could quit.

Karen does find pleasure in her friends as well as her pets: a dog and an exotic fish. When she talks of a dream day, her wants are modest. "I would get up early in the morning and drive to see my best friend in Springfield, Missouri. We'd go to a sidewalk café. Then we would go to the mall and shop for a few hours for clothes and goofy things that we don't need, but just have to have. We'd go to a nice restaurant and have appetizers and a bottle of wine. Then we'll go to a day spa and get the works done on us. We'll return to her house, sit out on the patio, and invite her neighbors over and grill outside. After dinner, we would play cards and catch up on old times."

As dreary as Karen Dunrack's life may be, it's important to note that she is well-off in comparison with the truly poor in many societies.

In India, for example, there subsists an underclass of women who perform the meanest and least desirable tasks imaginable, such as picking through trash and selling what they find, or working as "manual scavengers"—a euphemism for cleaning out the waste from houses without flush toilets. These women perform tasks that others refuse to do in order to make a little extra money per day, money that goes to feed their families.

Baby, a young woman from such a family, earns 75 rupees ($1.73) per month as a manual scavenger. The money is poor, but the way she is treated is even worse: people cross the street to avoid passing her, and "shopkeepers drop the rice to me; they won't touch me," she says.[5]

The Commercial Opportunity with Women Making Ends Meet

Yes, there is an opportunity with this segment, and it's not a cynical or exploitative one.

The woman Making Ends Meet has few resources and is very careful with her money, but she still needs to buy goods and services. She has well-established shopping patterns and thinks of Wal-Mart, Family Dollar, and other hard-discount outlets as her favorite stores. She is anxious about inflated food prices and the rising cost of living and is looking to get even more bang for her dollar. She would like value-engineered offerings that make it cheaper for her to live better. She also has a small pool of discretionary dollars, which she will spend on goods that bring her exceptional pleasure or that satisfy an immediate, sometimes impulsive need.

Women Making Ends Meet want to buy from retailers who respect them, who will provide reasonable amounts of credit on reasonable terms, and who offer alternative purchase arrangements. They want to receive value and performance for their limited dollars.

Key categories of interest to women Making Ends Meet: Cars, life insurance, investments, physicians, banking, low-cost entertainment, bargain staples, affordable treats.

Favorite brands of women Making Ends Meet: Kraft, Sony, Nike, Kellogg's, Coke, Adidas, Dell, Dove, Campbell's, Samsung.

LIFE STAGES AFFECT HAPPINESS

Life stage, economic status, social class, and educational level play a large role in women's satisfaction. We've found that, generally, women are hap-

V curve of satisfaction—from young to married to empty nester

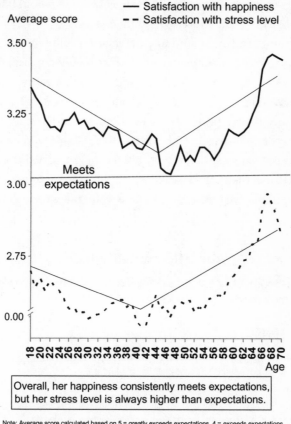

Average score

— Satisfaction with happiness
-- Satisfaction with stress level

3.50

3.25

Meets expectations

3.00

2.75

0.00

18 20 22 24 26 28 30 32 34 36 38 40 42 44 46 48 50 52 54 56 58 60 62 64 66 68 70

Age

Overall, her happiness consistently meets expectations, but her stress level is always higher than expectations.

Note: Average score calculated based on 5 = greatly exceeds expectations, 4 = exceeds expectations, 3 = meets expectations, 2 = below expectations, 1 = far below expectations; data smoothed over three years.
Source: Question Q28 of online survey; N = 11,747.

piest in their early years and again in their later years, with a pronounced dip in happiness in the long stretch of years in between.

Although women's time burden is heavy across all the life stages, they spend more time at their jobs before they have children. Single women and women without children are most likely to work outside the home and work the longest hours of all the archetypes. After they become mothers, women have more responsibility for the household. These trends are more pronounced in the United States than the overall survey data.

In addition to life stage, generational differences play a role in happiness. Younger women are more likely to work, and younger men are more likely to help at home. But across life stages, women would like their husbands or partners to help more around the house.

The greatest challenges tend to emerge at inflection points in women's lives. Managing finances, for example, becomes highly important for women when they are divorced and for older women after they retire. Achieving stability and managing stress become paramount when women have children.

Although women's priorities are different across life stages, women in most archetypes put others ahead of themselves. Single women are the only ones who rank themselves first, but once they get married they rank their husbands ahead of themselves. Children rank first for younger mothers, but once the children leave home, the husband again takes top priority.

Age Affects Everything

The survey findings show that women's behaviors and attitudes change significantly depending on what age and stage of life they are in.

OLDER WOMEN

- Work-life balance is not terribly important.
- They are not optimistic about their financial future.
- Most do not believe they will be happier in five years.
- They have more leisure time than younger women do—42 hours a week.
- They watch 50 percent more television than younger women do.
- They cook meals twice as often as young women do.
- A pet makes them extremely happy.
- They rely on their partner emotionally and economically.
- 76 percent think they are above ideal weight.

YOUNGER WOMEN

- Work-life balance is very important.
- They are optimistic about their financial future.
- Most believe they will be happier in five years.
- They rely on their partner emotionally and sexually.
- 57 percent of younger women think they are above ideal weight.

Commercially, women's unmet needs and purchasing behaviors are similar across life stages. Divorced women and widows have the greatest control of spending as they take on roles their husbands formerly played. Single women in the United States have greater purchasing power than women overall, largely because they are more likely to live on their own and therefore have less responsibility for other family members.

EVERY ARCHETYPE LOVES PETS

The needs and circumstances of the women in each archetype differ greatly, yet a few characteristics are shared by all. We were surprised to learn, for example, that the love of pets is approximately equal across all the archetypes. Half of the women we surveyed have some kind of pet—fish, dogs, horses, lizards. Eighty-three percent of these women list their pets as one of their greatest sources of happiness: 91 percent of Relationship-Focused women, 91 percent of Empty Nesters, 87 percent of women Managing on Their Own, 85 percent of women Making Ends Meet, 82 percent of Fast Trackers, and 73 percent of Pressure Cooker women.

Pets are included in many women's dream days and life goals, too— and the archetype they belong to strongly influences what they'd like to do for and with their pets.

"I'd wake up on an island with no one else around, take my dog for a swim in the ocean, read, have a massage, have dinner served to me under the stars. I'd then go back to bed with my book and my dog. The perfect day," says 37-year-old Allison from Australia, a divorcee who's Managing on Her Own.

"A dream day doesn't need money; just to be with my dog and husband is enough," says Tanja, 24, from Finland.

"Buy a large house, a vehicle, do something fun with my daughter and grandkids. Help my neighbors, my brother, and my mom. Have my cat bathed and groomed professionally," says Valerie, a woman Making Ends Meet in the United States.

"Spend the day hiking with my kids and husband, followed by dinner at my favorite restaurant. While I'm out for the day, a pet sitter grooms and bathes my cat and dog, and takes the dog for a nice jog," writes Pressure Cooker mother Laura, 38.

"If money were no object, I would like to open a dog shelter–charity.

Woman's Best Friend

Dogs are the world's most popular pet. In recent years, more and more women have become dog owners, and this has created many new dog-related commercial opportunities.

- Pet insurance is on the rise. In the United Kingdom, the number of dog owners with pet insurance increased by 17 percent. Premiums are rising accordingly, and are expected to increase by 58 percent by 2012.[6]
- In the United States, one in five employers allows pets at work, and more than 90 percent of these employers notice a positive change in the work atmosphere when dogs are in the office. "For me, it's much better than leaving him behind. If I'm late, I'm not thinking, 'I have a dog at home; I must get back,' and I feel safer walking home at night," says one employee who brings her dog to work every day.[7]
- Canine fashion is increasingly important to many women, especially the owners of small dogs. Louis Vuitton dog leashes, Burberry dog sweaters, and Pawlish (nail polish for dogs) are among the basics for doggy couture; there are also companies that custom-design dog clothes to match their owners' ensembles.
- An increasing number of affluent women hire interior designers to create a room specifically for their dog. Many of these rooms include flat-screen televisions, canopy beds, closets full of toys, and paw-print wallpaper. "If you live in a gorgeous home and have all these gorgeous accoutrements, do you really want to stick your dogs in a metal crate at night?" points out Susan Chaney, editor of *Dog Fancy* magazine.[8]

While I enjoy the corporate setup and relish a challenge, I do also feel contentment when in the company of pets," says Diana, 53, an Empty Nester in the United Kingdom.

ON INDIVIDUALS AND ARCHETYPES

Every woman is a unique individual. And every woman fits, more or less, into one of the archetypes.

Nearly all women are working and *have to work*. They have issues concerning physical and fiscal fitness. Many mention partners who do not set up dates, who fail to participate in chores, who don't listen, or who don't help enough. Many women feel underappreciated and unrecognized for their vital roles. They are concerned about their financial future. They feel no one is looking out for them and no one is teaching them, and their lifetime incomes suffer as a result of "childbearing breaks" in their employment. Women readers can grade themselves against the database: happiness, satisfaction, future economic outlook, time consumption, relationships at home and at work.

Companies that respond in full to dissatisfaction open a myriad of commercial opportunities. There is a great need to provide solutions that:

- Save time
- Make every experience fulfilling
- Participate emotionally in women's lives

The archetypes can be very useful to companies as they develop and market products and services for women. Imagine yourself as Zeus on the top of a mountain, the lightning bolts of your offering in your hands. Knowing the archetypes gives you a better chance to find the right individual and then to "own" her for life. You would create a richly imagined consumer. You would understand her latent dissatisfactions. And your company would respond with full resolve.

You would also realize that membership in an archetype is dynamic. A woman who is Relationship-Focused can very quickly find that her halcyon days of sleeping late, eating well, and taking romantic adventures with her boyfriend have turned into chore-filled marathons punctuated by short nights of not enough sleep. She has become, in short, a Successful Multitasker.

As we've seen, archetypes also overlap. A Pressure Cooker woman can also be a woman Managing on Her Own—trying to respond to all the demands of job and family (minus a spouse) and also confronting the realities of a reduced income and a fractured relationship.

This is why women's expectations of products and services are always changing and why their loyalty to a specific product, brand, or service can never be counted on. Women are unfailingly loyal to their responsibilities, to their families, and, as much as they can allow, to themselves.

No brand can expect to take precedence over those loyalties. However, any brand that enables a woman to better meet her obligations, that enhances her relationships, and that gives her back a bit of sweet time for herself will get her full attention, dollars, and a good word to her family and friends.

If you can please her pet, too, so much the better.

3.

Brands That Understand

In predictable ways, companies fail to respond to women's needs. The four R's: recognize, research, respond, refine. The ladder of technical, functional, and emotional benefits. Women buy using a value calculus. How the leaders set the tone: Do we listen? Do we respond? Do we invest? A woman wants you to reach out to her. She will tell her many friends about your winning moves and your failures.

S ome companies will be able to seize the opportunity—$5 trillion or more—to serve women better, but many will not. Those that fail will do so by making the following mistakes—the same mistakes that companies have been making for decades.

Poor product design and customization. They will fail to tailor their products to women's unique needs and challenges. They will deliver products as "one size fits all" or with only superficial customization. They will take the standard version and just "make it pink."

Clumsy sales and marketing. Their marketing will be based on outdated images or stereotypes rather than insights into today's women. Their sales or service delivery will not directly target women.

Inability to provide meaningful hooks and differentiation. Their innovations in products and services will provide no value or source of differentiation to women. They will not consider women as separate from the general customer population and will not think of women as several differentiated segments or archetypes.

Failure to develop community. These companies will fail to create a sense of community and empathy associated with a product or service, which is a source of differentiation and value for women. Personal connection and credibility are particularly important to key service categories and give brands "referral power"—women want to talk with other women about them.

SUCCESS AND THE FOUR R'S

The brands that understand women will avoid thinking at all about the "general population." They will never talk about the "market." They will focus instead on segments and segment needs. They will imagine an individual as their main consumer. They will ask, "What does Helen, Marie, or Joon want? How do we make the product or service real, affordable, within arm's reach, topical, a part of the solution for her life?"

To truly understand women and to seize the opportunity of the female economy, companies follow the four R's—recognize, research, respond, refine—particularly as they relate to women and women's needs.

Recognize. Female-centric companies recognize that women are looking for goods and services that leverage time, offer value, deliver comfort and pampering, are healthy, and are environmentally and socially responsible.

They recognize:

- The importance and influence of women
- Women's satisfactions and dissatisfactions
- The pressures and pleasures in women's lives
- The role that goods and services play in women's lives
- Characteristics women seek in goods and services

Let's follow the example of Westin Hotels & Resorts, a unit of Starwood. Westin recognized that women are important consumers and that women have particular interests and concerns regarding travel. "Today Westin guests are about 51 percent men to 49 percent women," Sue Brush, senior vice president of Westin North America, told us. "The target Westin consumer is a 'balance seeker.' Women who are very motivated and focused in their lives."[1]

Research. Female-centric companies conduct extensive research. They listen, empathize, and respond to women's dreams for themselves and their families. They build and constantly update enormous market research databases that give them a longitudinal view of attitudes, category use, responses to ideas for new products, and the unmet needs of their individual consumers.

They conduct research through:

- Intensive listening
- Analysis and understanding
- Analyzing current products and services

Westin's research showed that women were looking for a comfortable and relaxing environment with an emphasis on wellness. They wanted healthy menu choices, the chance to work out, and above all, a good night's sleep. Westin then focused its research on the components of the bed, evaluating more than fifty pillows, a hundred mattresses, and dozens of sheets and accessories. It tested many configurations before settling on a premium mattress and box spring, high-thread-count sheets and pillowcases, a duvet set, a hypoallergenic pillow, and decorative skirting.

Respond. Companies that understand women respond to what they learn from their research by offering simple, straightforward solutions that deliver the time savings women want along with emotional benefits women seek. These companies communicate with women in a way that resonates and builds relationships of trust.

They respond through:

- Design and development
- Testing
- Improvement and refinement
- Attaining perfect clarity on the value proposition
- Tailoring to segments and archetypes
- Being authentic and empathetic
- Making bold, not incremental, investments

Westin created the "heavenly bed" and made a commitment to offer this bed throughout its hotel chain. The company made a bold investment—by our estimate, the ensemble cost, at inception, about $1,010 per unit, in comparison with the $690 the hotel chain spent on a conventional bed at the time.

The launch resulted in increased occupancy rates in the Westin hotels that offer the "heavenly bed," produced a 5 percent improvement in the guest satisfaction index in those hotels, and revolutionized the industry. Many guests liked the bed so much that they purchased it from Westin at a retail price of $2,565. Said one guest, "I finally decided to buy a 'heavenly bed' because it seemed less expensive than moving into a Westin hotel." Today "heavenly beds" and the accessories line are a business of more than $20 million in annual revenue.

Haier, a "most admired" company in China, is another good example of a company that conducts extensive research and then creates a product based on its findings. Haier designs its refrigerators taking into account women's height and the length of their reach, and configures the compartments so that kids can serve themselves easily without having to ask Mom for help.

Refine. The companies that appeal to women constantly *refine* their products and services to respond to new research, changing conditions, and shifting sensibilities. Their product lines don't stand still—these companies are constantly searching for improvements in design, materials, and applications, and for ways to save users' time.

They refine by:

- Understanding the marketplace
- Merchandising
- Developing captivating displays
- Delivering authentic and nonstereotyped communications
- Creating communities

Following the success of the "heavenly bed," Westin continued its pursuit of health and wellness in the context of a hotel.

The bathroom came next, followed by the gym. Women, Westin discovered, wanted more privacy when working out than men did. "We created a few rooms in most of our hotels that have fitness equipment in the room," said Brush. "If you reserve a room with a treadmill in it, and you still don't work out, then you really have no excuse!" In many Westin rooms, Wii Fit is available. Then Westin expanded the "heavenly" concept to its spas. Its research showed that women wanted a retail component in the spas, and this finding led to a rapid expansion of the sales of Westin's White Tea line of candles, potpourri, and diffusers.

According to Brush, the focus on wellness and the success of the "heavenly" concept have led to higher satisfaction on the part of guests, high occupancy rates, and an ability to charge higher room rates: "Women are much more discerning than men, and are willing to pay more for wellness. In fact, our research shows that women will pay $11 more per night for Westin vs. $9 for men. If you can please the women, the men will follow."

The Ladder of Benefits

As companies focus on the four R's, they must also keep in mind the *ladder of benefits*: a durable, flexible concept that we defined in *Trading Up*, the first book in our series of explorations into the socioeconomic forces affecting how companies create products and why people buy them.

The ladder of benefits is highly relevant to an understanding of what women look for in goods in any economy and in every part of the world. There are three "rungs" on the ladder: technical, functional, and emotional.

Technical. Women look carefully for technical differences between products, in terms of design, technology, and materials. Subsumed within this technical level is an assumption of quality—that the product will be free from defects and perform as promised. Innovation driven by technical improvements provides the base layer for marketing claims.

Crème de la Mer, a superpremium skin cream, built its success on a technical innovation. In the 1960s, Max Huber, an aerospace engineer at NASA, suffered a severe facial burn when a chemistry experiment went awry. To speed the healing process, he began to experiment with various concoctions that he thought would help him heal and would minimize scarring. His breakthrough came when he discovered the unique properties of a variety of sea kelp growing in the Pacific Ocean off the coast of California, where he lived. Huber developed a fermentation process that combined the sea kelp with other natural ingredients and resulted in what he called a "miracle broth," which became the signature technical ingredient of the appropriately named Crème de la Mer.

Functional. Women do not prize technical differences as such. Rather, technology must contribute to superior performance. It's not enough to incorporate "improvements" that don't actually improve anything but are intended only to make a product look different from others or appear to be changed. Women want technical claims to translate into better functioning, greater convenience, and time savings. Functional benefits can be described in the consumer's own words and deliver real and specific advantages.

The formula worked for Huber, and he shared it with a few friends. Women found that the cream worked better than any other on the market. It made their skin softer, firmer, and virtually creaseless. The story of Huber's discovery spread by word of mouth, and he began to produce his crème in small batches and distribute it through his company, La Mer.

Emotional. The technical and functional benefits—along with other factors, such as brand values and the reputation of the company among women and society—must combine to engage the female consumer emotionally. Women are not fooled by products that make a shameless play for the emotions but fail to deliver on the technical or functional level. Many marketers make the error of rushing to emotional claims with no basis in technical and functional benefits. Consumers see this as a betrayal.

Over time, Crème de la Mer developed a cult following. People learned about the "miracle broth" and its recipe, which in addition to the sea kelp, included calcium; magnesium; potassium; iron; lecithin; vitamins C, D, E, and B_{12}; and extracts of citrus, eucalyptus, wheat germ, alfalfa, and sunflower. The ingredients had to be fermented for four months, with intense bursts of light and sound at various points along the way.

Women found an emotional benefit in Crème de la Mer, not only because it made them look and feel better but because they loved the story of the aerospace engineer who had developed a secret formula from one of the uglier natural ingredients, sea kelp—and because distribution was limited to a small number of those who were in the know.

The Value Calculus

All consumers, and women in particular, rely on a personal value calculus to assess every product or service from several perspectives. They consider its technical, functional, and emotional merits. They compare it with similar products they know about or can get information about. They gather knowledge and opinions about usage and satisfaction from many sources, especially their personal networks, and they consider how a purchase will affect their personal situation and their relationships with others. Finally, they put all these factors into an unwritten and even unconscious—but nonetheless rigorous—calculus, which enables them to determine the product's value to them at an any given moment and to decide whether its price justifies purchasing it. When the perceived value exceeds the asking price, the product will fly off the shelves. When the opposite is true, virtually no amount of sales and marketing activity will move it.

Coach is known for its ability to create products that make sense for women's value calculus—at the high end. This company pilots early production of bags in different colors and styles. It puts them into stores and watches closely to see how women respond to them. When an item or collection sells well, production quantities are immediately ramped up. When sales are poor, production is reduced.

But the value calculus differs from region to region and city to city. So every Coach store has a different assortment of products, aimed at the women of that area. The Madison Avenue store has a different assortment from the Northbrook, Illinois, store. The Naples, Florida, store has a different assortment from the factory store thirty miles north.

Each store gets a thorough review every month—what's selling and what's not; what categories get more shelf space; what categories get less shelf space. Coach is one of the great experimental vehicles in retail today.

IKEA, too, has a fine sensitivity to women's value calculus—at the lower end. IKEA's product range offers multiple options for every possible area of the home in different styles and at a variety of price points, all affordable relative to the products' quality.

Sometimes "Making It Pink" Works

According to Verizon Wireless, 71 percent of women make the decision about their family's wireless choices, including phones and service plans—and Verizon's research agrees with the findings of our survey. As a result, makers of smartphones are beginning to design and market their products specifically to women. Research in Motion, based in Waterloo, Ontario, has run ads for its BlackBerry phones in *Elle*, *Martha Stewart Living*, and *O*, Oprah Winfrey's magazine.

"You are not seen as a geek anymore if you have a smartphone," said Carolina Milanesi, research director at Gartner Group, as reported in the *New York Times*. "Women, including wives and mothers, need to keep track of their busy lives, too."

Creating smartphones for women involves making these phones smaller, sleeker, free of unnecessary features, rich in multimedia capabilities, cleaner-looking, *and* cheaper. Nielsen's research shows that women are more price sensitive than men but only half as likely to care about whether they have used a specific brand before.

And yet, some traditional characteristics of women's products still work with regard to electronics. The color pink, for example. RIM and Verizon Wireless decided to create a pink BlackBerry Pearl for a Valentine's Day promotion but discovered that getting the right shade of pink wasn't easy. They ended up with a subdued shade that would work in all kinds of settings—professional and social—where a woman might find herself. "It was the only color that was purely driven by the female audience," said Mark Guibert, vice president for corporate marketing at RIM. "Years ago the market was much more focused solely on function. Now there is more focus on lifestyle." So sometimes making it pink is the right approach. Just make it the right shade of pink.

Women use their smartphones to organize their business lives and their personal lives—as well as those of their friends and children. They use the notepad function of the iPhone to track restaurant and movie recommendations. They snap photos at concerts and family events, and post them on the Web. One woman used her iPhone to prove that she had been invited to a party at a nightclub even though her name wasn't on the list of invitees—she showed the bouncer the e-mailed invitation. According to Nielsen, two-thirds of women say they use their smartphones primarily for pleasure, whereas only 42 percent of male smartphone users say this.[2]

OPRAH WINFREY: UNDERSTANDING THE MORE THAT WOMEN WANT

No brand—for that is what she truly is—understands what more women want from their lives better than Oprah Winfrey.

Winfrey understands the multiple roles women play and the way they juggle their personal wishes with the wishes they have for their families.

She knows only too well their struggles with appearance, fitness, health, and weight. She has been a member of more than one archetype and seems instinctively able to understand and empathize with them all. She shares women's desire to create a better world as well as their cynicism about false or cynical marketing claims. She is also practical and sensible, and she talks about products and services and how they can help. She has known poverty and wealth, abuse and adulation. She knows that no matter how wealthy and successful one becomes, the fundamental challenges don't go away.

Winfrey is always connecting with her market. She has 300 customers present in her studio every taping day. She watches, listens, and pursues. She has a deep emotional connection. She operates on two planes: she takes her followers to a higher place—making a difference in the world—and offers practical, specific help on health, family, finance, and managing in the workplace. She is sympathetic, respectful, and engaging. She is willing to change the mix and provide drama, education, and titillation.

She has built a business worth $2.7 billion, based on exceptional insight into what women want and how they can get it. As of 2008, *The Oprah Winfrey Show* had been the number one talk show for twenty-two consecutive seasons, watched by some 44 million people a week in the United States and broadcast in 144 countries. In addition to the show, Winfrey's empire includes books and magazines, the popular Oprah's Book Club, radio shows, a TV and film production company, the Oprah Store, Oprah's Angel Network, two personal foundations, and an amazing network of affiliations and associations that span the globe and intertwine with an impressive range of industries, charities, and endeavors. She is reputed to be the richest African-American in the United States (although she herself does not make this claim and will not confirm it) and is often cited as the most influential woman in the world.

We found variations of Winfrey's motto—"Live your best life"—sprinkled throughout the 8,000 pages of comments we collected from women around the world, and we saw many more versions taped to refrigerator doors in the homes we visited during the course of our research. To women around the world, Winfrey is a welcome shot in the arm, urging them to complete their education, think big, and change the world.

Rebecca, a 42-year-old schoolteacher in a New York suburb, says, "I greatly admire Oprah because she went relentlessly after her dream and never stops moving and growing. She tells it how she sees it. There's no beating around the bush. She uses her wealth to help others less fortunate and to call our attention to where our help is needed in the world."

Winfrey's distinct form of public confession as therapy has earned the name "Oprahfication." Winfrey leads the way by making her own confessions on camera, about topics including money, love, abuse, relatives, pain, illness, weight gain, and weight loss. Because she is willing to reveal so much about herself, her guests follow suit. But the show never devolves into the kind of over-the-top confessions of *The Jerry Springer Show* and others like it, thanks to Winfrey's intelligence, her seriousness of purpose, her signature smile, and her pealing laugh, which serve to keep the balance between revelation and entertainment.

Winfrey's range of interests is deep and broad. Her empire includes endeavors in all media, and she addresses an encyclopedic range of topics including:

- *Spirit*. Self-knowledge, inspiration, body image, emotional health.
- *Health*. Wellness, disease prevention, weight loss, exercise, nutrition, disease management.
- *Style*. Fashion, hair, makeover, makeup, skin, body.
- *Relationships*. Couples, dating, sex, parenting, family, friends, abuse.
- *Home*. Decorating, home improvement, outdoor living.
- *Food*. Recipes, menus, party planning, eating out.
- *Money*. Personal finance, debt, career, parents and kids, real estate, couples.
- *The world*. Environment, health, global issues, culture and travel, education, people and politicians.

Winfrey's empire continues to expand. In 2006, she signed a $55 million, three-year deal to launch a channel and host a show on XM satellite radio (which merged with Sirius in 2008 to become Sirius XM Radio). Oprah Radio is a channel "dedicated to helping you live your best life" and featuring shows hosted by a number of her expert friends and colleagues. In 2008, Winfrey and Discovery Communications announced plans to create OWN: the Oprah Winfrey Network, a multiplatform media venture designed to entertain, inform, and inspire people to live their best lives.

OWN is scheduled to debut in 2010, and to be received in more than 70 million homes.

As Winfrey has built her company and expanded her activities, she has steadily remade herself as well. From being a radio news reader, television news anchor, and featured talk show host, she has now become a major philanthropist and one of the most influential people in the world.

She wields power in many ways. She is a phenomenon in the publishing world. Her book club can make a book a success, whether it is a new title or a classic. Book publishers say that when a book is chosen by Winfrey's book club, the incremental sales are 500,000 to 5.5 million additional copies. When she selected John Steinbeck's *East of Eden*, first published in 1952, it climbed to the top of the best-seller lists. If Winfrey says, "Read this book," millions of people go out and buy it.

She is a political force. Her support of Barack Obama is considered one of the critical ingredients in his defeat of Hillary Clinton in the hard-fought race for the Democratic nomination. She initiated the National Child Protection Act, known as the Oprah Bill, which established a national database of convicted child abusers. *Vanity Fair* says that Winfrey "has more influence on the culture than any university president, politician or religious leader, except perhaps the Pope."

The women in our survey confirm what the media tell us. Winfrey is loved for many reasons:

- "She makes the world a better place just by being in it and doing what she does."
- "She's not afraid to be revolutionary and always tries to bring out the best."
- "She's a great advocate."

Oprah Winfrey is also a woman who gives back. She is one of America's top fifty philanthropists, having given away an estimated $303 million just through her personal foundation and another $80 million raised through her Angel Network. The Oprah Winfrey Foundation offers educational grants for children and their families throughout the world. The Oprah Winfrey Leadership Academy Foundation supports her Leadership Academy for Girls in South Africa. Winfrey's Angel Network is a

They Love Oprah Winfrey in Saudi Arabia

Nayla, a young Saudi homemaker, reveres Oprah Winfrey. "I feel that Oprah truly understands me," she says. "She gives me energy and hope for my life. Sometimes I think that she is the only person in the world who knows how I feel."

Nayla is not the only Saudi woman to feel a special connection to the American media mogul. When *The Oprah Winfrey Show* was first broadcast in Saudi Arabia in November 2004 on a Dubai-based satellite channel, it became an immediate sensation among young Saudi women. Within months, it had become the highest-rated English-language program among women 25 and younger, an age group that makes up about a third of Saudi Arabia's population.

Some Saudi women say that Oprah's assurances to her viewers—that they can take control in small ways and create lives of value—help them find meaning in their often cramped and usually veiled existence. "Oprah dresses conservatively," explained Princess Reema bint Bandar al-Saud, a co-owner of a women's spa in Riyadh called Yibreen and a daughter of Prince Bandar bin Sultan, the former Saudi ambassador to the United States. "She struggles with her weight. She overcame depression. She rose from poverty and from abuse. On all these levels she appeals to a Saudi woman. People really idolize her here."

The Oprah Winfrey Show, with Arabic subtitles, is broadcast twice each weekday on MBC4, a three-year-old channel developed by the MBC Group with the Arab woman in mind. The largest-circulation Saudi women's magazine, *Sayidaty*, devotes a regular page to Ms. Winfrey and copies of her magazine, *O,* which is not sold in the kingdom, are passed around by women who collect them during trips abroad.

"Oprah is the magic word for women here who want to be heard," says one of her loyal fans.[3]

public charity that inspires people to make a difference in the lives of others. The Leadership Academy and Angel Network have spent about $50 million for education, advocacy for women and children, and community building.

All of Winfrey's work is designed to further her stated mission: "To be a catalyst for transformation in people's lives, to help them see themselves more clearly and to make the best choices they can using stories, real people's experiences, information and ideas. Our intention is to create moments in which people can connect to the truest sense of themselves and build from there."

Winfrey has accumulated an estimated $2.7 billion in net worth by helping women get more of what they want.

P&G: DELEGATING THE CLEANING ROUTINE

No matter how successful, wealthy, and influential women become, they still keep a careful personal eye on the cleanliness of their homes. On one of her shows, Oprah Winfrey said, "It is my dream to have a home that is always neat and clean so I wouldn't wince when someone does a drop-by visit." And she is not alone.

Our research into home cleaning shows, beyond the shadow of a doubt, that the triple challenge of time has permanently changed this routine. A woman still has responsibility for a healthy, hygienic home, but she no longer does the deep periodic cleaning of every inch of the house that was typical ten or twenty years ago. Her routine now involves spot-cleaning in the bathroom and kitchen, cleaning everything else only as needed, and delegating cleaning chores, when possible, to her husband or the kids.

The greatest beneficiary and possibly the principal architect of this change is Procter & Gamble, and at its heart is the Swiffer Sweeper, one of P&G's most surprising and unlikely successes. Our consumers tell us that sweeping or cleaning the floor is one of the toughest and most relentless tasks, and it never ends: as soon as a household member or pet walks across a newly cleaned floor, the routine begins all over again. For some women, a clean floor is a very personal statement about pride, love, quality of care, and engagement.

Swiffer is a sweeper fitted with a disposable wet or dry cloth that traps dirt, dust, and hair. Consumers tell us Swiffer Sweeper is better than sweeping or mopping, because it literally lifts dirt up and captures it rather than pushing dirt around as brooms and mops—those primitive devices—do. Swiffer Sweeper is lightweight, easy to use, and remarkably effective.

A. G. Lafley, the CEO of P&G, a master at drawing insights from qualitative research, and a man who relentlessly travels the globe doing his own version of in-home research, describes the success this way: "The beauty of Swiffer is there's a standardization of the process. So there's basically a handle, an implement, and there's a cleaning cloth. Some are wet. Some are dry. Some are shaped in a funny way so they can dust. And some are electrically aided. But it brings much more predictability to the process. [A woman] likes the fact it's convenient, it's not too backbreaking. They're very easy to manipulate. It's easy to dispose of."[4]

Swiffer Sweeper had first-year sales of $200 million in the United States.

It has expanded into a variety of forms and shapes; has captured share from mops, brooms, and electric and electronic cleaning systems; and has made itself useful in several additional ways, including cleaning furniture. It is supported and protected by extensive patents.

P&G is a bold and persistent competitor. It has consistently expanded into new categories (from its origin as a candle maker to soap, paper, cleaning, beauty, healthcare, and beyond). When P&G is successful, this expansion means that incremental sales do not cannibalize existing product lines. At its size and required growth rate, it has no choice but to take this approach. Swiffer Sweeper is a good example of expansion. P&G had no tradition in the mop and broom business, but its research highlighted significant consumer dissatisfactions. Sweeping "stirs up" dirt, and mopping is a hassle. P&G understood further that the person doing the cleaning in a household is time-starved and stressed out. It identified and licensed a product, developed by a Japanese competitor, that seemed to fill the bill.

P&G launched Swiffer Sweeper with the intention of creating a revolution. It created buzz through copromotions, demonstrations, and "tell a friend" coupons. It followed with a media campaign that defined "five stages of clean," revealing them one at a time in the first round of advertising. It created a series of line extensions, including Max (extra-large), Wet, WetJet, Mitts, Dusters, Swiffers for all surfaces, SweeperVac, and Dust & Shine furniture polish. All the while, it has continued to improve the core product with new technical features, such as deeper ridges in the sweeper pads, that have led to functional benefits (faster and deeper cleaning) and even greater emotional satisfaction.

Lafley sees Swiffer Sweeper as an example of the power of understanding. "We're very much attuned to [a woman's] needs, her habits and practices, what she can afford, and what she really needs and what she really wants. I try on a regular basis to get into stores, not just alone, but also to shop with women when they are doing their weekly shopping. I try to get into homes whenever I am in emerging markets, I'm always in homes. When we are in homes, we prefer to do the job with them so we can see what they do and talk to them about what they are doing and what we can do better."[5]

"We knew that cleaning certain surfaces was a dirty, ugly task," says Lafley. "With Swiffer it's a relatively easy, simple, and hygienic task, because when you're done, you slip the cloth off, and it's disposable. We didn't see the end-vision of what the Swiffer lineup of implements and cleaning cloths would be. We were thinking about floor cleaning. Now we're thinking about all the surfaces in the home. A whole new way of cleaning."[6]

P&G and the Four R's

P&G pursues the four R's relentlessly and almost automatically.

Recognize. P&G has always recognized the value of attracting women consumers and leveraging their insights at all stages of product development. The company recognizes that women have different needs across ages, incomes, geographic regions, and archetypes; and it segments its offerings to respond to these needs. From its beginnings as a soap and candle maker, P&G understood that it was a company serving women as they emerged economically and demographically. In the last decade it has made the transition to understanding that the margin it can charge for products is a function of the amount of emotional appeal it can deliver. (And how well this appeal relates to technical and functional benefits.) It has built innovation around increasingly tight definitions of segments: age, income, lifestyle, family composition, work process, and psychographic type.

Research. Regarding its investment materials, P&G says, "We invest more than $2 billion a year in R&D, nearly twice the level of our closest competitor, Unilever, and roughly equal to the combined total of our other major competitors. Virtualization is enabling P&G brands to codesign products with consumers. . . . Consumer modeling and simulation saved P&G about seventeen years of design time in the last year alone."[7] P&G seems to have a voracious appetite for understanding consumers through primary research. Participation in these efforts is expected of all P&G employees, from entry-level brand associates to the CEO.

Respond. Disruptive innovation creates new categories, new segments, or entirely new sources of consumers. These are innovations that address consumers' needs no other brand or product has met. Virtually all of P&G's billion-dollar brands were created with disruptive innovations.

P&G technologists have been responsible for several products that revolutionized their product categories and spawned many imitators:

- Tide, heavy-duty synthetic detergent
- Crest, cavity-prevention toothpaste

Leslie Wexner: You Can't Sell to Women
as If They're Men Wearing Skirts

Leslie Wexner, the 71-year-old founder and chairman of The Limited, says the best technique for understanding what women want and what they will buy is simply to observe.

"I've been selling to women since 1963. Women, even as little girls, care much more about appearance then men do. Some women will have 24 different shades of lipstick in their drawer. Men do nothing like that. You can't just sell to women like they are men wearing skirts. You have to understand the differences, the differences in mind-set. Women stare at themselves in the mirror. When a woman tries on a pair of jeans, she looks at herself. She cares deeply about her appearance. You have to understand why fashion is sexy. You see it with little girls and how they play with dolls."

Leslie Wexner has been one of the most prolific inventors in retail history. He started The Limited, started Express, invented Bath and Body Works, re-created Abercrombie, cloned Limited Too, morphed Victoria's Secret from one store into a global icon, and turned the Victoria's Secret offshoot Pink into a $1 billion brand. His legacy is over $20 billion in annual retail sales, many spun out from his empire and run as independent companies.

As a 21-year-old graduate of Ohio State University living in Columbus, he worked part-time at his parents' dress shop. "I saw the differences then," he said. "The fashions were different then, of course. But when a woman tried on outfit after outfit you could see it. Women want to be striking and beautiful. Cosmetics is a case study. There is no equivalent of makeup for men."

Wexner says the key to success is the ability to project and understand and have empathy for the consumer: her life, her life stage, her goals and ambitions.

"Narcissism, sex, and beauty are real whether it be Cleopatra or Angelina Jolie. In history, women had enormous influence. Today they are rising to absolute power. They are the most valuable consumers. Guys are rational and cheap. Women are willing to spend on becoming more beautiful, even in a recession."

Wexner says apparel has lost its emotional appeal as the world has shifted to a more casual lifestyle. He has experienced forty years of apparel price deflation and sees the survivors as low-price, fast-fashion houses like H&M and Zara.

"The fashion cycle is less important. People are looking for different choices for emotional content. Every woman still wants to be as sexy as she can be."

Wexner's latest experiment is the recrafted Bendel chain. He has been tinkering with the model for years and concluded that the best way to grow it is with fashion accessories at the core. "We just opened the model store. It's a tightly edited assortment. The goods have high emotional value. Women love it. Goods are flying out the door. If they buy during a recession, you can only imagine what it will do during the upside."[8]

- Pampers, disposable diapers
- Pert Plus, first haircare product that combined cleaning and conditioning
- Actonel, osteoporosis therapy that reduces the incidence of spinal fractures
- Crest Whitestrips, teeth-whitening strips

Refine. At its core, P&G is a relentless competitor, constantly developing new products, refining existing ones, and shedding those that no longer have potential for growth. It focuses on its biggest brands and provides full support to dominate advertising, promotion, and in-store merchandising. It is willing to make dramatic bets, acquiring high-margin, high-growth businesses and aggressively reducing overhead costs to pay for the acquisitions. It uses its geographic infrastructure to make the acquisitions pay out. It takes process discipline to a high level, applying this discipline across marketing, sales, productivity, and operational programs. It will, in a very methodical way, spin or sell off brands that don't contribute, earn below-average margins, and provide fewer opportunities for growth. The result is a portfolio of twenty-two brands with $1 billion in annual sales or more.

GERBER: SUCCEEDING BY LISTENING TO MOTHERS

The baby food producer Gerber knows how to create and maintain a lasting emotional bond with its customers—especially the Pressure Cooker women, and most of all the Successful Multitaskers. Take, for example, its most recent ad campaign, which features mothers-to-be in delivery rooms, being coached along in their contractions while quiet yet inspiring music plays in the background. The effort, called "Anything for Baby," generated an outpouring of emotional responses from women across America. The commercials quickly found their way onto YouTube and the blogosphere, where entire communities of women sprang up around them to watch, rewatch, and comment on the joys and terrors of motherhood.

"I don't know about you, but when I saw this I found myself barking out a totally involuntary sob of gut-punched emotion," blogged one new mother.[9] Anne Mohl, vice president–infant nutrition marketing, said, "Before, ads showed bucolic orchards and farmers to reassure moms of the quality and safety of Gerber baby foods. But we weren't leveraging an emotional bond with moms as much as we should have. The new campaign celebrates moms, all the hard work they do for their babies. Gerber is there to be her supporter."[10]

Resonant though the ads are, however, they're not the primary reason that Gerber has enjoyed category leadership for nearly eighty years. The actual reason is the company's consistent practice of listening to mothers, and delivering products and services that accurately address their desires and concerns. Gerber continues to expand its product line in keeping with the company's ongoing and intensive research into what mothers want for young children. Gerber's ability to maintain a high standard of quality and dependability in its products, while simultaneously adapting to meet changing demands and emerging trends, has made it a market leader and a household name.

Gerber has been a steady innovator over the years—starting with its line of strained peas for babies in 1928; introducing small glass jars in 1960; and, in 1990, launching Graduates for Toddlers, a line of fruit puffs, chopped vegetables, and other foods that are easy for toddlers to manage and require little if any cleanup.

When Kurt Schmidt took over as CEO of Gerber in 2004, the company had an approximate market share of 75 percent, but its growth was slowing, largely owing to a drop in the birthrate. Schmidt realized that the company had enormous untapped potential, particularly in the Graduates for Toddlers line. He recognized that women were having fewer children, often later in life, when their earning (and spending) power was at its peak and their life experiences would be likely to influence their views on child rearing and nutrition. He put more resources behind product development and marketing for the toddler foods, emphasizing the convenience and dependability they offered to busy working moms. Over the next few years the toddler line grew significantly, accounting for 39 percent of Gerber's overall growth by 2007.

In 2007, having taken notice of Gerber's continued category leadership as well as its growth spurt since Schmidt's arrival, Nestlé bought Gerber for $5.5 billion, 15.7 times earnings before interest, taxes, depreciation, and amortization (EBITDA), and a 2.8 sales multiple. Nestlé bought a global brand with iconic status, 100 percent awareness, 97 percent purchase pene-

tration, and 82 percent market share in the United States. It also holds leading positions in Mexico, Central America, and Poland.[11]

As part of Nestlé, Gerber is expanding even further. In August 2008 it
introduced the Gerber Graduates for Preschoolers line with seven products
ranging from fruit twists to microwaveable lunch and dinner entrées.[12]

A startling number of young children in the United States are overweight, and this number has doubled in the last twenty years. And according to a recent study published in the *Journal of the American Dietetic Association*,
sponsored by Gerber and known as the FITS study (Feeding Infant Toddler
Study), many children under 2 are consuming an unhealthy diet: up to a
third of children under 2 consumed no fruits or vegetables in a given day,
according to the survey. Nine percent of children 9 months to 11 months old
ate fries on the day of the survey. For those 19 months to 2 years old, more
than 20 percent had fries. Hot dogs, sausage, and bacon also were staples
for many children—7 percent in the 9-to-11-month group, and 25 percent in
the older range. More than 60 percent of 12-month-olds had dessert or
candy during the day, and 16 percent ate a salty snack. Those numbers rose
to 75 percent and 27 percent by age 19 months.[13]

Many mothers told us they felt uncertain about what to feed their
young children once they were on solid foods, and many more admitted to
feeling guilty about feeding these children whatever was fastest or easiest;
but they said they were facing a constant battle against time, a tight budget,
and picky eaters. For many of these Pressure Cooker moms, the Gerber Graduates line makes their lives a whole lot easier while relieving their guilt
about their children's nutrition.

One mother of two children, Megan Sontz, 37, is a devotee of Gerber.
Because she is a middle-school science teacher, Megan's days are filled with
grading, planning, and communicating with students' parents in addition to
caring for her own children and running her home while her husband works
full-time. The Sontz children—a boy age 3 and a girl of 10 months—are at
very different stages of development, and it takes all their parents' energy to
keep up with them. The hardest thing of all, according to Megan, is getting
them to eat properly. The Gerber baby foods were smooth sailing, but the
transition to solid foods has been "nothing short of a pain," Megan says.

"The Gerber Graduates for Toddlers line really takes the guesswork
out of solid foods," she continues. "Both of my kids really like these meals,
and I like that they're really quick to prepare. My 10-month-old wakes up

from her nap hungry and screams until she has something to eat. These meals are ready in thirty seconds. And the puffs are amazing. The star shape is really well thought out. It allows the baby a very easy way to pick it up and my 3-year-old loves them, too. They keep my babies occupied so we can eat meals, clean up, and attend to other things. They are easily supervised and cleaned up. They dissolve so well that there is no mess!"[14]

Megan was delighted when she learned that the Graduates line is extending to preschoolers. "Frankly, the best thing about it is that they're in the same aisle as the other Gerber foods." Megan laughs. "My son is basically guaranteed to like them because he's liked all the other Gerber foods. I'll know he's eating food that's good for him and in the right proportions. And grocery shopping with two young children in tow is enough of a nightmare without strolling up and down the aisles looking for something my 3-year-old won't throw on the floor, so this is going to save me a lot of time and aggravation."

The acquisition of Gerber has taken Nestlé to the number one position globally in baby meals and drinks. Total Gerber (Baby/Toddler Foods) market share is 82; Graduates market share is 89 percent in the United States.

Gerber illustrates the power of focusing on a segment of women. If you can engage them about their deepest concerns, create a relevant product response, and launch the product with authority and conviction, you can expand your domain. Growth at constant or higher margins drives enterprise value.

This is what listening and responding to women can accomplish.

PART II

The Key Categories

Food. Fitness. Beauty. Apparel.
Categories of Greatest Dissatisfaction:
Financial Services and Healthcare

4.

Food

Answering the Daily Question "What's for Dinner?"

Food is both a pleasure and a challenge for women. Even primary categories like food hold rich opportunities for transformation. Companies can add value, improve time savings, increase the health, safety, and ego benefits. Women worldwide do most of the food preparation for their families. They want suppliers to combine healthy choices, convenience, and affordability. Women see food as adventure and education.

WOMEN AND FOOD

Food presents a pleasurable problem to women. Women say food is their greatest source of satisfaction and the top category in which they will trade up. Meals offer opportunities for connection with family, friends, lovers, and potential lovers. Providing meals is one of a mother's most fundamental obligations and most constant duties. Sharing a meal is one of the most primary behaviors.

Though some sociologists and social commentators predict that—because of our fast-paced, fractured lifestyles—the family dinner hour is a thing of the past, our survey results did not bear that out. Ninety percent of women say they prepare and eat at least one meal a day at home, and 82 percent eat together as a family at least once or twice a week. Eight-seven percent of these women feel that they are competent in the kitchen. Forty-one percent say they have above-average cooking skills, and 4 percent rate themselves as gourmet cooks.

Women want food to taste delicious, look and smell wonderful, and also be nutritious and healthy. They want variety, ease of use, and convenience. Mothers think of food as fuel to help their children grow and thrive. Wives try to serve food that will help keep their husbands fit and healthy. And women love food that delivers a sensuous experience, delivers the nutrition they need, and doesn't get them in trouble with the bathroom scale.

When asked to choose among a list of things that make them happy, 67 percent of the women in our survey selected food—just ahead of sex, at 66 percent. Women in three segments—single women, empty nesters, and divorced women—said that food is their number one source of happiness.

Each archetype or segment has a particular take on food. Singles cook less but indulge more. Pressure Cooker moms must balance the expression of love through food with the time they have available to devote to meal preparation. Fulfilled Empty Nesters are particularly concerned with the connection between food and health and social sustainability.

When we asked women around the world to describe their "dream day," they were likely to mention food as an important part of it. "I would prepare a picnic and we'd share it at a wonderful beach. At the end of the day, we'd have dinner at our favorite restaurant, and then sit by a campfire, sharing warmth, conversation, and laughter," said an American woman, age 62. A 32-year-old Argentinean woman said that her day would start with a "super American-style breakfast," proceed to "lunch in an open-air restaurant," and end up with "coffee at a bookstore."

As much as food brings pleasure, however, it can also be a chore. Every day, women everywhere face the same old question for themselves and from their families, "What's for dinner?" For many women, preparing dinner is a nightly drama that rarely wins applause. Every ten minutes of food consumption at home requires five or ten times that amount of time in preparation and cleanup—planning meals, making lists, shopping, cooking, setting and clearing the table, and washing up. Working women like Nicole Green have to squeeze food-related chores into tiny pockets of time—on the way to work, while waiting for a child at an after-school activity, on a Sunday afternoon.

Our research shows that, around the world, 88 percent of women have sole or shared responsibility for grocery shopping and 85 percent for meal preparation. American women in all age categories spend at least seven hours per week on grocery shopping and cooking, and that number increases to eleven hours for married women with children. Even though drive-through outlets, takeout and delivery services, microwave dinners, prepared foods, frozen pizza, and other time-saving and convenient forms of food have become staples of modern life, women still feel tremendous responsibility for providing meals that are healthy, taste good, satisfy everyone, and fit the family budget.

Food is also one of the consumer's important budget items (just below home and transportation expenses), one that can be adjusted but never eliminated. So women are constantly looking for the right combination of convenience, affordability, delight, and nutrition.

Jeannie Clark: Family Foodie

Jeannie Clark finds tremendous satisfaction when a meal she prepares—whether it's a sit-down dinner with the whole family or just the items she packs in a lunch box—brings smiles to the faces of the people she loves most. Shakespeare wrote that "music is the food of love," but Jeannie Clark might argue that food itself is the food of love.

Jeannie, 36, is an elementary school teacher, a fit and slender woman with animated gestures, a bright smile, and short blond hair. She lives in Florida with her husband, Roy, a plumbing contractor, and their two kids: Kimberly, age 9; and Justin, age 5.

Jeannie considers herself something of a foodie and would like nothing better than to spend her days browsing through cookbooks, shopping for ingredients, cooking wonderful meals, and lingering over them in the evening with her family. That life, however, is not in the cards—at least not at the moment. Like many Successful Multitaskers, Jeannie is so busy that she doesn't have the time to conduct research into food products or to do a lot of complicated cooking. However, she still wants to serve her family good-tasting, nutritious meals as often as she can, and she is bound and determined not to cave in and take the easy route of fast food and too many packaged goods. "I believe that what we feed our kids is what they become. If they eat junk, they get hooked and that's what they'll do for their whole lives. I can help them make better choices."

Jeannie's ally in her fight for the right foods is Whole Foods. Even today, twenty years after its founding, Whole Foods still comes up with a winning formula for women who really care about food. As Jeannie puts it, "Whole Foods offers a complete approach to taking care of the family, wellness, and healthy eating."

Jeannie's day looks pretty much like that of Nicole Green, although she is not so much of a Fast Tracker. She gets up earlier than Nicole—the alarm usually goes off at 5 A.M.—and then fixes the kids' breakfast, drops them off at school, and drives about eight miles to the school where she teaches. After a day of teaching, she picks up the kids and returns home, where she spends what's left of the afternoon cleaning the house and preparing dinner. Roy also starts early—he's usually out the door by 6:30 A.M.—and works long hours, arriving home around 6 P.M. The family eats dinner—yes, as our research shows, most American families *do* eat dinner together regularly—around 6:30. After dinner, Jeannie works on her lesson plan for the next day, grades papers, and gets the kids to bed. Around 11, Jeannie and Roy, unlike Nicole and Peter, usually spend half an hour together—talking or perhaps watching a bit of television. That is usually the first and only moment that the two have some quiet time together. Jeannie rarely gets any time completely to herself—for a cup of tea or a quiet glass of wine, or to read a book or watch a show.

The Clarks lead a busy life, but it is a less stressful life than the Greens'—there is less striving, less need for perfectionism, less tension between husband and wife. They live in a development in southern Lee County, Florida, in a house which they bought in 2002 for $350,000. Even after the worst of the housing decline in 2008, the house had still appreciated in value by about 12 percent. They are settled in their neighborhood, and the house is big and well-situated enough that they have no plans to move before the kids leave home. The Clarks' annual household income is $120,000, which puts them solidly in the top quintile of households in the United States. Roy's business is doing well—the world will always need plumbers, and he's good at his work—and Jeannie feels secure in her job as a public school teacher. They are reasonably certain that their family income will continue to grow, that their house will slowly appreciate in value, and that they can put away enough money to help their kids with college when the time comes. Retirement is still a good three decades away, and Jeannie is confident that she'll have a decent package and that Roy may be able to sell his business or at least save enough money to make them comfortable when they are no longer working full-time.

Back to food.

In the fall of 2008, Jeannie invited us along on a shopping trip to a Whole Foods market near her home. Unlike Nicole Green, who does her grocery shopping in twenty-minute bursts, Jeannie shops less often and spends forty-five minutes on each trip. She has been shopping at this particular market since they moved into the neighborhood, and she still looks forward to her visits there. "I know that people think Whole Foods is too expensive or too PC. I don't see it that way. To me, Whole Foods is more than a grocery store. It's an adventure. A place to learn. Everything I pick up teaches me something about diet, good food, and healthy choices."

Jeannie led the way into the market, and we found ourselves in a bright, appealing environment, brimming with well-displayed merchandise. Our first stop was the fish counter, where she greeted the fishmonger by name.

"Hi, Leon, what's good today?"

"I have some nice Chilean sea bass, Mrs. Clark. I know you like that. But have you guys tried tilapia? It's on sale today at $7.99 a pound."

There follows a discussion about the qualities of tilapia, whether children would like it, and how it might best be prepared. Leon hands Jeannie a recipe card that includes three ways to cook the fish—an oven-baked version with a bread-crumb coating, fried with Creole seasoning, and broiled with a mustard topping. Leon says that he likes to marinate the fish in a hot Tabasco sauce and then grill it outdoors.

The fish looks good, the recipes are appealing, and the price is right, so Jeannie decides to go for the tilapia. They pick out the fillets together, and Leon weighs out a little over a pound and a half of fish. Jeannie nods, and he wraps it carefully.

On to the produce section.

It would not be an exaggeration to say that Jeannie is somewhat obsessed with fruit and vegetables. She takes a deep breath as we enter the produce area, stops, and looks around at all the choices before getting down to work. She quickly buys the basics she needs: lettuce, tomatoes, a cucumber, apples, and pears. Then she considers the avocados. "I love avocados. They're high in monosaturated fat, which is not so great if you have a lot of fat in your diet, but we don't eat much red meat or other fatty foods, so it's OK. Besides, they have more potassium than bananas and lots of vitamin B." She smiles. "They had an avocado expert in here last week and I learned a lot about them. Besides, I *am* a schoolteacher. I like learning these things."

Jeannie picks up an organic avocado and checks the price. "Ouch, $2.49 each!" She debates with herself and then decides to splurge. "It's a dollar more than the nonorganic variety. But I only need one. I think we can swing that!" After a few more stops—for cereal, bread, peanut butter, and other items—we take a detour to the cheese counter, another of Jeannie's favorites. There is a special display today of parmigiano reggiano, a variety imported from an Italian family dairy; it costs $27.99 a pound. The cheesemonger hands her a sliver and Jeannie takes a taste. "I love it. Too many people think of parmigiano as a grating cheese for spaghetti. I love to eat it straight. It's made from pure unpasteurized cow's milk." Even so, Jeannie passes on the cheese. "It's just too expensive. One dollar more for an avocado is one thing. Half a pound of this would cost five dollars more than a domestic brand, which also tastes really good. The kids won't notice. Roy might, but he'd agree with me."

We pass a sign on the wall that states the Whole Foods approach to its business: "Our goal is to sell the highest-quality products we possibly can. We define quality by evaluating the ingredients, freshness, safety, taste, nutritive value, and appearance of all of the products we carry. We are buying agents for our customers and not the selling agents for the manufacturers." There is more about how Whole Foods chooses products free of artificial preservatives, colors, flavors, sweeteners, and hydrogenated oils, and how it gives preference to organically grown foods and food that supports health and well-being. "We appreciate and celebrate that great food and cooking improve the lives of all of our stakeholders. Breaking bread with others, eating healthfully and eating well—these are some of the great joys of our lives."

Jeannie shrugs when we point out the sign. "Well, I'm not usually very big on corporate pronouncements like that. But, in Whole Foods' case, I actually believe it. I see this store as a partnership between the company and the customers. They believe in the importance of food. They love it like I love it."

Still, Jeannie is not without reservations about Whole Foods. She is acutely aware that its attention to sustainability and health comes at a price and that it is so expert at merchandising that she is often tempted to buy things that aren't strictly necessary. "Even though we have a good household income, that doesn't mean I can go crazy shopping. I need to keep our food expenditure under $200 a week. But the food presentations here are so beautiful and the staff is so friendly, it's far too easy to go over budget. That's why I always write out a list before I come and force myself to stick to it."

So, as much pleasure as Jeannie took in her circuit around the store, she was very careful about what she actually put into the cart. She murmured to herself as she pushed her cart along, keeping a running tally of the number of items she had purchased and a rough estimate of the cost, and always keeping a watchful eye on her list.

"I buy as much fresh and healthy food as I can within my budget at Whole Foods. But I don't usually buy staples or commodities, like rice and flour, paper products, and household cleaners. I can get all those things much cheaper at Wal-Mart or at Publix. Plus, there are some foods that Roy and the kids really want, like certain kinds of cereals, that Whole Foods doesn't carry."

As we headed for the checkout, we passed a section devoted to yoga. "I'm thinking about doing yoga at home. I just don't have enough time to get to class as often as I'd like. But if I had a video, I'd have no excuse not to exercise." So she decided to splurge on a yoga DVD even though it wasn't on her list. "I couldn't buy that at Wal-Mart or Publix," she said. By our calculations, the DVD, which was produced by a Whole Foods subsidiary, added about $6 in gross margin to Jeannie's cart, bringing the total gross margin to about $55.

Jeannie Clark, like so many other multitasking mothers, despite her skepticism of marketing claims and her general disregard for brands, has completely bought into the Whole Foods story—even if some items are too pricey and even if an item is not on her list. Problems with food contamination at other stores make her particularly grateful for Whole Foods' approach. "I think of shopping at Whole Foods as buying food insurance. I know that they are looking at the quality. They're making sure the producers haven't added anything bad to what should be good. I trust that their organically grown products actually are organic and free from artificial preservatives, colors, and flavors. Whole Foods promotes organic, local, sustainable agriculture. It is a company that does good."

WHOLE FOODS: AN EARLY UNDERSTANDING OF WOMEN'S FOCUS ON HEALTHY EATING

Whole Foods has understood the relationship of women to food since its founding. Today, despite rapid growth, some difficulties with acquisitions, an emphasis on private-label products that some women resent, and a reputation (somewhat undeserved) for inflated prices, Whole Foods continues to be the market of choice for three core segments: young Fast Tracker women who often purchase prepared foods for lunch or dinner; affluent Pressure Cooker moms; and women Managing on Their Own who are very concerned with health and nutrition.

Whole Foods has always been more than just a business. It was founded by John Mackey, a college student studying philosophy and religion at the University of Texas in Austin. Desperate for a girlfriend, he thought he might meet some interesting women at the university vegetarian co-op, so he joined up. "I was in my early twenties and open to alternative lifestyles. I thought, 'I bet you get a lot of attractive, interesting women in a vegetarian co-op.' "[1] He was right. He met a woman named Renee Lawson Hardy. They dated, dropped out of school, scraped together $45,000 from family and friends, and opened a health food store that they called SaferWay—a dis on the Safeway grocery chain. It was the first health food store in Austin or, for that matter, in Texas, or so they claim.

There wasn't much space at the store, so Mackey and Hardy stored food products in their apartment. This eventually got them kicked out, and they decided to live at the store. Since they did not have a proper bathroom with a shower, they used the hose from their Hobart dishwasher as a shower.

In 1980, John and Renee partnered with two friends (and rivals), Craig Weller and Mark Skiles, to merge SaferWay with Clarksville Natural Grocery. That led to the opening of the original Whole Foods Market. At 10,500 square feet and with a staff of nineteen, the store was large relative to the typical health food store of the day.

Less than a year later, on Memorial Day 1981, Austin was hit with its worst flood in seventy years. Whole Foods' inventory was destroyed, and many of its fixtures and much of its equipment were damaged. The losses came to about $400,000, and Whole Foods Market had neither enough cash to rebuild nor insurance coverage to fall back on. But in just that one year of operation, Whole Foods had created a loyal following. Friends, customers, suppliers, and neighbors arrived to help clean up, repair the equipment, and get the store back in operation. It reopened in less than a month. And Whole Foods has been that kind of company ever since: a movement as much as a retailing operation.

Whole Foods caught a wave of growth and tied itself to the fortunes of three groups of women: urban professional female singles, affluent mothers, and women over 55 attempting to secure a healthy future by following a special diet. As dedicated as these women are to Whole Foods, they all shop—as Jeannie Clark does—at many stores for groceries and household products. Whole Foods is the place to buy fresh meat, poultry, and organic fruit and vegetables. Commodities are better bought elsewhere. They don't think of the store by its derisive nickname—"Whole Paycheck"—and in fact they believe that the prices are "not that much higher" than at other stores and that the products are worth the extra money.

Fast Trackers, especially, buy into the company's claim of "highest quality, least processed, most flavorful and natural foods possible—unadulterated by artificial additives, sweeteners, colorings, and preservatives." They respond to a labor force that really seems to enjoy working at the company and consistently earns Whole Foods its *Fortune* ranking as one of the best 100 companies to work for. Affluent moms visit Whole Foods to buy fresh produce, meat, and fish. Empty Nesters, many of whom are on special or restricted diets, love Whole Foods for its quality, variety, and careful labeling. Singles tend to visit the store more frequently than women in other segments, often eating prepared meals there or buying these meals to take home for dinner. One devotee we met, for example, visits the store nine or ten times per month and spends about $20 each time.

Seventeen percent of Whole Foods' customers account for about 45 percent of total store visits and 30 to 35 percent of sales. Of the Whole Foods shoppers who spend $200 a month there, 76 percent are female.

Although Whole Foods has been successful at attracting and retaining female customers, it is not an entirely satisfactory case study of value creation.

The company has certainly become a leader in the natural food industry, and has done so largely by executing a business strategy known as the roll-up—purchasing dozens of small players and regional chains and incorporating them into the fold. These include Wellspring Grocery, Bread and Circus, Mrs. Gooch's, Fresh Fields, Bread of Life, Nature's Heartland, California's Food for Thought, Harry's Farmers Market, Select Fish, and Fresh and Wild.

With each new acquisition, Whole Foods rebranded the stores, installed its own systems, upgraded operations, improved quality, and built sales. The process has enabled Whole Foods to grow to a chain of 270 stores, including outlets in the United Kingdom and Canada, generating $8 billion in annual sales, while maintaining a 34 percent gross margin, which is very high by grocery store standards.

Not everything at Whole Foods has been, or continues to be, brilliant business. A number of the acquisitions have been controversial and have produced less than stellar results. The purchase of the Wild Oats chain, for example, required Whole Foods to take on $700 million of debt, much of it at variable interest rates and involving various fees and covenants that seemed reasonable prior to the financial crisis of 2008 but looked less tolerable thereafter.

Wild Oats brought Whole Foods into fifteen new markets, but the synergies promised in cost reduction, purchasing scale, and distribution leverage have yet to fully pay out. The acquisition was on-again, off-again, thanks to government intervention. Although Wild Oats has effectively been absorbed, Federal Trade Commission activity on the deal is still pending. Whole Foods' stores in the United Kingdom generated annual losses of $18 million in 2007. It built stores in the center of London at peak rents. The Wild Oats acquisition continues to dilute earnings.

For suppliers, Whole Foods can be a challenging customer. The company is demanding about ingredients, processing, packaging, and labeling, and knows how to deliver gross margin for Whole Foods but not necessarily for suppliers. It is a "value"-driven company. It places a strong emphasis on private-label brands with skinny manufacturer margins and sources a significant share of products locally directly from farmers. In these ways, Whole Foods is remarkably like Wal-Mart.

The economic environment of 2008 presented Whole Foods with a problem as a retailer, even though total sales continued to grow as a result of space additions. The value of Whole Foods, however, depends on sustained same-store growth and expansion into new markets. The strategy worked well for a time, and the company's market value reached $8 billion in July 2006. But overly rapid expansion, the outlay of a great deal of cash for acquisitions, and leveraged deals like the one for Wild Oats combined to make Whole Foods look vulnerable, and its market value fell to $1.4 billion at the end of 2008.

Although total sales continued to grow, comparative store sales, the ultimate measure of performance, were flat, and cannibalization of old stores by new stores had a negative impact. Not surprisingly, analysts blasted the management team at Whole Foods for making bad investments in nonperforming real estate, overpaying for acquisitions, and ignoring the details of cost structure, cash flow, and operating leverage.

For Whole Foods to continue to create value, consumers must continue to increase their income, increase their appetite for good and healthy food, and be willing to pay premium prices for what Whole Foods offers. But as the economy worsened in 2008, consumers had less money to spend. As a result, the company began emphasizing value and price, both of which challenge the economics of high-cost players like Whole Foods.

Whole Foods initiated a program called the "Whole Deal" and promoted—with coupons and budget recipes—the ways that Whole Foods could become part of the consumer's solution to tough times and tightened belts. It pushed its 365 private-label brand harder than ever, offered more case discounts, and sold more products in bulk. It also decided to focus on smaller stores—about 35,000 square feet—and cut back the size of its new stores accordingly. The smaller stores, the company believes, can deliver the products that women want, can achieve higher sales per square foot, and are more appropriate in lower-density geographic regions.

Although the economic crisis of 2008 may have ended the era of seeming infallibility for Whole Foods, the company's story is far from over. It is likely to close some stores, relocate and remodel others, open new stores offering lower prices, and pay closer attention to its use of capital. But Whole Foods has too good a core business to go away. Count on Jeannie Clark and millions of women like her—apostles of healthy eating and adventurous shopping—to remain loyal, convert others, and keep visiting Whole Foods for its brilliant combination of pleasure, obligation fulfillment, learning, and value.

What Is It About Breakfast?

Breakfast holds a special place in the hearts of women around the world. In their survey responses, especially those about "dream days," they mention breakfast often. It is generally the most informal, intimate, and pleasurable of meals. It does not have the complexity or expectations (or expense) associated with dinner, or the banality and often purely functional nature of lunch. Breakfast is also wonderfully linked to sleep, bed, bathing, and, often, sex.

A few quotes from the survey:

"I would start with breakfast in bed. After eating, my partner and
I would slowly make love."

"I would take a leisurely bath, put on my new outfit and have my driver
(I would have a driver!) take me to the finest
restaurant for breakfast."

"I would meet my mother for a late breakfast and tea, served on a terrace
overlooking a glorious and lush garden, complete with homemade
baked goods and strong tea served with silverware and bone china,
and then take a walk through the garden."

"McDonald's has the best coffee and biscuits. I love them.
I could eat breakfast foods all day long."

"After a long bath, I would have a nice breakfast served to me,
followed by a massage, pedicure, and manicure."

"I would have breakfast in bed with my partner and
spend an hour or two reading the papers or a good book.
Then I'd have a bubble bath and put on brand-new clothes."

"I would sleep until I awoke—no alarm clock. I would have
a delicious breakfast with eggs over easy, pancakes, sausage,
and real maple syrup."

"I'd get up at six in the morning, walk along the beach, come home,
and my partner would cook me a fabulous breakfast."

"After waking up and being pampered and attended to by my staff
I would have a luscious breakfast. Then I would jet off to an island
for a vacation, taking my staff with me."

THE OPPORTUNITY IN FOOD

Women's deep engagement with food translates into a willingness to spend serious money in food- and cooking-related categories—including ingredients, meals away from home, and cooking equipment.

As much as women love food, they have far less time to prepare meals than they had in the past. They are often overwhelmed by choices. Their work responsibilities can make shopping difficult. They want to be able to create healthy meals that don't require a dozen exotic and hard-to-find ingredients and that don't take half a day to prepare: meals that taste good enough to appeal to their tastes, which have been refined by reading cooking magazines and dining out when they have time. And, oh yes, why can't shopping be an enjoyable experience rather than a soulless trek down endless aisles of jars, cans, and boxes?

Across all life stages and segments, women say they will trade up to get the kind of quality they want in the food they purchase for consumption at home. And women in many of the segments will also trade up to get higher-quality food when they buy meals outside the home. Married women without children, in particular, say they will spend more at restaurants that offer superior-quality food. Married women with children and empty nesters are less likely to trade up on restaurant meals but will spend more to get better-quality kitchen appliances. There may not be enough time to take the family out for a meal, but at least cooking at home can be made as enjoyable as possible!

In short, delivering food of the kind that women really want is one of the largest and most essential business opportunities of the female economy.

TESCO: CONVENIENCE ABOVE ALL

Whole Foods answers the question "What's for dinner?" in one successful way, but there are many women who are not so taken with food as an adventure and are less concerned with organic ingredients and local produce than they are with convenience and value. For these women, Tesco, based in the United Kingdom, has come up with an innovative and welcome alternative for purchasing what they need: its stores are essentially one-stop destinations for almost all household items—groceries and nonfood essentials as well, including books, furniture, gasoline, and financial services.

Tesco offers a variety of retailing formats to meet the needs of particular communities. The Metro stores, approximately 7,000 to 15,000 square feet, are designed for busy population centers—such as Covent Garden in London—where food and prepared meals are the focus. Tesco's Giant Extra stores, of 60,000 square feet or more, are one-stop shopping destinations that stock larger items and items sought by suburbanites: garden furniture and electrical equipment are sold alongside personal care and children's supplies, and of course groceries, groceries, groceries.

In all its stores, Tesco's mix of grocery items is extensive and usually features several of its private-label brands. These include Tesco's Kids line, its Value selection, and the "Free From" range of foods, created for people with food allergies and intolerances. Tesco's Free From products contain none of the ingredients that affect most people who have food allergies, such as gluten, wheat, and milk. There are more than 150 products in the range, packaged with the Free From logo—a purple disk and yellow lettering. All of Tesco's own-label foods, not just the Free From line, have an allergen information box on the back of the pack so the customer can check to see if there are any ingredients that might be troublesome to her or her family.

Banking is perhaps the most intriguing of Tesco's diverse range of products and services, but you can also find books, CDs, and DVDs; PC, photo, and gaming gear; phones; home electrical supplies; furniture and kitchen products; home and garden products; do-it-yourself and auto supplies; jewelry and watches; sports and leisure gear; toys and games; baby and toddler products; clothing; optician services; and travel services.

Tesco Personal Finance Services offers savings accounts, credit cards, and car insurance. In 2003 it was the most successful new entrant into the United Kingdom's financial services market. Apparently, customers feel comfortable conducting their financial affairs with Tesco, largely because they trust its name in groceries. Surprising logic, perhaps, but logic nonetheless.

Tesco understands that every minute counts for its time-pressed customers, the majority of whom are women and are not fussy about how they interact with the store—in person or online. Miranda Cardew, 41, for example, manages a busy household in London. She's married, is raising four children, and works two days a week. She does most of the household chores herself, as her husband works long hours. When she does have time to shop, she prefers spending her time in "nice markets or delis," but not in the supermarket. It is for women like Miranda that Tesco created its Web site.

"I order a weekly delivery via the Internet," she says, "and supplement it with a box of organic produce and meats from a local shop."

Tesco.com, launched in 2000, sells a huge array of groceries, wine, books, flowers, toys, and hundreds of other nonfood items, from gasoline to electronics, as well as a number of services including a large number of health and weight loss products and services—such as diabetes screening and smoking cessation programs, dial-up, broadband, and financial services. As a result, Tesco has a 70 percent share of the online grocery market in the United Kingdom. The convenience makes it easy for customers to spend more money than they might in the physical store—regular online customers in fact spend $600 to $1,400 more per year than store-only shoppers.

Whether at its stores or online, Tesco builds customers' loyalty through its Tesco Clubcard, which enables the estimated 14 million active cardholders[2] to receive rewards, such as discounts and coupons. Tesco uses the information gathered from its cardholders to classify customers into segments—not a mere six segments (like ours) but *twenty-seven* lifestyle types, including the adventurous foodie and the gourmet wine buyer. The women we surveyed don't seem to mind being classified in this way. A 47-year-old loyalist who took part in our survey says, "Tesco always delivers great value for money. Even their Value products range taste great. Tesco also has the added bonus of providing a loyalty scheme which we have used to get free entertainment and holidays."

Tesco has experienced astounding growth since its founder, Jack Cohen, opened a grocery stall in East London in 1919. It became a private limited company in 1932 and floated its first stock in 1947 at 25 pence per share. Since then, Tesco—like Whole Foods—has pursued a strategy of acquisition, steadily acquiring hundreds of stores throughout England. The Leicester location was declared the largest store in Europe in the 1961 *Guinness Book of World Records*. Annual sales exceeded £2 billion in 1982. In the mid-1990s, the company began expanding internationally, and it now operates in twelve markets in Europe, Asia, and North America. It has leading positions in Ireland, Poland, Hungary, Slovakia, Thailand, and Korea. In the United States it is a fairly new arrival: its first Fresh and Easy market opened in Phoenix, Arizona, in 2007.

In the United Kingdom, Tesco's more than 280,000 employees make it the largest private employer, but more than half of its selling space is now outside the country and more than 160,000 employees work in the international divisions of Tesco, serving 28 million customers, generating £13.8 billion in sales, and producing £700 million in profits.[3] From 2003 to

Denise Morrison: The Values of Soup

Denise Morrison, president, North America Soup, Sauces, and Beverages, for Campbell Soup Company, understands that today's women want products to reflect their own personal values and that, in food, this means good nutrition and good taste. "When we designed our Select Harvest soups, we were looking for low calories, less sodium, clean labels, whole grain pasta, no MSG. It was a direct response to all the negatives. We wanted to give consumers good food for their family that is convenient, nourishing, and affordable."

To do so, Morrison followed the four R's. She recognized the size of the opportunity and seized it as primary for Campbell's. She conducted deep ethnographic research and focused on two key segments of women: working mothers and older women without children. She reviewed thousands of recipes before testing the Select Harvest sub-brand. "Select Harvest is designer soup for women."

She initiated a comprehensive upgrade of the condensed soup business. It aimed at growth and has delivered, breaking a seventeen-year decline for the company's core high-margin soup business. She's doing it again with the V8 brand and with Italian sauce. "We have focused on the needs of women for wellness, quality, convenience, and value. We're helping them make simple meals that take less time to prepare."

Morrison knows well the challenges of being a working mother trying to make ends meet. "I know what it is like to live on a budget. I ate chicken thirteen different ways. I take that attitude to our products, to our marketing. I know what it's like to be a working mother. You get pulled in fifty different directions. I used to help my daughter with her papers, editing and faxing from the Marriott Courtyard when I was traveling. It's a struggle."

Morrison takes the values she gained in childhood to work with her every day. Dennis Sullivan, Denise's father, was an executive with AT&T. He and his wife Connie raised four daughters, all of whom now work in business. Both parents taught their kids the value of education, goal-setting, hard work, and discipline. Sullivan would roust the girls out of bed at 6 A.M. to exercise together. He expected Denise to read a book a week and write a report for him. "He would say, 'The author has two years of research in this book and you can get it all in a week!' That's the way he raised us."

"We were encouraged to have a greater purpose," says Morrison. "I'm not working here only to make soup. I want to nourish people's lives." [4]

2008, Tesco's sales growth increased 17 percent, contributing to its annual total shareholder return (TSR) of 14 percent.

By tapping into so many simple but persistent consumer needs at once, the Tesco brand has become so powerful that it has reached beyond the food aisles where it started into many aspects of women's lives. Tesco saves women the irritation of running around to accomplish many different errands—and, as a result, Tesco has outperformed the market. The company leverages its trusted brand to continually improve the shopping experience and expand its role in people's lives. Tesco noted in its annual report, "We try to make our customers' shopping trip as easy as possible, reduce prices where we can to help them spend less and give them the convenience of shopping when and where they want—in small stores, large stores, or online."

AMY'S KITCHEN: AFFORDABLE HEALTH ON THE RUN

Whole Foods is the food brand with the most devoted apostles; Tesco provides convenience that women greatly appreciate; Amy's Kitchen has found another successful take on the food market: healthy, affordable, fast food with enough variety to appeal to women's interest in learning and enough taste to score reasonably well on sensuality.

For women with little time to do virtually anything related to food—shopping or cooking—Amy's Kitchen has created a healthier, greener alternative to takeout pizza, frozen dinners, and prepared meals laden with salt and fat. "Amy's offers a great variety of products, and I like all of them," says Danali, a 55-year-old woman who participated in our survey. "There are ethnic varieties, frozen foods, canned foods—all made from organic ingredients and always tasty." With a household income of about $42,000, Danali considers it important that "the price is reasonable, too."

A husband-and-wife team, Andy and Rachel Berliner, started the company in California in 1987, when their daughter, Amy, was an infant. The concept came from their own lifestyle: they wanted quick, convenient meals made from natural ingredients, and they figured that other people would want the same. "There's nothing like fresh food, but when you don't have time, at least we want people to feel good about having to eat convenience foods," Andy Berliner told *BusinessWeek*.[5]

Amy's 150 varieties of vegetarian frozen meals—all certified as organic—include canned soups and sauces, breakfast burritos, and potpies. More than 50 percent of the vegetables that Amy's uses in its products are grown within 200 miles of the company's production facilities. All-natural recipes appear on the packaging. The Web site features diet plans, recipes, and tips for healthy living, as well as guidance and support for a vegetarian lifestyle.

The eponymous Amy herself, now a college student, writes a blog about organic food and the healthy lifestyle.

Not only are Amy's Kitchen products organic; they consistently win taste tests, especially those conducted by women's magazines. In 2008, *Body + Soul* chose Amy's veggie burger as one of the best for the barbecue season. Magazines like the healthy appeal of Amy's Kitchen, too. The January 2008 issue of *Women's Health* named three Amy's Kitchen products among the 100 best packaged foods for women.

And Amy's Kitchen does not limit its "green/eco-friendly/organic" focus to the meals themselves—it is on a quest to become a fully sustainable company. The company uses paper rather than plastic trays. Its cartons are made from unbleached boards with no poly coating on the inside, where it might come into contact with the food, and a clay coating on the outside so that no chemicals will leach through the board. Every package has recycling information printed on it.

Women say they like Amy's Kitchen because its products fulfill many of their wants and needs. With prepared food, there is typically a trade-off between health and convenience. This brand enables women to feel good about the meals they choose for themselves and their families. It nicely balances their obligations and their aspirations—they can be good mothers and meal providers, and also feel that they are contributing to the welfare of the planet.

Amy's Kitchen has been very savvy about how it prices, presents, and retails its offerings. Although the company charges a premium for its products, it packages them in such a way that the per-package price is comparable to that of products from competitors. And rather than sell only through premium channels, such as organic or health food stores, Amy's Kitchen has various distribution channels, including supermarkets and warehouse club stores. Women need not go out of their way, or make an extra trip, to find them.

Amy's Kitchen has been one of the first to enter the organic foods category, and it continues to grow. The company, which is still family-owned, achieved a compound annual growth rate (CAGR) of 20 percent in 1987–2005. In fiscal year 2007, the company reached $80 million in revenue. The brand is sold in ten countries, and Amy's Kitchen plans to expand into Latin America and Asia. It seems to be poised to continue successfully tapping the need for healthy, tasty, easy-to-prepare, eco-friendly meals.

No wonder the Web site EveryWomansVoice.com, on March 11, 2008,

---

Recipes from Food Providers Make Women's Lives Easier

Since the majority of women in our survey take sole or shared responsibility for grocery shopping and meal preparation—a daily obligation—they appreciate any kind of assistance they can get. The food companies that we profiled oblige by making recipes available. These help people use the company's products and further build brand loyalty. Providing recipes is a very effective way for companies to create "habituation"—get themselves fixed in the customer's purchase cycle, become seen as a family staple, and achieve longevity in the household.

Tesco prints a magazine that is distributed in the stores and posted on tesco.com, with a cookbook section listing seasonal recipes. A separate magazine, *Real Food*, is devoted exclusively to recipes.

Whole Foods gives out seasonal recipes in booklets about such topics as party planning and guides to a particular kind of produce. The recipes on its Web site promise "healthy, wholesome cooking ideas," and give nutritional analyses and special diet information. It also distributes a weekly video podcast cooking show, "Secret Ingredient."

Though Amy's Kitchen specializes in prepared meals, its Web site lists several recipes in its breezy LemonSlice section, hosted by Amy Berliner, the company's namesake and daughter of the founders, Rachel and Andy Berliner. The recipe section, called the Lunchbox, states its goal as giving healthy meal ideas. "Whether that means opening up a box of Amy's, or getting a little creative with some of Amy's great foods, we can help." Customers are also invited to send in recipes.

---

chose Rachel Berliner, cofounder of the company, as a "Woman We Love." "It's easy to admire Rachel and the rest of the Amy's team for their great-tasting and healthy products, but it's their commitment—to keeping Amy's a family operation, to using sustainable practices, to supporting organic farmers, to keeping their customers in mind all the time, to raising consciousness about the benefits of eating healthy foods—that makes them stand out!"[6]

ALWAYS ANOTHER MEAL TO PREPARE

A large percentage of women feel that they do not have the relationship with food they would want to have. They must make too many compromises and trade-offs. Pressed for time, they succumb to the lure of fast or packaged food. Pressed for money, they settle for less quality. Pressed for knowledge, they accept food that does not meet their standards or align with their values. Pressed for energy, they fall into a routine of cooking the same old thing.

The companies profiled in this chapter perform well on the four R's. They all have recognized the importance of women in their category, have done considerable research into the wants and needs of their archetypes, and have responded with distinct offerings. Whole Foods, despite its recent focus on value, gives the highest priority to freshness and flavor, variety and adventure, and organic criteria and sustainability, and sets prices accordingly. Tesco delivers on convenience. Amy's Kitchen takes an interesting path that combines a bit of both. When it comes to refinement, Tesco seems to be the winner. This retailer keeps adding items and offers several distinct ways to buy. Whole Foods is struggling a bit when it comes to refinement: its move to smaller stores suggests a retreat from its traditional focus on growth and ever-increasing store sizes and product selections. The refinements at Amy's Kitchen are so far primarily about product variations; but refinements to the business model may be in the wings—perhaps dedicated Amy's Kitchen stores?

The opportunity remains large. There are, no doubt, better ways to make shopping easier and faster for those who don't have time to shop or don't like to. Ingredients could be bundled to make shopping and cooking easier. Women want value-added components that improve taste, variety, and healthy attributes as well as exotic ingredients at lower prices. Like Jeannie, they look for guarantees of freshness, safety, and pure ingredients. They also want to make connections with food producers around the world who ensure social responsibility and encourage philanthropy.

Most of all, women seek new, better, and more answers to one of the world's oldest questions: "What's for dinner?"

5.

Fitness

Still Looking for a Holistic Solution

Women want to be thin, but healthy; fit, but not necessarily buff. There are three main approaches to a better body: fitness without bodybuilding; a network of support; and packaged diets and total food replacement. Women in the vast middle market require a special lens: low cost, easy solutions, broad access. Twice as many women think they are overweight as actually are. Women constantly struggle with their health, weight, and fitness and are eager for a better way. They represent an untapped opportunity.

WEIGHT AND FITNESS

You can never be too rich or too thin" is a statement variously attributed; but whoever first said it, the sentiment has resonated in women's minds for decades. Still, just as the perspective on being rich has evolved over the years (having a lot of money without giving back is no longer admired), the value of "thin" has also changed. Just being thin, without accompanying fitness or overall health, can be as disturbing as it is appealing, given the prevalence of eating disorders among girls and women and the popular (largely media-driven) obsession with looking thin.

Today, women still want to be thin—and 68 percent of our respondents believe they are significantly or slightly higher than their ideal body weight—but they are likely to be concerned about their bodies in a more holistic way. They think about weight in relationship to overall fitness, physical health, and mental and spiritual wellness. Although the statistics about increasing obesity, both in the United States and in other countries around the world, have received a lot of attention, some research suggests that there are not always direct negative connections between overweight and compromised health. According to a study published in 2008 by Mary-Fran Sowers, a professor of public health at the University of Michigan, almost one-quarter of adults whose weight is considered "normal," or approximately 16.3 million people nationwide, have displayed one or more of the risks usually associated with being overweight—such as high blood pressure and high cholesterol. And slightly more than half of overweight adults, or about 36 million people, and almost one-third of obese adults, 19.5 million people, were deemed metabolically healthy.[1]

So science and the emotions sometimes part ways. For women, fitness is a particularly complicated issue, tied as it is to body weight and feelings about their own attractiveness. Only 25 percent of the women we surveyed believe they are extremely or very attractive; 26 percent say they rarely or never feel beautiful. Still, most women are not interested in the kind of gym-centered, limits-testing fitness activities that appeal to many men. Nor do they really want to look like Madonna.

It is hard to stay fit. It is hard to access fitness facilities: most of them are expensive and are not designed for women. The result is that the fitness industry—although it is so fragmented as to scarcely deserve the name—includes several approaches to fitness for women, none of which is perfect and all of which cause significant dissatisfaction. As a result, women try one approach after another—diet plans, exercise regimes, healthcare memberships, yoga classes, home equipment, spa programs, health retreats, and, for some, medical treatments and even surgical procedures. There is a high rate of recidivism. Weight goes up and down. Gym memberships go unused. Exercise equipment gathers dust in the cellar.

Women constantly look for ways to gain all the benefits that can come with exercise: weight control, diet management, greater energy, better appearance, disease prevention. But they don't want to abandon their greatest source of satisfaction, food. Nor do they want to spend hours and hours, which they don't have, on exercise. Nor do they want to sign up at a gym that is filled with grunting men, who eye them in their spandex, and who leave sweaty imprints on the benches and exercise mats.

Given the need, the dissatisfactions, and the emotional intensity involved, the health and fitness, nutrition, and weight loss industry could expand almost infinitely.[2]

Lisa Bennet: The Mirror Is Not My Friend

Once or twice a day, Lisa Bennet, 38, feels a pang of sadness, guilt, and regret. It can quickly pass, or it can send her into a gray mood that lasts for hours, sometimes days. Two things reliably trigger the pang: the full-length mirror in the bedroom and the box of doughnuts in the staff room at work. Lisa, at five-foot-four and 158 pounds, is about twenty-eight pounds overweight. According to government standards, in other words, she is obese.

Otherwise, Lisa is quite satisfied with her life. She lives with her husband, Frank, and two children—Ashley, age 12; and Frank, Jr., 9—in Mountain Grove, Missouri, a town of some 20,000 people about forty miles east of Springfield, with a median household income of $22,330. Lisa enjoys her job as a technician in a veterinary practice, and Frank works as a driver for the local gas utility. Both children do well at school, academically and socially. Lisa leads an active life, especially on the weekends, when she goes fishing with her husband and attends her kids' softball games and gymnastics tournaments. Although the Bennets never seem to have as much money in the bank as they'd like, they always pay their bills on time and have no debts aside from their mortgage. Lisa is a Pressure Cooker mother, who falls more into the Struggling for Stability than the Successful Multitasker subsegment. Like so many other women in similar circumstances, Lisa feels that she and her family are average, middle-class Americans, getting by with good humor and good values. All things considered, she doesn't have much to feel bad about.

Except for her weight. Lisa is one of more than 35 million American women who are overweight. Sixty-four percent of the women in our survey say they are overweight.

And what used to be thought of as a distinctly American phenomenon is now a worldwide issue. Statistics compiled by the World Health Organization (WHO) show that, although the United States has the highest percentage of overweight women, women around the world are putting on extra pounds. Weight is a major issue in developed countries such as the United Kingdom, Canada, and Germany, as well as in developing countries such as Mexico, Russia, and Brazil. Even China, India, and Japan are not immune. (In 2008, Japan instituted a national standard for healthy waistlines. Citizens aged 40 to 74 whose waists measured above the limit—33.5 inches for men and 35.4 inches for women—would receive information about dieting and would be expected to slim down.) The combination of sedentary jobs, large portion sizes at meals, more tasks to accomplish than there are hours, and the resulting stress and often compensatory eating habits, has produced an alarming prevalence and rapid rate of weight gain worldwide.

Lisa has not always been overweight. "What kills me is that I used to look great. I put on a few pounds in college, but throughout my twenties I maintained a pretty healthy weight. I gained twenty-eight pounds when I was pregnant with Ashley, and I have never been able to lose it." Lisa misses her former figure, but the worst of it is the guilt she feels. There are so many diets, gyms, workout regimens, and products available, she says, that it seems as though losing weight should be easy, but all the methods seem expensive, inconvenient, and ineffective to her. "Obviously they work for some women or else [the companies] wouldn't stay in business. Those women must somehow know which diet or program to choose. I just don't. It makes me feel I have no one to blame but myself for being overweight. That really gets me down."

Lisa shares her disenchantment over the methods of weight loss available to her with a vast number of women. Despite their concerns about their weight, fewer than half of the women we surveyed say they exercise once a week or more. "I don't have enough time to exercise," many women say. And, "I can't find a plan that works for me."

Even Nicole Green, the quintessential multitasker who manages to cram everything else into her eighteen-hour days, is at a loss when it comes to exercise. She's not overweight, so this is not quite such a pressing concern for her as it is for Lisa, but Nicole still longs for more physical activity. "I bought a treadmill four years ago, but the only place we had to put it was in our bedroom. And the only time that I could use it was when the kids were asleep, either before they woke up or after they went to bed. But the thing is so loud—thump, thump, thump, thump, thump—the second I got on it, the kids would wake up. I'd hear them yelling at me, 'I can't sleep!' So now it sits in the corner of the bedroom and we hang clothes on it."

Plan B for Nicole was to try to take a walk early in the morning, alternating on-duty days with her husband. "We agreed that I'd take a walk one day while he got the kids ready for school and he could go out the next day.

But we could never follow the schedule. If one person didn't want to get up one morning, the other wasn't necessarily prepared to walk. It just fell apart very quickly."

Now the Greens are considering plan C. "We fixed up the basement. It used to be really disgusting down there. I didn't want to go down unless I was wearing a toxic waste suit. But now it's a usable space. Nothing fancy, but clean and fine. So that's where the treadmill is going to live, and my plan is to use it in the morning. The only problem is that for me to get up at 6 A.M. and get down there for a half hour on the treadmill, I'll have to start going to bed earlier. And to go to bed earlier, I have to do fewer things after the kids go to sleep. I just don't know if that's going to be possible."

Daily exercise is an essential part of weight loss and is beneficial to overall health and emotional well-being as well. Leading weight loss scientists say that women who weigh 125 pounds and want to maintain that weight should not consume more than 1,500 calories a day without exercise. If you exercise vigorously for thirty minutes per day, however, you can consume up to an additional 300 or so calories. But women—especially those who are out of shape, like Lisa—say that exercise is, by and large, uncomfortable, inconvenient, and exhausting. "When you're getting by on six hours of sleep, and you have more chores than you can do, and no money for help, it can all be overwhelming. When I do have extra time, the last thing I want to do is hit the gym and get all sweaty and sore."

Dietary options are also less than ideal. Although most women we spoke with told us they buy some low-fat and low-carb foods, they also told us that it was virtually impossible to cook three balanced, healthy meals for their families each day. They rely on prepared meals and dine out more than is healthy, but they feel it's their only practical option.

Lisa pays close attention to what she eats, but her time and options are limited. "My lunch is too often a fast-food meal—burger, fries, soft drink—and that can be as much as 1,000 calories. Fresh fruit is expensive. Good salads are hard to come by at fast-food places. Frozen vegetables don't taste very good. And don't even get me started on dining out. At restaurants the portions are ridiculously big and you can't get information about the number of calories you're consuming. I figure a serving of pasta at my favorite Italian restaurant is around 1,300 calories. Add a glass of wine to that and a cannoli and you're over your daily allowance with just one meal."

I DON'T EVEN WANT TO TALK ABOUT IT

When we spoke to women about their weight, we found that many of them find it hard to even talk about the subject. They feel embarrassed, sad, and helpless. Roughly 15 percent of adult women say they are on a diet at any given time. Many of them are yo-yo dieters. They stay on a strict diet just long enough to get down to a target weight, then go off the diet, start eating as they ate before, and gain all the pounds back within weeks. Hundreds of women we surveyed listed "becoming overweight" among their greatest fears, just as "losing weight" was one of the most frequently listed goals.

We also found that a high percentage of the women we surveyed have a distorted body image. Although 64 percent of our survey sample think they are overweight, only about 32 percent actually are, according to their body mass index (BMI), which we calculated from the heights and weights they reported. They describe how difficult it can be to think about their weight realistically, especially in a society—and a consumer market—that favors thin, perfectly shaped women.

Women make a direct connection between their weight and their success in life. When they are dissatisfied with their body image, they cannot help feeling that everybody they meet is dissatisfied, too. They worry that their weight holds them back from finding love, moving forward in their careers, meeting interesting people, and living a balanced, healthy life. And in many ways they are right. Being overweight does indeed present significant threats to health and wellness; the risk of heart disease and diabetes increases significantly in overweight people. And, increasingly, research supports the claim that thinner, more attractive people are more likely to be promoted at work. Women want to be healthy and attractive; they want to feel confident and in control of their bodies and their lives. The problem is simply that among the countless workout and diet options, so few seem to be worth the money and effort that many women either try them all and see disappointing results, or are discouraged from even trying.

I Feel Like the "Before" Picture

"I always feel like the 'before' picture. I feel invisible. When I go shopping
for clothes the store clerks ignore me. No one will hold the door for me.
People think I'm fat and therefore must be lazy. I've tried every diet.
I've just never been able to lose the weight and keep it off."
—*Sarah, 48, Chicago*

"The pressure to be thin is huge. Being out of shape makes me
angry with myself. I feel lazy and isolated. I used to be attractive;
now I always feel I need to hide."
—*Cecilia, 24, Memphis*

"I am scared that others don't like my body. I have submitted myself to
a rigid diet for many years now and I am still overweight. I am scared to
die young because of my physical problems."
—*Lucia, 37, Italy*

"My goal is to achieve my ideal weight so that I feel healthier,
so I can play with my kids without getting exhausted."
—*Gabriela, 32, Mexico*

THE WEIGHT LOSS INDUSTRY

The desire for fast, easy weight loss regimens has fueled an increasingly global industry of exercise facilities and equipment, home-delivered food, and nutritional supplements. There are hundreds of providers of each of these, ranging from the dubious and cheap to the effective and extremely expensive, and including everything in between. In addition, women face a dizzying array of books, magazines, commercials, Web sites, and blogs, listing their options, telling them what works and what doesn't, and contradicting each other from one month to the next.

Nevertheless, diet and exercise remain incredibly lucrative businesses. The United States diet food marketplace—which is dominated by female consumers—is worth approximately $10 billion, growing in high single digits every year, and we estimate the worldwide total at $20 billion. The health club industry generates revenues of about $14 billion. There is an immense opportunity for growth and niche fulfillment in both categories, particularly for companies that can cater to women successfully. There are three basic concepts in the diet and fitness industry that have proved to resonate with women, and companies that adhere to any combination of these concepts have demonstrated how profitable the market can be: fitness without bodybuilding; providing a network of support for fitness and weight loss; and convenient food replacement.

Convenience, value, and effectiveness are the most basic elements of these concepts. The diet programs and workout regimens that have achieved the greatest success are those that are easy to follow, that an average middle-class woman can afford, and that produce the results an overweight woman wants to see.

CURVES: FITNESS, NOT BODYBUILDING

Curves has succeeded with a very simple concept: cheap, fast exercise routines, without guys leering, available in a convenient location. The goal at a Curves gym is not to create six-pack abs or fannies taut as trampolines, but to shed a few pounds, increase cardiovascular health, and tone up a little.

Curves occupies a distinct space in the fitness industry. There is certainly no shortage of gyms and health clubs in the world; in the United States alone, there are about 24,000 health clubs listed in the Yellow Pages, plus nearly 3,000 YMCAs and thousands more independent personal trainers.[3] But numerous as they are, most of these gyms fail to offer all the things women most desire in a weight loss regimen: convenience, effectiveness, and value.

In the superluxury segment, there are health spas, such as Exhale, that offer a wide range of classes, as well as a menu of spa services and personalized care options that promise to keep a woman's morale up while they help her lose weight. At a starting rate of $124 per month, however, an Exhale membership is out of reach for most middle-class females like Lisa Bennet. There are dozens of middle-range clubs, such as Lifetime Fitness and Bally Total Fitness, but these places are designed for people who are serious about working out and know their way around the Nautilus machines and free weights—a description that does not fit most working women who just want to slim down enough to get back into their favorite skinny jeans.

Curves Fitness Centers, on the other hand, deliver on all three core desires. Curves are fitness centers for women; more specifically, these no-frills workout spaces are geared toward middle-aged women of average build and weight who are not particularly interested in working out for the sake of working out. Curves has demonstrated an excellent understanding of its target clientele and an unparalleled ability to address the specific needs expressed by women everywhere.

Curves was founded in 1992 by Gary Heavin. Heavin's mother had died at age 40 from a variety of health complications that largely resulted from her weight, and he decided he would devote his life to fitness and women's health. He realized that conventional gyms were not designed to meet the needs of middle-aged, overweight women, and that these women needed a workout space to call their own. "Conventional gyms look more like night-clubs than health clubs," Heavin says. "Women weren't comfortable there. Perhaps the aerobic bunnies were, and women looking for a date, but our sisters, mothers, and grandmothers weren't comfortable."[4] Heavin opened the first Curves in Harlingen, Texas, and it was a runaway success. Three years later, in 1995, Heavin and his wife began selling Curves franchises. Today there are some 10,000 Curves worldwide. Membership fees average about $40 a month.

"Curvers," as Curves members sometimes call themselves, run the gamut of women: low-income and affluent; highly educated and high school dropouts; single, married, and divorced. They come to Curves not only for simplicity and affordability but also for convenience. Curves franchises are usually located in central, commercial locations—on a busy street or a strip mall, close to a supermarket, a nail salon, a Laundromat. Women can combine a trip to Curves with a stop at a drugstore, or sneak in a workout while the kids are at soccer practice or another after-school activity.

Curves Delivers Technical, Functional, and Emotional Benefits

Curves distinguishes itself with several technical features.

First and foremost, it is a women-only facility—there are no men present to be flirted with, or to stare at your cellulite, or to hog the good machines, so there is no way to get distracted by chin fat or a bad hair day or how you look in a tank top and tights. The atmosphere is pleasant. The reception area is filled with encouraging posters, informative articles, and instructions on how to stretch properly. The workout space feels bright and airy, thanks to the large windows and walls painted in cheerful yellows, pinks, and blues. Third, the workout itself is highly structured, with a circuit of sixteen machines, each of which works a different muscle group. Women who are new to working out don't have to learn to use the machines or waste time fiddling with weights and adjustments. They simply spend thirty seconds on each machine in sequence. You can complete two circuits in half an hour and burn as much as 500 calories in that time. Upbeat music plays constantly, interrupted only by a female voice instructing members to move to the next machine. Curves suggests that, for tangible benefits, women do the double circuit three times per week. The Curves staff stands by to track your progress and does so by measuring inches lost rather than pounds, to give women a clearer idea of what they've achieved.

These technical features translate into functional advantages: women save time, achieve noticeable results without having to become bodybuilders, and are satisfied enough with the process that they are less likely to quit than they are with other programs. They find friends among the members. They feel as if they are part of a community.

These technical and functional benefits of the Curves experience add up to a real emotional boost for most Curvers. When we talk to women in Curves, they tell us that it creates an overwhelming sense of achievement. They amaze themselves; they feel they're transforming their bodies.

Jackie Spence, 47, joined Curves after her psychiatrist recommended exercise to fight her depression. "Joining Curves is the best thing I have ever done. I would even go so far as to say it has saved my life because without it, I really doubt that I would still be here today. . . . That was the summer of 2005 and I really haven't looked back since. I have lost about 16 pounds and toned up about 25 inches from across my body, but for me it was never about weight. Curves means so much more to me than that and I actually get quite emotional talking about it. I have self-confidence and I am happy."[5]

Janet Campbell, a mother of one, had been a member of Curves for a year before she was diagnosed with breast cancer in 2006. She kept going to the gym as often as she could, before, during, and after her treatments. "At one point I was going every morning just because I needed something to do to take my mind off the cancer. I kept going right through the radiotherapy and the people were all great because they never really mentioned it, even when I lost all my hair. I would never have gone to the gym at that time if it hadn't been ladies only. And now I have finished my treatment and—fingers crossed—the cancer is gone, I am still going to Curves."[6]

Sally McLean reported on her experience with the Curves three-month challenge: "Yes, despite being inherently lazy and preferring a bottle of wine and Chinese food to a liter of water and vegetables, I have done the unthinkable. I have lost 12 inches in three months. That's a FOOT." Skeptical at first, she was willing to give Curves a try after visiting the gym and seeing that the women there "looked pretty comfortable exercising and chatting away to the staff. None of them seemed close to collapse, which was something I had always associated with gyms." She was very impressed with her results, and especially with the staff member who measured her and coached her, saying that they never failed to be encouraging and supportive, with none of the tough-guy bravado and "just deal with it" attitude so often seen in personal trainers.[7]

Vincenza Sousa is 35 years old, a mother of two, an elementary school teacher at a Catholic school in Toronto's Little Italy, fit and trim-looking but nevertheless unhappy with her body. In short, she is a typical woman trying to stay in shape while juggling her family and career. So when a Curves franchise opened recently in a basement studio near her school, Sousa was keen to try it out. "I loved it," she said after finishing her first thirty-minute workout at the College Street facility, one of more than eighty in the Toronto area. "I've tried other gyms but always felt really self-conscious. If you wanted help you had to spend a lot of money on a personal trainer. Here, I can set my own pace and get it all for $40 a month."[8]

Another important feature of the Curves approach is that the company offers an entrepreneurial opportunity that is very attractive to many women. The smaller locations, lean operations, and lower investment requirements make it a comparatively low-risk option for women who are venturing into entrepreneurship, with a potential for very high returns: Curves franchises generate an average of $145 per square foot, compared with $50 per square foot generated by their competitors. It's a low-cost, low-overhead model that allows Curves to break even on 200 members and to become very profitable with only 400 members per month, who can reliably be recruited in a town with as few as 10,000 inhabitants. A Curves franchise pays a royalty to the parent company with a cap of 6 percent of annual turnover. "I don't want to penalize my franchisees for doing well," says Heavin. He does not do aggressive marketing to find franchisees. "We wait for the right people to come to us, through word of mouth." When women join Curves as members, they generally meet the owner, who is often on-site, and they feel as if they are participating in a win-win situation—they're getting fit physically and helping another woman do well financially.

The Future of Curves

With nearly twice as many locations as the next-leading workout facility (the YMCA), Curves is conveniently accessible to women almost everywhere in America and, increasingly, around the world. As of 2008, there was one Curves franchise for every two McDonald's in the country, and the number is still growing. The company now has 9,300 clubs in the United States and operates in seventy countries; its locations include Canada, Europe, South America, the Caribbean, Mexico, Australia, New Zealand, South Africa, and Israel. Expansion in South Africa has been remarkable: the first gym opened its doors in 2005 in Pietermaritzburg, and today there are sixty-nine, with thirty-two more under construction. Japan—despite the fact that weight has not traditionally been seen as an issue there—is an increasingly profitable market for Curves, with 700 locations. Gary Heavin announced in January 2008 that Curves Japan will open 400 to 600 new clubs a year over the next few years. Curves Japan currently has about 160,000 members and aims to attract some 1.6 million, or approximately 3 percent of Japan's adult female population.[9] Heavin also announced Curves' intention to move into China, India, and Russia within the next couple of years.

In November 2007 Curves International and Rodale, a trusted provider of health and wellness content, announced the launch of www .CurvesComplete.com, an online weight loss subscription service based on Gary Heavin's book *Curves: Permanent Results Without Permanent Dieting*, which became a best seller on the *New York Times* list. "Helping women achieve their fitness and weight loss goals is what Curves is all about, and the launch of CurvesComplete.com adds another dimension of support," said Heavin. "People now have the option to track their weight loss online, and best of all, you don't need to be a whiz at technology to use our service."[10]

Unfortunately for Lisa Bennet, the Curves clubs closest to Mountain Grove are in Springfield, about forty miles from her home. "That's just too long a drive. I know I'd never do it."

WEIGHT WATCHERS: A NETWORK OF SUPPORT

If Curves is a gym that functions like a supportive community, Weight Watchers—a well-established, trusted, $1 billion brand—is an even more expansive network of support for women who want to get healthier and thinner.

Founded in 1963 by Jean Nidetch, the company began with the premise that women are social creatures and would be more successful at maintaining a healthy diet with the support of like-minded friends. Nidetch was an overweight New Yorker who was frustrated with the failure rate of fad diets. She wanted a more sustainable plan and formed a support group of friends with similar weight loss goals who could help her stay on track. Calling themselves Weight Watchers, this group met weekly, shared progress, and ultimately spread by word of mouth into a national and then a global brand. Measured in sheer loss of pounds, Weight Watchers is the most successful weight loss formula in history. It is also a public company with a $1.6 billion valuation.

Weight Watchers consists of two main pillars of dieting: meetings and diet "points." Convening for one hour per week, the meetings are an open forum where members can share their ideas, tips, and fears about dieting; commiserate about the trials and pitfalls; and celebrate successes. There are also informational sessions on health, diet, and weight loss and confidential weigh-ins with meeting leaders. The program is affordable, at under $10 per week. It's convenient, with more than 50,000 weekly meetings across the globe: any member can find one at a place and time that accommodates her schedule.

The company's points program is just as straightforward. Weight Watchers assigns point values to every food—two points for an apple, thirteen points for a cheeseburger, and so on—and allows members to eat whatever they want within their allotted range of points for the day, between twenty and forty points, depending on what each woman weighs and what her target weight is. The diet offers choices and freedom: members don't need to buy specialty foods; they must simply learn portion control, and the conveniently laid-out points system makes this easier. It is both less demanding and more satisfying to think of a meal in terms of "points" rather than "calories." The emphasis is on learning how to develop a sustainable lifestyle. Interestingly, Weight Watchers, like Curves, devised an alternative to the standard metric. Curves tracks inches, not pounds. Weight Watchers thinks in points rather than in calories.

The Weight Watchers program offers a number of options to make participation easier. Some women are not fans of the points system; instead, they can use the Core Plan, which offers an "allowed foods" list from which they can eat all they want. There are online meetings available if a member can't go to a live one. Members can track their progress, find recipes, and participate in forums at the company's Web site. There are weekly and monthly payment options, too.

Molly, a 55-year-old participant in our survey, told us that Weight Watchers changed her life. "I tried every diet and bought every book," she said. "My weight would go down and then my weight would go up. I was beside myself. I actually thought my husband was going to leave me. I was forty pounds heavier than when we got married. He was two or three pounds heavier. I was sad, depressed, and anxious. Then my company offered Weight Watchers as a benefit and I jumped at it. The points were easy to get a handle on. I still was able to occasionally indulge. But I could see an end that was really going to work. I've been a Weight Watcher for two years and I'm ready to look at myself in the mirror and smile."

The heart of the model is support and sense of community. At a Weight Watchers meeting you will typically find a group of twenty to thirty women (and perhaps a few men), all at different stages of the weight loss experience. Some are just beginning; some are well on their way to achieving their goals. Meetings are run by "leaders," former members who have found personal success on the program and can effectively share tips, experiences, and best practices. Women who successfully lose weight and maintain their new weight on the program are designated "lifelong members." They can attend meetings free, indefinitely. Many become meeting leaders.

More than 90 percent of members of Weight Watchers are women. Nearly 1.5 million women worldwide attend a Weight Watchers meeting weekly. Ninety-seven percent of members say they would recommend Weight Watchers to their friends, and 60 to 70 percent of new members are referrals from current members. There were nearly 63 million attendees recorded worldwide in 2007. The average age of a woman in Weight Watchers is 45 to 47, but participants range from teenagers to seniors. Additionally, Weight Watchers currently has close to 600,000 online subscribers, an increase of nearly 100 percent from three years ago. There are more than 1 million paid circulations of the *Weight Watchers* magazine, which was launched in 2000.

The brand has relevance worldwide. Although North America represents the majority of sales (about 65 percent), the company operates in thirty countries, including the United Kingdom, Germany, Australia, Italy, Sweden, and Mexico. In 2008, Weight Watchers partnered with Group Danone to bring a program to China. The diet programs are tailored to each geographic region: different point values suit local tastes and nutrition profiles. Marketing and educational materials are also adapted for each country's culture.

Weight Watchers has withstood the test of time and has remained an industry leader through tough times, including the low-fat craze and the use of fen-phen in the 1990s and the popularity of the Atkins Diet. Growth in licensing and Internet revenues remains robust, illustrating that the extendability of the brand equity is real, recognizable, and difficult to replicate.

NUTRISYSTEM: MANAGING FOOD INTAKE

The traditional prescription for losing weight remains the most effective one: exercise and control the diet. NutriSystem focuses on the diet by providing ready-made foods that help reduce the consumption of carbohydrates.

NutriSystem is the grandmother of weight loss food. The company's model is all about convenience: food is premade and delivered to the home, saving a huge amount of time and eliminating decision making. The company was founded in 1972, but its current—and extremely successful— incarnation as a diet plan that delivers food to the customer is only about a

A Surprise Winner with Women:
The Nintendo Wii Fit

Traditionally, video gamers have been young and male, but Nintendo wanted to attract a broader audience. Its Wii was designed to be a highly active gaming system. With a wireless controller and interactive games, many Wii games require players to stand, work their arms and legs, and move around to play effectively.

Although Nintendo did not specifically target female purchasers, women of all ages have discovered Wii Fit and hail it as a stroke of calorie-burning genius. It has four categories—yoga, balance, strength training, and aerobic exercises—each of which offers a wide variety of activities and levels. The game also includes charts and graphs to track goals such as weight loss, proficiency levels, and improved flexibility. The $90 system comes with a pressure-sensitive plastic slab and sophisticated exercise and fitness tracking software. Players enter their height and then stand on the Wii Balance Board to let it read their weight for an accurate body mass index measurement. Then players do basic balancing tests to get a general indication of fitness level.

The Wii Fit's pièce de résistance is its fun factor. Your Mii, the 3D caricature that you create of yourself, mimics everything you're doing onscreen. Many of the programs also include other Miis, like training instructors or jogging partners. The number of exercises and games available to each player grows with time and practice, so the workouts don't get stale, and curiosity acts as an incentive to keep going. A user who stops using Wii Fit for a few weeks or months might return to find that the training instructor has a dramatic new haircut or has been replaced. The new trainer shakes his head despairingly at the erstwhile absentee before beginning the session.

Jane Higgins, a 57-year-old flight attendant for American Airlines, received Wii from her fiancé for Christmas. "I love it," she told us. "I do the yoga; I can feel it tighten my sides. I do it every night that I'm home."

In Canada, more women than men now buy and use Wii, and Nintendo cites Wii Sports and especially Wii Fit as the reason. Wal-Mart boosted its Mother's Day sales by advertising Wii Fit as a time-saving workout for moms.[11] The game has sold more than 14 million copies worldwide since December 2007, and it has been continually sold out in stores across the United States and Europe since its launch in May 2008 and April 2008 respectively.

decade old. After operating weight-loss centers, both corporate and franchised, for years (greatly reduced in number in 1993 after the company was thrown into involuntary bankruptcy, and subsequently closed all corporate centers in December 1997), NutriSystem reinvented itself in 1999 with nutrisystem.com. Since then, the company has built a strong business selling prepackaged foods to participants through direct channels including the Internet, QVC, and phone sales.

The shift has been successful: annual revenues approached nearly $750 million in 2007—up from only $14 million in 2003—or a CAGR of more than 160 percent. Membership has also skyrocketed. In 2007 there were just shy of 1 million new members, compared with fewer than 25,000 in 2004.

Technically, the plan is grounded in science. It is based on the glycemic index, which emphasizes low carbohydrate intake and consuming several smaller meals per day to reduce hunger throughout the day by keeping blood sugar levels consistently higher.

Above all, NutriSystem is designed to be easy and convenient. The design speaks to the busy woman: delivered meals have a long shelf life, and can be quickly prepared in the microwave or by simply adding water. The program provides the foods with the appropriate nutritional values and directs the consumer to add in fresh grocery items that will help with weight loss—about one to two pounds per week. The meal cost averages $7 to $11 a day.

Published customer surveys say 91.5 percent of NutriSystem customers chose it over other programs because of the ease of prepared meals, 81.5 percent liked having food delivered right to their door, and 79.6 percent said the program was easy to follow. The programs are also tailored to meet the needs of different groups: different meal options for men and women, a "silver" program tailored to older men and women, and options for diabetics and vegetarians.

NutriSystem also provides, at no additional charge, support from its Nutrition and Dietary Services team; weight loss coaches who are available to members via phone or the Internet; and online weight loss tools, including a meal planner, daily food trackers, exercise DVDs, an interactive Mindset Makeover Manual, and a recipe book. This range of resources gives women a chance to discuss their goals and concerns with a live person, but also gives them anonymity to deal with their issues. Marketing campaigns are also tailored to reach women across different groups. Ads feature a combination of testimonials from "normal" program members and from celebrity spokespeople. Female spokespeople are mostly actresses, TV personalities, and models, most of whom are moms: Marie Osmond, Jillian Barberie, Danielle Fishel, Zora Andrich, and Tori Spelling.

NutriSystem is predominantly a U.S. business, but its global relevance is growing. It was launched in Canada in January 2008, and there are plans for rollouts in Japan and the United Kingdom by 2009. In 2007, NutriSystem delivered $728 million in revenue at a 21 percent operating profit. It invested about $163 million in its marketing message—75 percent on television. Although NutriSystem has a very high percentage of men relative to other weight loss companies (about 30 percent of its customers are men), women still represent the vast majority of its sales. NutriSystem advanced its model in 2008, opening distribution at Costco at heavily discounted prices and experimenting with home-delivered food of a much higher quality. NutriSystem works because the provision of three meals a day plus dessert creates discipline regarding food consumption and total calories consumed.

FITNESS AND WEIGHT LOSS: THERE HAS TO BE A BETTER WAY

Companies like Curves, Weight Watchers, and NutriSystem create apostles for their particular approach and build a business model with high operating leverage. They know precisely who their target consumer is and how to reach her. They know how long she is likely to stick with the program and what ancillary and supporting products and services she will be interested in purchasing. Because tastes and preferences in food and fitness change rapidly, these companies continuously track shifts in what influencers such as Oprah Winfrey and others are doing (or not doing) to keep fit. They make their products and services available in whatever form or through whatever channel they believe their consumer finds most convenient and effective. The most successful companies make their businesses a franchise opportunity so the owners become apostles and word of mouth spreads organically and rapidly.

The future winners will be able to create $1 billion businesses that help women eat and exercise properly, control their weight sustainably, lower their healthcare expenses, and improve their quality of life.

Women like Oprah Winfrey (who declared 2009 her "year of hopefulness" during which her goal would be to achieve the "weight her body could hold, and be healthy and strong and fit"[12]), and Lisa Bennet, and millions of others have shed far too many tears over the state of their bodies. They would dearly love to be able to look at themselves in the mirror and see a woman who is healthy and strong and fit. This is one of the great unfulfilled market hopes for women today.

6.

Beauty

The Next Product Needs to Do It!

Women seek beauty that combines physical appearance, fitness, health, and wellness. Science and technology play a major role in beauty products and services. The beauty industry has exploded in size, number of brands, and types of delivery channels. Women always hope that the next thing will bring a better answer. Markets are elastic. You compete for scarce disposable income across categories. Every day, a woman makes painful trade-offs between herself and family members. She wants you to reach out to her. She will tell her many friends of your winning moves and your failures.

Diana Beck devotes more time to the quest for beauty than most women do. A look inside her medicine cabinet reveals almost everything one needs to know about the current state of the beauty industry.

Start with the fact that it's not really a cabinet and there isn't actually any medicine in it. We're talking about a set of peach-colored shelves behind frosted-glass doors that line the wall above Diana's sink in the bathroom. Inside, we do not find aspirin, cold relievers, tampons, or prescription drugs. We do find:

- Skin exfoliant, for everyday use ("Deflakes and reveals smoother skin.")
- Skin exfoliant, gentle, for use when skin is dry ("Especially in cheek area.")
- A plastic bottle of skin toner ("Tightens pores and removes excess oil.")

- A glass bottle of antiaging serum ("Repairs visible signs of aging.")
- Brightening cream ("Boosts skin clarity and transparency.")
- Facial moisturizer, concentrated ("Replenishes and nourishes the skin.")
- Facial moisturizer, light ("Refreshes and hydrates the skin.")
- Night cream ("Rejuvenates skin while you sleep.")
- Makeup remover ("Cleanser, toner, and face and eye makeup remover.")
- Eye cream, moisturizing ("Reduces the look of fatigue.")
- Eye cream, to reduce puffiness ("Deflates puffiness and improves elasticity.")
- Body moisturizer ("For all-over rich skin texture.")
- Hand cream ("Tones, moisturizes, and softens, without a greasy feel.")
- Cream to treat calluses ("Smooths skin of the feet and prevents formation of calluses.")

And that's just the skincare regimen. If we open another set of frosted-glass doors, we find Diana's makeup products: three blushes; two bronzers; a sparkling powder; five eye shadows; three eyeliners; two lip liners; five lip glosses; four bottles of nail color; a nail foundation coat, topcoat, and nail corrector pen; six lipsticks; a lip contour cream; and a lip plumper. Not to mention haircare products and sun protection lotions, as well as a basket of tools and devices, including makeup brushes, eyelash curlers, an eyebrow kit, tweezers, a massage brush, fingernail clippers, and scissors.

Diana, 41, is a charming, vivacious woman with brown eyes and shoulder-length dark brown hair. She lives with her husband, Andy, in a two-bedroom apartment on the Upper West Side of Manhattan and works full-time as a lawyer. She is, as you might guess, extremely well-groomed—with meticulous hair, perfectly manicured nails, and subtle makeup.

Diana has a basic beauty regimen that varies only slightly from day to day. "I always use the foundation, concealer, blush, eye makeup, and lip gloss. Sometimes I will use one shade of eye shadow. Sometimes I'll contour two or three complementary shades. Sometimes I apply lipstick before I leave home. Sometimes I'll put some on while I'm riding the subway. Depending how my skin feels, I'll go for a heavier moisturizer or cream."

Diana, like many women, splurges on beauty products and services. She spends about $1,500 annually on the skincare, makeup, and bath products that fill her medicine cabinet. She spends another $3,500 a year for beauty services, which include a weekly manicure and pedicure, weekly hairstyling, a monthly hair coloring, and occasional facials and massages. Total spent: $5,000 a year. And some years it can go much higher.

"I would much rather spend money on beauty products than on clothes. You can spend the whole day shopping for clothes and not come back with anything you like. If you do find something that works it goes out of style in a year. It's very frustrating. With beauty products I feel that I'm doing something good for me. Taking care of myself. When I go out wearing anything new it makes me feel confident and beautiful. It's a lot easier and cheaper to get a new lipstick than a new jacket, but they both give me the same good feeling."

AN ANCIENT AND ULTRAMODERN INDUSTRY

Women have always sought ways to get the good feeling that comes from enhancing their natural looks and have employed inventive methods over the centuries to do so. Ancient Egyptian women colored their eyelids with kohl, a fine powder made with antimony, a bluish metallic substance. Women of the Roman empire smoothed out blemishes with herbal remedies. Japanese geishas crafted elaborate hairstyles with *bintsuke*, a wax derived from soy.

Today, the art of beauty has become fused with science and technology and offers a wide array of organic and inorganic complex compounds (e.g., peptides, alpha hydroxy acids, antioxidants, coenzymes, Retin-A) and a huge variety of delivery methods (such as gels, creams, emulsions, muds, salts, masks, scrubs, exfoliants, and toners) to enhance attractiveness, improve health, and counteract the effects of aging.

And beauty is no longer just a matter of looking good on the surface. As with fitness, women think about beauty holistically, as a radiance that results from a combination of physical health, inner calm, and attractive external appearance. Knowing that they look good has a powerful and positive effect on women. It makes them feel more confident, engaging, and attractive.

Spending time and money on beauty rituals not only helps women feel more beautiful but can be a first step in anticipation of a coming event or a reward for personal achievement. As Dagmar, a single working mother in Germany, put it, "I like to treat myself with spa products. The shower is the only part of my day that is truly mine, when I'm not responsible for anybody else. I look forward to it every day, and I like to make the most of it."

Most women have at least one favorite brand or product, a secret weapon that makes them feel especially fine and polished. Fiona, a 41-year-old British working mother, described her favorite brand as follows: "Clarins helps me feel a little bit pampered and special every day."

For most women, buying a new beauty product is an exciting and happy experience, so it's not surprising that beauty is the category in which women say they are most likely to splurge on themselves. Women who spend as much as they can on beauty report feeling more satisfied (54 percent), successful (46 percent), and powerful (31 percent). In contrast, women who spend the bare minimum on beauty report feeling less satisfied (38 percent), successful (26 percent), and powerful (12 percent).

In addition, women who list beauty as a priority also report lower levels of stress despite working longer hours. There appears to be a "virtuous cycle" here: women invest in feeling and looking their best, and this investment leads to higher levels of satisfaction and happiness in their lives.

But for most women, feeling beautiful is easier said than done. Only 7 percent of the women we surveyed said they always feel beautiful; 68 percent said they only sometimes, rarely, or never feel beautiful. Yet it's not for lack of trying: virtually all women surveyed devote at least some of their time, energy, and money to their personal quest for beauty.

Although most women say they will splurge on beauty products, our research shows that they also have fundamental dissatisfactions concerning this category and the way the industry is evolving that keep them from spending as much as they might.

Over the past ten years the beauty industry—with revenue of approximately $200 billion in 2008—has seen spectacular growth of 8 to 10 percent annually, fueled by the proliferation of brands, both large global brands and small innovators; dramatic technical innovations; new distribution channels; and the industry's expansion well beyond its traditional base of cosmetics and skincare to include bath, body, sun protection, self-tanning, haircare,

hair color, beauty tools, salon and spa services, and dermatological procedures such as micro-dermabrasion, laser therapy, and injected drugs such
as Botox and Restylane.

As the industry has grown, the big players—including Estée Lauder,
Lancôme, and L'Oréal—have found themselves competing more and more
with smaller niche players. We see this across all segments of the U.S. market—in color, skincare, and fragrance. At the same time, the growth and
technological advances of the mass brands—Olay (owned by Procter & Gamble) and L'Oréal in particular—have increased the availability of beauty products and brought their prices down, a combination that has brought more
women into the beauty market.

As more and more brands have emerged, and as brands have created
more new products and variations, the beauty category has exploded with
choices and become harder and harder for women to navigate. The typical
mass retail store offers hundreds of SKUs (stock-keeping units) of color cosmetics, and a department store or specialty beauty retailer may carry close
to 1,000. There are hundreds of competing products, offering a bewilder-
ing array of formulas, new technologies, and active ingredients, and a long
list of claims about the benefits of each product. Even the most enthusiastic
and experienced shopper can be overwhelmed by the selection. Typical la-
ments: "I feel challenged when looking for skin products because there is
so much to choose from!" "Some of these stores can be very stressful and
overwhelming."

L'Oréal: The Advantages of Range

L'Oréal delivers at every price point and in every channel, using a stream of
technology innovations to move the market.

With worldwide sales of $25 billion annually and operations in more than
sixty countries, L'Oréal delivers variety, scope, innovation, and accessibility.
Among the largest players in the beauty industry, L'Oréal is unique in its size
and reach. Its product portfolio spans brands from mass-market to superpremium, and includes products appropriate for virtually every age and need.

L'Oréal started out with a single innovation: hair coloring. In 1907, Eu-
gène Schueller, a French chemist, adapted techniques used to dye fabrics
to create a safe, permanent coloring for human hair. Schueller called his

product Auréole and sold it to hairdressers across Paris, where it achieved immense and continuing popularity. In 1909 he founded Société Française de Teintures Inoffensive pour Cheveux (meaning, roughly, the French Society of Harmless Hair Dyes), which became L'Oréal.

Schueller refined his product; broadened his sales operations to the Netherlands, Italy, and Austria; hired a staff of chemists; and expanded into other beauty products—including the world's first soapless shampoo and the first sunscreen. Despite the continuing product innovation and sales in other European markets, L'Oréal remained primarily a prestigious Parisian company. Even in 1970, despite forays into the United States with the acquisition of Cosmair, 85 percent of sales still came from Europe, with 50 percent of total sales and 60 percent of total profits coming from France alone.

L'Oréal's transformation into a truly global company came through strategic acquisition and extension, beginning with the purchase of a French soap manufacturer, Monsavon, in 1934. In 1964 the company acquired several brands: Lancôme (upscale perfumes and cosmetics), Vichy (exclusive pharmacy skincare), and Garnier (mass-market haircare), which continue to play important roles at the company today. The 1980s brought ownership stakes in Ralph Lauren Fragrances and Helena Rubinstein, as well as the purchase of Redken.

This pattern of acquiring brands and companies accelerated in the late 1990s to transform L'Oréal into a truly global player. In 1996, the company acquired Maybelline—a brash, colorful U.S. cosmetics company—to build its presence in the United States and to strengthen its position in the mass market worldwide. Maybelline was one of more than twenty strategic acquisitions by L'Oréal between 1996 and 2008, worth more than $4 billion in total, including the major pharmacy brand La Roche-Posay; professional haircare lines Kérastase and Matrix; as well as small cult brands like U.S. Kiehl's and Japanese Shu Uemura; and Skinceuticals.

Even as L'Oréal went for scope, it continued to focus on innovation. L'Oréal spends twice the industry average as a percentage of total sales in research and development, resulting in over 500 patents in 2007 alone.[1] Thanks to its ability to cater to and innovate for women at all levels, L'Oréal delivered four points of margin enhancement between 1997 and 2007. Sales grew at more than 10 percent annually from 1989 to 2007, and L'Oréal now maintains a leading share (first or second place) of the global market for beauty across all segments. L'Oréal wins through its global reach, price, and channel segmentation, by offering a stream of real technical innovations and achieving scale and clout at retail.

THE URGENCY OF THE NEW

The proliferation of brands and the stepped-up pace of innovation have given women more choice and, as a result, a tendency to always be on the lookout for the next new thing. Women frequently report that they change products although they are not necessarily dissatisfied with the products they are currently using. The promise of newness attracts women and keeps them trying new things, particularly if the new technology or product comes from a brand they already trust. In skincare and color cosmetics, for example, well over 200 new skincare products are launched each year, 30 percent of sales come from products launched that year, and many of the new products will not survive more than three years.

This constant churning contributes to the high cost of doing business in the beauty category. A major new skincare product takes two to three years to develop and consumes large quantities of research and development resources. Beauty is a hit-driven industry—a small number of products are expected to deliver most of the revenue and profit for the entire line, and they are the ones that get the most support during and after a launch. If one of these featured products has a disappointing launch, it can depress the profitability of the entire line.

The economics of launching a product are particularly brutal in fragrances. Of all beauty products, a fragrance is the one most likely to be a gift, so sales are heavily skewed to the fourth quarter. Every holiday season about fifty new prestigious fragrances are launched, so companies must spend millions of dollars to break through the clutter. Because of the high advertising costs, combined with the development costs of the "juice" and the bottle that contains it, the investment in a new fragrance is so significant that the vast majority of new fragrances lose money.

Further, over the past decade the number of new fragrances launched annually has been staggering, exacerbating an already overly fragmented market. More often than not, sales of new fragrances peak in the launch year, and then sales fall off a cliff. The top-selling fragrances—Chanel No. 5, Beautiful, Pleasures—are the same as they were five years ago. There hasn't been a new "classic" created since Clinique introduced Happy in the 1990s.

Olay: Your Mother Loved a Very Different Brand

One of the reasons women continually try new products is that the social context within which beauty is defined changes continually. Driven by trends and tastes in the media and key influencers, new styles, looks, and shades emerge, take on currency, and then quickly fade away again.

Olay, a brand of Procter & Gamble, has proved time and again that it understands what women are looking for in skincare. The company has continually introduced new products that incorporate up-to-the-minute advances in technology; it has also entirely reinvented itself in order to better address the needs of its customers.

Olay today is a $4 billion global brand with $1 billion in annual sales. It is one of the brands that understand how women feel about skin and skincare, and it has morphed from being a low-end product with a straightforward purpose, used by about 2 percent of the population, to being a high-end product with a wide variety of applications that has 40 percent household penetration. One of the reasons the company has been so successful is that it has constantly improved and refined its product. Oil of Olay was an early user of nonwoven technology to create a product called Daily Facials, which enables you to give yourself an acceptable equivalent of the facial you would receive at a fancy spa.

Olay's greatest claim to fame is its breakthrough antiaging skincare line, Olay Regenerist. The 1.7-ounce jar of Daily Regenerating Serum, the cornerstone of the Regenerist regimen, sells for $18 and is advertised as the next-best thing to cosmetic surgery for making skin look younger. The Regenerist line is composed of some twenty-four products, including micro-sculpting cream, micro-exfoliating wet cleansing cloths, a micro-dermabrasion and peel system, and a filling and sealing wrinkle treatment. Each product costs between $15 and $25, and women are encouraged to buy any combination of products to create their own customized skincare.

Olay is a textbook example of a company that operates by the four

R's—and it is characterized by continuous evolution, expandable space, covering most core segments, changing the game, and transferring technology from specialty to mass.

Regenerist was created in 2003 after the research and development teams at Olay redoubled their efforts to deliver powerful antiaging products to address lines, wrinkles, and skin texture without irritating the skin.[2] According to the Olay Web site, "this luxurious cream has the highest concentration of our signature amino-peptide complex infused with intracellular fortifier and a touch of precious marine proteins. Intracellular hydration regenerates volume and shape across skin's 10 million surface cells, progressively lifting and micro-sculpting." This mouthful of quasi-science may be confusing, but the cream seems to back up its promise by improving skin tone and decreasing the appearance of fine lines, at least temporarily.

Olay remains a favorite with women of all archetypes, because it delivers a unique combination of technology, low prices, convenience, and prod-

---

Olay: A Favorite Brand Around the World

"It works and is an affordable luxury. I am very comfortable with it.
Its products are elegant, soft, and give a nice effect."
—*Naima, 32, United Arab Emirates*

"Olay. Simplicity. Quality. Delivers on its promise.
Products are easily attainable and affordable."
—*Gemma, 27, Australia*

"I started to use Olay because it is what my mom used when I was little.
I love using it to this day because it makes me feel good, and in the last
six months I have received four compliments on my skin."
—*Amber, 31, United States*

"The variety of products takes in almost all needs of facial care.
It cleans my face, moisturizes, revitalizes, etc.
I have not found anything in its line that I do not like."
—*Audrey, 58, United States*

"I like Olay soap because it's inexpensive and doesn't dry out my skin."
—*Li Shiao, 19, China*

uct lines that address a woman's most serious skincare concerns, including antiaging, body cleansing, body moisturizing, facial cleansing, facial moisturizing, specialty treatments, and sunless tanners.

Robin Burns: The Beauty Secrets of Lamps

Robin Burns, one of the leaders of the beauty industry, started her career in the lamp department at Bloomingdale's. "I thought it was going to be terrible," she told us. "Why lamps?"

Turns out she was wrong. She learned how to select, buy, and import merchandise from all over the world, especially the Far East. The lamps she sold—a pot from Portugal, Afghanistan, or India, with a shade from China and assembled in Long Island City—taught her about product creation. Take intriguing ingredient A, add complementary ingredient B, put them together in a compelling package, merchandise them with sophistication and differentiation, and people will buy. This is the formula that Robin has applied throughout her career.

The lamps became Bloomingdale's signature pieces, one-of-a-kind products presented in spectacular displays so exotic and glamorous that even celebrity shoppers couldn't resist them. When Jacqueline Kennedy Onassis came in one day, Burns waited on her.

Robin discovered that she had a talent for merchandising, which could be applied to any Bloomingdale's product, not just lamps. She went to India to commission reproductions of Seurat's and Van Gogh's paintings on decorative pillows and created a model room that had the look and feel of an art exhibit. Her inventory sold out almost immediately.

Her formula worked so well that her boss pushed her to apply it to the beauty category, starting with men's fragrances. "I knew nothing about men's fragrance," she said. "So I asked my boss what it would take for me to be successful. He said, 'Nothing. Everybody wants to launch a fragrance product with Bloomingdale's. But if you want to know what it takes to be great, that's a different story.'"

She learned quickly—working with Chanel, Clinique, Ralph Lauren, and Estée Lauder—and then came a blockbuster hit, the launch of a little-known fragrance called Giorgio Beverly Hills. The brand was catapulted to national attention, thanks in large part to one of Burns's merchandising ideas—to include a Giorgio scent strip in every Bloomingdale's catalog. Before long, she was running the women's fragrances and cosmetics departments, too.

The year Burns turned 30, she was lured away from Bloomingdale's by Minnetonka, the licensed fragrance company of Calvin Klein. The Minnetonka company was small and losing money when she arrived. The licensor, Calvin Klein, was working the apparel business and had lost faith in the potential for a fragrance business.

Robin bet that the best way to rescue the company's underperforming line of fragrances was to come up with a startling innovation—the Obsession brand. With Obsession, Robin brilliantly followed her formula: ingredient A plus ingredient B, great package, sophisticated merchandising. Obsession had a memorable tagline, "Passion without reason"; impressive store displays; and an overt selling approach. It worked. By the time Robin left Minnetonka, Calvin Klein cosmetics were big and profitable.

For the next twenty years, Robin applied her formula in the beauty industry. She became president and CEO of Estée Lauder USA, where she helped manage its first transition from a family-owned company to a public company. Lauder became the graduate school of the beauty business by combining marketing skill, sales, channel management, and financial controls. Robin became recognized as a pioneer of high-visibility merchandising.

She was recruited as CEO of beauty products at The Limited, parent company of Victoria's Secret and Bath and Body Works. There, she captured the power of integrated retail, with control of all aspects of the in-store experience. Victoria's Secret fragrance became an instant hit by piggybacking on the store's existing clients and store infrastructure. The fragrance got store prominence, instant distribution, sales staff endorsements, and "suggested sell," and delivered margin accretion to the retailer.

In 2006, Robin founded Batallure Beauty with Sam Ghusson, a former colleague at Calvin Klein, to fill a market niche for fragrance and cosmetics lines tied to vertical fashion retail brands. She knew that retailers were eager to maximize their productivity per square foot with their own private-label beauty items, such as cosmetics, haircare, and fragrances. They needed an easy way to outsource the creation of these products. With her industry expertise, Burns and her business partner realized they could provide everything from research and development to packaging. Among Batallure's first clients were Abercrombie & Fitch and Ann Taylor.

What Robin Burns learned through creating and selling lamps laid the foundation for her long, successful (and continuing) career in product development, merchandising, and management—and a deep understanding of what women want from products and services.

THE ROLE OF TECHNOLOGY

Although technological innovation has long played a role in the development of beauty products, the past decade has seen an explosion in the development and application of raw materials technology and innovative delivery systems in cosmetic formulas, with active ingredients ranging from chemically produced vitamins such as Retin-A and tocopherol to naturally occurring plant-based ingredients such as sea kelp, algae, nut butters, and fruits with natural acids.

One of the major stories in beauty has been the phenomenal growth of facial skincare products into a $20 billion category worldwide. Antiaging skincare formulas, in particular, have reached the high and low ends of the market. Whereas the shelves used to be lined with products whose purpose was to moisturize the skin, now there are formulas containing elements such as sun protection, skin lifting creams, and capillary strengtheners—all designed to prevent, or at the very least disguise, aging.

At the top of the range is Swiss-based La Prairie's Cellular Cream Platinum Rare antiaging moisturizer, which sells for $1,000 for a 1.7-ounce jar; the jar itself is made of Swarovski crystal. The cream contains a trace of platinum, which, according to the company, "recharges the skin's electrical balance and protects the skin's DNA."[3] Despite the high price, customers lined up at luxury retailers such as Saks and Neiman Marcus to purchase a jar when the product was introduced in October 2008.

The development of new compounds and formulas—including Action Liposomes in 1986 and Pro-Xylane in 2006—enables brands to continue to command premium prices and provide superior technical benefits for which women are willing to pay more.

Shiseido: A Venerable Brand Stays
Modern Through Innovation

Shiseido, today one of the leading global beauty brands, traces its roots to the scientific and technological advances of the late nineteenth century. In particular, Shiseido owes its early growth to the vision of Arinobu Fuku-hara, who in 1872 had been the chief chemist of the Japanese navy.

For about 200 years, starting in the mid-1600s, Japan's leaders had kept the country secluded from external influences. This isolation came to an abrupt end in 1854, when Admiral Matthew Perry, backed up by the U.S. Navy, opened the gateway to Japan. Soon a wide variety of modern goods and innovations—including guns, manufacturing machinery, and scientific principles—had been introduced to Japanese society.

In 1868, just before Shiseido was born, the Meiji restoration began in Japan, signaling an important shift toward closing the gap between Japan and the West, even when it meant breaking with Japanese tradition. Fuku-hara admired Western-style pharmaceuticals even though traditional herbal medicines were the norm in Japan. Concerned about the quality of the pharmaceuticals sold to the public, he focused on research and development and opened Japan's first Western-style pharmacy.

Fukuhara's early commitment to Western scientific principles led to product innovations and investments in science. In its transition from pharmacy to beauty company, Shiseido introduced Japan's first fluoridated toothpaste (1888) and Carmine, a medicated cosmetic to treat acne and whiten the skin (1937). Shiseido continued to invest in the science of beauty through its Shiseido Research Center, created in 1939, bringing researchers from different departments together at a single location; the Institute of Beauty Sciences formed in 1953; and in 1989, a partnership with Harvard Medical School to conduct research on skin and aging.

In the early years, Shiseido broke with tradition and incorporated some Western influences, introducing skin-toned face powder (Kaede and Hana) when all other Japanese face powders remained white. However, as Western influence became more prevalent, Shiseido also reconnected to what was Japanese. In 1917 it created Japan's first original fragrances, inspired by Japanese scents (rather than copying Western scents), and in the 1970s it used a Japanese model to promote makeup most suitable for Asian eyes.

After selling exclusively in Japan for eighty-five years, Shiseido began expanding and growing internationally, first in Asia, then in America, then in Europe. Today, the company's largest region for sales remains Japan, at 64 percent. Slightly over 14 percent of sales come from Asia and Oceania. Europe also accounts for just over 14 percent of sales, and the Americas deliver about 8 percent. Operationally, Shiseido manufactures its products globally (with four factories in Japan, three in France, four in Asia outside Japan, and three in the Americas) and employs 40,800 people around the globe: 26,100 in Japan and 14,700 overseas.[4] Today, Shiseido has $7.235 billion in annual sales (at ¥100/dollar) and is the largest Asian beauty company, thanks to its combination of science and innovative ideas about how to serve its market.

A PROLIFERATION OF CHANNELS

All these beauty products, tumbling out of the industry in a constant stream of new forms and variations, have also become much more available to women around the world through a wide variety of channels. The most common and dominant retail formats for cosmetics—the department store counter and the drugstore—have steadily been losing share to emerging concepts.

There are the specialty stores that sell a variety of brands, such as Sephora and Ulta, as well as stand-alone stores that offer only a single brand: MAC, Kiehl's, Fresh, Origins, and L'Occitane.

The specialty retailer Sephora works because it provides a complete assortment of brands stocked in open displays so women can try them before buying. The stores offer a no-pressure atmosphere; there are no manufacturers' reps working in the store; no one jumps out at you to urge you to buy. Sephora has realized double-digit sales growth in each of the past five years, and it has been a growth vehicle for its owner, LVMH, despite initial skepticism when it began to roll out. Sephora continues to expand its presence globally.

Television has also become an important format for selling beauty products. The trend for beauty brands sold on television started with newer niche brands such as Bare Escentuals, but it is no longer just about new brands—the big, established brands have taken note and now view television as a viable format. QVC has expanded its beauty offerings. Sephora has formed a partnership with HSN to showcase several of its lines. Infomercials for beauty products are on the rise in the United States and Japan. Even venerable Estée Lauder appears on QVC to sell its Prescriptives and Bobbi Brown brands.

These direct channels work well for several reasons. Above all, they are convenient; women do not have to leave home to buy products. The direct channels also offer education; consumers can learn about the benefits from the experts hosting the shows, and from other consumers who call in to share their views. Women can gather information on their own terms at their own convenience, without having to directly interact with a salesperson who may be focused on commissions or less knowledgeable than she should be. A woman can also order and purchase items covertly; no one has to know that she is buying antiwrinkle cream. More and more women also turn to online sites to try new products or replenish their favorites, and although penetration is still low, it is on the rise.

Direct sales have also become an important channel for the sale of beauty products. Natura has become a force in the Brazilian beauty market because of its direct sales, a format similar to that used by Mary Kay and Avon in the United States. The direct selling model works well in the developing markets, partially owing to lack of a retail infrastructure. Avon has had its fits and starts in the more mature U.S. and U.K. markets, but its rapid double-digit growth in Latin America and eastern Europe has been remarkable. China has also shown early, strong potential. The model works so well in these geographic areas because, in bringing access to high-quality products, the direct sales approach also presents women with an opportunity to earn income by being a sales rep. Consumers get to interact with other women to buy their product, and can do it from the comfort of their own home. This is a model that leverages the power of relationships. Equally important, women can earn money by selling the products they love. Avon calls itself "the company for women"—women as consumers, women as sales representatives, and yes, the company has a woman CEO.

INJECTIONS AND PROCEDURES: THE BLEEDING EDGE OF BEAUTY

As the beauty industry has evolved from a source of cosmetics and basic skincare products, it has gradually embraced specialized treatments, regimens, and medical and surgical procedures.

Today, women account for 88 percent of the cosmetic procedures performed in the United States. Since the FDA approved Botox for cosmetic use in 2002, this has reigned as the number one nonsurgical treatment, with medical professionals performing nearly 4.5 million procedures in 2006 alone. By injecting small doses of botulinum toxin between a patient's eyebrows, physicians can temporarily paralyze facial muscles, eliminating wrinkles for up to four months.

Allergan, the biologics company that created Botox, originally researched the substance as a treatment for fluttering eyelids, crossed eyes, and other disorders such as cervical dystonia (spasms of the neck or shoulder muscles). Although many patients profit from the medical applications of the drug, Botox is best known for its cosmetic benefits.

Botox and other, similar nonsurgical treatments appeal to many women as an affordable luxury and a personal investment. Patients cite many reasons for choosing to undergo elective cosmetic procedures, including a desire for a more youthful appearance, a better self-image, and more attention from men.

Furthermore, the rapid normalization of cosmetic procedures in general—propelled by shows such as *Extreme Makeover, The Swan,* and *Dr. 90210*—has prompted women to speak more openly about these topics, which were previously taboo. The spa industry has successfully capitalized on this trend, with revenues of $10.9 billion in 2007; and "medical spas" offering chemical peels, Botox injections, and other antiaging services have proliferated. Many women now view nonsurgical procedures as a way to bond with their friends. Botox parties have become mainstream but rarely resemble the popular Tupperware parties of the past.

In some cases, brides have even been known to give the gift of younger-looking skin to their bridesmaids before the big day. Kacey Knauer, a 35-year-old bride-to-be who decided to host an evening at the TriBeCa Med-Spa for her bridal party, explains the reasoning behind her decision: "Giving them a bracelet isn't as special as spending an evening together. Plus, as you get older, everyone is more conscientious about their skin and appearance. Giving them something for themselves—as opposed to something that they'll never wear again—is more meaningful."[5]

Other women who use Botox or dermal fillers consider the enhancement a necessary part of their professional careers. Whereas men who show signs of aging are often assumed to have more wisdom and authority, women are not similarly perceived and frequently attempt to minimize such signs.

"I've had numerous Botox injections in my forehead and my brow, lasered spidery red veins on my face, and had silicone injected into a deep crater above my brow," a 46-year-old pharmaceutical representative explains. "I work with a younger generation of women. Their average age is probably 28 to 38. Even my manager is in her early 30s. I'm the mommy of the bunch, but I'm trying really hard not to look that way."[6] Kathleen Hudson, a 57-year-old marketing consultant from Virginia who receives Restylane or Juvéderm injections, has a similar viewpoint: "If you're in the business world and you want to be competitive with the younger people, you need to stay on top of your game," she says.[7]

Despite its popularity, some people express concern that the trend has gone too far. Botox parties, Botox walk-in clinics, and Botox spa services strike some women as excessive and, in some cases, potentially dangerous.

Nonetheless, the number of Botox injections performed each year continues to increase; and even in the midst of an economic downturn, Allergan estimates that its 2009 profit on earnings will still grow by 5 to 12 percent largely thanks to Botox sales. Since results wear off after four months, repeat customers fuel revenues, and with the increased normalization of physician-assisted beauty regimens, that customer base is likely to expand.[8]

DISSATISFACTIONS WITHIN THE RICHNESS OF OFFERINGS

One result of this enormous growth and expansion of the beauty industry is that women's brand loyalty has dissipated, and women have become continual switchers, triers, and seekers—always with an eye toward the new, interested in claims of greater efficacy and the benefits of new technologies, and intrigued by trends, fads, and changes in the beauty zeitgeist.

Customers are also dissatisfied and restless with regard to channels. Women in our survey tell us that department stores, in particular, are characterized by overly insistent salespeople and by a deluge of overly expensive options. "I hate the high-pressure environment. The salespeople are all over you. It's crazy." They may get lots of attention, but good advice is harder to come by. "With department store shopping, there is a regret factor. You buy it because they say you need it. Often you don't." In drugstores and mass retail outlets, women are generally not pressured to buy anything, because there is rarely a salesclerk in sight. When salesclerks can be located, they may or may not have knowledge about specific products. "Shopping at a mass retailer is strictly a do-it-yourself enterprise. The clerks don't know anything. There aren't enough samples."

One consequence of these dissatisfactions is disengagement—women simply give up on beauty products. Pressure Cooker women are particularly susceptible to disengagement. Even Diana Beck, whose medicine cabinet is now chock-full of beauty products, was so overwhelmed when her son was an infant that she all but stopped buying and using cosmetics. "I felt tired and schlumpy all the time. I'd wear sweats around the house and never bother to dress up. Sometimes the whole day would go by and I wouldn't even have time to wash my face."

But when Diana was getting ready to return to work, she snapped out of her slump. She threw off her sweats, got dressed up, and went on a shopping spree. "I started to feel attractive again. I had big dark circles around my eyes, and a makeup artist at one of the stores totally transformed them. I came home resolved to lose the rest of my extra weight before going back to work. I really didn't want to be one of those women who just totally let themselves go."

DOVE: BEAUTY FOR "REAL" WOMEN

The definition of beauty is always evolving in every culture, and it has changed significantly over the past twenty years. As health and wellness have taken on a greater importance, beauty has expanded to mean both inner and outer beauty. A holistic approach is also an inclusive approach— women need not be perfect to be beautiful—and the skincare brand Dove built a highly successful campaign on this idea.

Dove has been a favorite among women since its launch by Unilever in 1955. The brand features soap, cleansers, and moisturizers aimed at women, emphasizing moisture-rich formulas and ingredients that are safe and gentle on sensitive skin. In 1979 a dermatologist found that Dove was significantly less irritating and less drying than ordinary soaps. Sales of Dove soap improved dramatically, and by 2003 Dove had won more than 24 percent market share.

In 2004, Dove launched a new ad campaign that all but attacked the mainstream media and traditional advertising for their misrepresentation of women's image. The "Campaign for Real Beauty," launched in 2004, advertises to—and with—"real" women who do not fit the stereotypical and unrealistic image of "perfect" beauty. Dove's stated goal is to permanently and irrevocably change the paradigm of female beauty. Commercials for Dove products feature average women of all ages and body types, rather than models. The Web campaign includes a series of short films chiding the beauty industry, from weight loss products and superthin supermodels to plastic surgery. The Web site includes sections on being "pro-age" and spreading self-esteem among young girls.

The ads became something of an Internet phenomenon, with each commercial being viewed on YouTube millions of times. The immense popularity of the ads led to a unique grassroots spin-off campaign. A nationwide contest in Canada was launched, asking women to write letters to their own bodies; the thirteen winning articles were adapted into a stage play, *Body and Soul*, with the winning writers in the leading roles. No direct reference to Dove was made in the play, but free Dove products were handed out at some performances. Meanwhile, the video *Evolution*, a short film exploring how the image of beauty has become distorted, had 13 million hits on YouTube.

"We have really found the sweet spot to get consumers engaged with the brand, and it is such a wonderful place to be in, as a brand," said Alison Leung, a marketing manager for Dove. "We have people calling us saying they want to raise money for the Dove Self-Esteem Fund [a charitable organization launched by Dove to fund self-esteem programs], and it does not take money."

Robert Levy, president of BrandSpark International, a marketing firm in Toronto that compiles an annual research study for its Best New Product Awards, noted that "many women made comments about the fact that Dove cares about women," citing a "general halo" around the Dove brand. "It was quite unusual, because consumers rarely talk about the impact of an advertising campaign."[9]

The campaign has clearly struck home with women who are weary of unrealistic beauty ideals. In a 2006 global study by Dove, 91 percent of women aged 50 to 64 said the media and advertising need to do a better job of representing realistic images of women over 50. The company has experienced double-digit growth every year since the launch of the "Real Beauty" campaign—in a category that generally grows 2 to 3 percent annually—and annual sales now top $3 billion globally, making this the number-one-selling cleanser in the world.[10]

Certain aspects of the "Real Beauty" campaign have been criticized for being self-righteous or overblown, but Olivia Johnson, who contributed to planning the campaign, said, "Dove is putting its head above the parapet and it is too easy to have a pop at it. When we carried out focus groups among women, they were delighted to think they didn't have to be perfect. There is a terrible tendency among marketers and the elite to be snooty, but women still seem to be genuinely pleased."[11]

WAITING FOR THE NEXT BREAKTHROUGH

So, as fast-growing as the beauty industry is, and as much money as women spend on beauty products and services, consumers tell us they still have not found adequate solutions for a host of issues that trouble them: dark circles under the eyes, unwanted facial hair, clogged pores, hair loss, heat and chemical damage to hair, oily skin, visible pores, dry skin, and so on. What's more, no single company has been able to create a range of products, a retail outlet concept, or a portfolio of services to bring together solutions for all of women's beauty wants and needs in one offering.

Perhaps this is because the industry is still operating with the "hit" model, chasing the extraordinary margins that can result from a big winner—some players earn in excess of 30 percent of operating profit. According to a 2008 survey by the YWCA reported in *Boston* magazine, the average woman spends $100 per month on beauty products, and this can add up to a lifetime total of $60,000.[12] But a large percentage of women, like Diana Beck, spend much more. If a woman averages $5,000 a year for fifty years, that's a lifetime total of $250,000. According to our research, the spending is highly concentrated: 30 percent of American women—Diana among them—spend 70 percent of the dollars in the category.

It may also be because beauty is an industry dominated by male executives trying to guess what more women want. Surprisingly, this most

Underlying skin and hair problems drive women's "real" need for beauty products and services

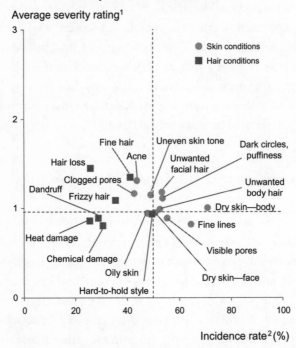

Incidence and severity
of key skin and hair conditions

Average severity rating[1]

● Skin conditions
■ Hair conditions

Fine hair
Uneven skin tone
Dark circles, puffiness
Acne
Hair loss
Unwanted facial hair
Clogged pores
Unwanted body hair
Dandruff
Frizzy hair
Dry skin—body
Heat damage
Fine lines
Chemical damage
Visible pores
Oily skin
Dry skin—face
Hard-to-hold style

Incidence rate[2] (%)

1. Respondents who experience each condition rated severity on scale of 0–3; 0 = do not consider an issue, 1 = consider a minor issue, 2 = consider a moderate issue, 3 = consider a major issue. 2. Incidence among higher-income target population between the ages of 22 and 60 = single/divorced/separated/widowed women with HH income ≥$50K or married/living with partner women with HH income ≥$75K; Target population = 28% of female population reporting income and 44% of total spend (products and services) among female population reporting income.
Source: BCG/Harris online omnibus survey, May 2007; N = 652 (target population only); BCG analysis.

fundamentally female of industries—beauty—has a long way to go in improving how women contribute, shape, and lead it. Women are particularly passionate about the beauty industry, and it has a larger share of women at entry levels than other industries do, but it has a difficult time maintaining women's participation into the executive and leadership levels. The answer may be to recruit more women to executive roles and—even more—to use the four R's in some novel fashion to better serve women.

Hope springs eternal when it comes to beauty. Women of the world are waiting for a category transformer that combines products, services, and holistic wellness. Fortunes have been made serving this market, and new fortunes are waiting to be created. But beauty is not for the faint of heart— it is a ruthlessly competitive field in which the winners must meet women's never-ending demand for products that meet their need for the new and that make them feel young, vibrant, and beautiful.

7.

Apparel

Always Hunting, Never Satisfied

Most women are not size six and don't like to be reminded of the fact. Suppliers that provide a "fit" guarantee will earn loyalty and save time. The growth is in fashion that is affordable. A woman is always looking for the "next" thing. Companies that sit still will get swallowed up.

As we have seen, women go to great lengths to eat well, hold their weight in check, and keep their skin, hair, and face smooth and beautiful. But all their efforts come to naught if the clothes they wear don't reflect the image of themselves they want the world to see. A woman's size six figure and perfect skin are of little use if she looks as though she just rolled out of bed or if her clothes are ill-fitting or inappropriate.

And most women in our survey are not size six. The pressure of work, family, and chores puts exercise and personal nutrition on the back burner. They are therefore, on average, size fourteen or larger. They find shopping for clothes a reminder of their failings. That's a primary reason why expenditure on personal consumption has shifted to fashion accessories (belts, purses, shoes, jewelry) and beauty products.

Today, women's fashion—including apparel, accessories, and shoes—is a global industry with $47 billion in annual sales. Women need clothes that suit the many roles they play: business or business-casual clothes, comfortable but nice clothes for running errands around town, sturdy but inexpensive clothes for doing housework and caring for the kids, fun and sexy clothes for going out with friends or partners. All these clothes must also reflect a personal style, be age-appropriate while avoiding the dreaded "mom jeans" look, and satisfy the individual's value calculus.

To meet this combination of needs in any item of clothing is no small feat, both for the companies that produce clothes and for the women who buy them. The average American woman spends approximately 400 hours per year shopping for clothes (for herself, that is; many women also do the shopping for their husbands and children) and spends a large percentage of those hours searching for tops and bottoms, lingerie, coats, shoes, belts, and handbags.

Shopping trips fall into two basic categories: shopping for a specific item—a top in a specific color to match an outfit, or a replacement item such as new black pumps to replace ones that are worn out—and shopping with nothing in mind, hoping to stumble across a perfect outfit by chance. For a given shopping trip, however, there is only about a 50 percent chance that a woman will find something she really loves.

By and large women love to shop, but all too often the experience results in a letdown. The clothes don't fit right, or are aimed at a younger (or older) demographic, or are too expensive. Styles and trends change so quickly that when a woman does find a style or a piece she likes, chances are she'll never find another one like it. These frustrations—as well as the persistent joy in shopping that comes from the thrill of the hunt and the satisfaction of finding the perfect item—are expressed in more than half of our survey respondents' "dream days":

- "My fiancé and I would go out for a nice breakfast; then we'd head to the mall and go on a shopping spree. We'd get a whole new wardrobe. Then we'd go to sleep on the most comfortable bed in our new and comfy PJs."
- "Spend the morning shopping for clothes, shoes, jewelry, and items for my home, then lunch, then an afternoon of relaxation at a day spa."
- "Go shopping and buy tailor-made clothes from my favorite stores, books from the local bookshop, gifts for friends, DVDs."

- "I would like to be happy with myself and my surroundings. I would like to continue wearing nice clothes and having a few statement pieces to reflect my personality. I would like to fall in love, get married, and raise a healthy family."

Fashion brands that succeed in winning women's business and loyalty are those that maintain a consistent style but also offer an ever-changing variety of merchandise. They serve a wide demographic, and their clothes serve a number of a woman's overlapping needs. Banana Republic and H&M are two such companies.

BANANA REPUBLIC:
SEEING THE OPPORTUNITY IN BOTTOMS

Pants are the foundation of the female wardrobe, and women spend more on two-legged bottoms—including pants, slacks, and jeans—than on any other apparel category, including dresses and skirts, tops, sweaters, and outerwear. Women in the United States between the ages of 24 and 28 are especially big buyers of pants and jeans, spending more than $1.5 billion each year on them, or about 28 percent of their total apparel budget.

But, despite the importance of pants, women in the age group 24 to 28 have not been well served in this department. Most specialty retailers—including American Eagle, H&M, Abercrombie and Fitch, Express, and J. Crew—target younger women, between the ages of 14 and 23. Department stores and mass marketers—including Target, JCPenney, Wal-Mart, Macy's, and Nordstrom—overwhelmingly serve older women, age 39 and above.

But one U.S.-based specialty retailer, Banana Republic, saw the dissatisfactions that women had with pants and shopping for pants and also recognized that women in the key mid-twenties age group—including Fast Trackers, Relationship-Focused women, and some Pressure Cooker women—had been overlooked.

Banana Republic developed a strategy that has made it one of the world's leading retailers of women's pants, particularly for women in their peak pants-buying years, the mid-twenties.

The Many Elements of Fit

One woman in our survey defined her dream day quite differently from most other women. Rather than describing a leisurely breakfast with her family or a nice dinner out with her husband, she said, "I would hire someone to custom-make pants for me."

The primary problem women have with pants is fit. Women have very high expectations of pants and complex requirements for them:

Best-feature optimization. Simply put, pants should make a woman look as good as possible by enhancing those physical attributes that she considers her strong points.

Silhouette management. Looking good is essential, but not looking bad is also critical. The pants should conceal or minimize any physical characteristics that a woman considers her flaws or less-than-stellar points.

Physical comfort. Comfort has to do with how the garment feels against the body. Texture and fabric play key roles, along with cut and style.

Movement with the body. How do the pants work with the body as the wearer walks, sits, and moves throughout her day? Not only does the movement of the garment affect comfort; it also removes anxiety and doubt about whether it might tear, split, pop open, or otherwise fail to perform as required.

But there is more to fit than the physical. Women are also looking for "style fit," which means that they want the garment to deliver in other, less tangible ways.

Brand fit. Women come to trust certain brands to create and edit a portfolio of styles. Usually, a woman has four or five brands that she will consider as long-term contributors to her wardrobe.

Personality fit. Women are acutely sensitive to brand image and identity and will not buy a brand whose personality does not fit their own.

Occasion fit. Women give credit to certain brands for their particular understanding of the rules that accompany given occasions and social situations. Women overwhelmingly wear clothes that they describe as "business casual"—which typically means casual pants worn with a dress shirt or knit top—or "casual," which usually means jeans worn with a wide variety of tops including tees and polos.

Women are constantly working to create a balance of the two types of fit. They have an idealized style image—a vision of the way they would love to look—and also a style comfort zone in which they feel natural and most comfortable, and the two can easily be at odds. What's more, women often look for crossover clothing—items that fit their style at work and that they can also wear to an after-work social event without having to change. "I like Banana Republic," one woman told us, "because I feel I can always go in and find something that fits my need—whether it is for work attire or a date that night."

Banana Republic has been particularly successful at delivering this balance and versatility by creating a limited number of style "families," each with its own distinct physical fit and signature. Each family is offered in a variety of styles and fabrics so that a woman can round out her wardrobe within a single family. And the physical fit of the family, especially the pants, varies very little, even as new styles are introduced over time. So if a woman knows she looks good in pants from the Martin family—a classic fit that sits just below the waist—she knows that a new pair will fit her just as well. This makes shopping for pants much easier, more reliable, and less stressful, and, above all, it saves time. Women can go directly to the display of the pants family they want—always clearly marked in the retail locations—and can also feel confident enough about the fit to buy additional pairs online. "BR always has the same 'standards,'" one woman wrote. "That allows me to feel comfortable buying pants via the Internet."

How Women Learn About and Shop for Pants

Even when a woman finds a pair of pants that fits her physically and also suits her style—and even when she identifies a brand like Banana Republic that she trusts and will return to over and over again—that does not mean she has solved the pants problem. There is still the question of fashion, trends, and changing styles. Women tell us they value "newness" and are highly sensitive to the refreshment of a brand or a retail outlet. They will quickly abandon a store that doesn't seem as if it has been recently refreshed. Some brands and their stores, they say, seem "almost forgotten" and "lost."

Generally speaking, women are motivated in their shopping for apparel by outer-directed concerns, that is, how others see and judge them; and therefore they want to be seen as aware, current, and appropriate. This is in contrast to men, whose motivations are primarily to avoid shopping if they can, to preserve the status quo, and not to look foolish in the company of other men.

Achieving the balance between physical fit and style fit, and keeping up with changing fashions, is not easy, and women find that they have to shop at a broad range of stores to buy garments that satisfy both needs. This need to shop at many stores, although it stems from a fundamental dissatisfaction—not enough pants that fit; so little time—ironically enables women to engage in an activity that many genuinely enjoy: shopping for clothes.

Women, therefore, not only shop at more stores than men do but also shop much more frequently, and as a result are very quick to understand what a store has to offer and whether it has the potential to satisfy them. So Banana Republic's success is built not only on the product, but on the way the company communicates about the product and presents it in stores.

Women look to a very wide variety of sources in order to learn about fashion and its purveyors—remember that women pride themselves on learning and have proved themselves expert learners. They look to each source for very distinct purposes. They will scan fashion magazines and the general media for education about how to build a wardrobe, accessorize well, find cheap chic, or get inspiration for new looks and combinations. They talk with (and observe) peers and colleagues, to help them shape expectations about what is and isn't appropriate in certain social situations and also to establish "guardrails" for personal style—bounds beyond which they do not wish to trespass. A woman looking to update her style keeps an eye on what celebrities and actors in television shows are wearing, especially those who bring high fashion into the mainstream and provide aspirational style. And she assesses television advertising because it tends to bring a brand to life by addressing the two distinct relationships most women have with an apparel brand: as a brand they actually wear and as a destination where they shop.

Men, by contrast, tend to look to role models and key influencers within their circle, at work and in their community—who rarely are fashion leaders or risk takers—to learn about new styles and trends before they adopt anything personally. Men often look to their wives or significant others to play the role of a fashion editor who is trusted to interpret and recommend styles to them and keep them from making bad choices or falling for weird combinations. Women often act as purchasing agents for their husbands and boyfriends.

For women, learning continues right into the store. In fact, women see the window display as an important source of information. If the silhouettes and styles shown in the window do not seem to be likely candidates for a balanced fit, a woman may skip the store altogether. Or she may conclude that only one department of the store is worth visiting and will bypass the rest without a second look.

The store environment and layout are also key factors for women who are shopping for pants. Although some stores, like Anthropologie and upscale boutiques, are organized in a way that appeals to the emotions and makes shopping there an adventure of discovery, Banana Republic chose to organize its offerings in a primarily rational, functional way, with the intention of making the visit as efficient as possible. Young women in the age group 24 to 28, especially what we call the Fast Trackers and Pressure Cooker women, do not have hours to linger.

Color plays a significant role in women's apparel. Men feel most comfortable with a neutral palette of colors, although they will sometimes buy a strong-colored garment to refresh the grays, khakis, blues, browns, and whites. But the color is usually confined to one item only—a brightly colored shirt or pair of socks. Women love to play and work with color. They use it emotionally, to create or communicate a mood and to emphasize the more stylish parts of their wardrobe. They employ it rationally, as well, as a tool to manage variations in seasonal attire or to create a look for a particular occasion or situation.

Because women pride themselves on their color skills, they will judge a brand on how well it creates and combines colors in particular products and collections. When a brand fails to show mastery of color for a specific style or trend, women tend to give it low marks for color authority. Lack of color expertise reflects poorly on the image of a brand as a whole.

The Price-Value Equation for Pants

Women operate with a flexible price-value equation when it comes to pants. They usually walk into a store with a defined price in mind, but they tend to use it more as a guideline than as a fixed amount that is not to be exceeded.

Because they have usually done a fair amount of research before they

Women Say That Banana Republic Is a "Favorite Brand"

"Everything fits well; they put outfits together for you;
most things match each other and are versatile;
the clothing lasts and usually doesn't go out of style overnight."

"I always find looks that make me feel professional and put together,
and that fit well."

"It's just the character and appeal I want to have.
It makes me feel professional and more my age."

"Allows me to look and feel good for a fair price."

"Very classy, fits well, and is high quality."

"Great product, good fit, nice price, consistent."

"Fashionable, perfect for every day, and affordable."

"It has a variety of fits to suit every body type."

"Simple but sophisticated; moderately high price point but still affordable."

"I live in a big city and I feel their clothes communicate that
they are stylish and urban."

shop, and because they shop frequently, women are rarely surprised by prices. But their expectations about price vary, depending on the item they're looking for and the role it will play in the closet. Women are willing to make many trade-offs as they pursue the best possible item at the best possible value. They will accept lower quality for a pair of pants that meets the fit criteria extremely well. They will abandon a favorite brand name for an item that fits as well but comes at a better price.

Banana Republic has created a good price-value balance through a combination of factors. It has used fabrication, in particular, as an important way for women to assess tangible features that contribute to value. In a highly competitive market, fabrication—the construction and detailing of a garment—is seen as a factor differentiating brands.

The Four R's and Further Lessons from Banana Republic

Banana Republic recognizes the wide demographic of women who need comfortable, good-quality clothes that they can wear to work, but that they can also be comfortable in when juggling their other roles. It successfully targeted the group of women most in need of clothes, particularly pants, that fit their bodies, personalities, and daily needs.

The company put a great deal of research and resources into designing its signature standard fits of pants. It factored in different body types, the activities that women do on a daily basis, and the fabrics and stitching that created the desired lines. It also researched women's value calculations to determine what price point would be appropriate for its offerings.

It responds to the continued desire for new colors, styles, and outfit combinations while still maintaining a fit that enhances each woman's body type. Banana Republic's clothes are always up-to-date, but there is a consistent and classic tone to all of them.

Finally, Banana Republic continually refines its offerings, factoring in changing style trends, color palettes, and body types.

Within those general practices, Banana Republic offers a number of more specific lessons:

1. *Know your customer.* Understand why the customer shops at your store and what she is looking for there, and then deliver it. Banana Republic saw that the mid-twenties woman was underserved and that she wanted well-made, versatile casual and business casual clothing—especially pants—that met all her fit criteria.

2. *Consistency is key.* You can become a trusted brand by offering consistent fit, quality, and store experience. The company created families of clothing that offer a variety of options for physical fit as well as style fit. These helped women understand the brand offering and made it easier for them to find their fit and save time doing so. However, consistency does not mean sameness or lack of change. It means consistency of fit and style but with regular refreshment.

3. *Simplify.* Customers have a variety of needs and limited time to meet them. Add value by simplifying their experience. Banana Republic has done this particularly well through simplified store

organization, in-store signage and education, and the limited number of product families. It edits the assortment to make choice easier.

4. *Cover all end uses.* Meet all customers' needs that you can credibly fill and provide a one-stop-shop for fashion needs. Even as Banana Republic has simplified, it has to put together a number of items within each family that go together to meet a wide variety of situations.

The Waning Social Function of the Mall and Department Stores

Female-focused specialty stores like Banana Republic are often located in malls (although many are on city shopping streets), which were created following a long tradition of retailing for women that began with the department store.

When F. W. Woolworth opened his first five-and-dime store in Watertown, New York, in 1878, he revolutionized retail in this country and, eventually, the world. The store carried a huge variety of everyday items—from cookware to baseballs to clothing—all at prices lower than those in the small, single-category shops that then dominated the retail landscape. With everything they needed so readily available, and at such low prices, women found that shopping at Woolworths was a pleasure rather than a chore. They began shopping in pairs and with groups of friends. Nathaniel Fowler, a pioneer in the advertising industry, advised his clients to aim all their ads, even those for men's clothing, at women. "Woman buys, or directs the buying, of everything from shoes to shingles," Fowler wrote in 1879.

Woolworths also opened a new avenue of employment for women as salesclerks. Especially for working-class, uneducated women, clerking offered work that was more respectable than running a factory machine or serving as a domestic. And store owners found that female clerks made shoppers feel at home and less intimidated about asking for assistance. By the turn of the century there were 56,000 "Woolworths girls," most of them in their early twenties.

Woolworths helped to transform retailing in England, just as it had done in the United States. During the reign of Queen Victoria (1837–1901), the English typically thought of shopping as a wasteful, indulgent, possibly immoral, even disorderly, female activity.[1] But as the era waned, emancipated women would not be denied access to the many commercial and cultural delights of London's West End—restaurants, hotels, exhibitions, museums, theaters, and women's clubs—and increasingly could be seen, unaccompanied by men, strolling the streets together, sometimes even alone, and examining the goods and services on offer.

The growing acceptance of women's shopping in London, along with the success of Woolworths, caught the attention of another American retailer, Harry Gordon Selfridge, who had been an executive at Marshall Field's in Chicago and is credited with coining that central phrase of American retailing, "Only X more shopping days 'til Christmas!"

Selfridges, the store, opened on lower Oxford Street in March 1909. The building was a palace of retail, with elegant restaurants; a library; reading and writing rooms; special reception rooms for French, German, and "colonial" (American) customers; a first aid room; and a "silence room," with soft lights and deep chairs. Staff members were trained to be on hand to assist customers, but not to aggressively sell the merchandise. Selfridges featured twenty-one of the largest plate-glass display windows in the world, behind which Selfridge and his staff created fabulous scenes of goods in various settings, which turned Oxford Street into a kind of movie set combined with a fashion show.

Selfridge tapped into, and pushed forward, the idea of shopping as a social activity, a pleasure, and primarily one pursued by women—and one that was classless, in a society trying to break free of its rigid class structure. Selfridges helped make shopping seem a respectable and important social function and make women feel personally comfortable and safe. Here was an oasis where one could escape the drudgery of the kitchen and the insularity of the home, a showplace where one could encounter an exciting array of products and services, and a public arena where women could walk freely, take tea with friends, and mix with strangers from around the world, without fear or shame.

Today, most women work outside the home. They need no excuses to meet with female friends in restaurants or other public places. They have little time to linger over tea in department store salons. And their tastes in food have progressed well beyond the department store lunch counter. So, for women, the social role of the department store and the shopping mall has virtually vanished. And as it has, both retailing formats have suffered.

THE H&M STORY: VERTICAL ARCHITECT OF CLOTHING

Banana Republic has built its success on a consistent business casual style that has variations to suit every woman's taste and body type. On the other hand, H&M, the Stockholm-based fashion retailer, has taken an entirely different approach to addressing women's needs: fun, trendy clothes and a shopping experience that's virtually guaranteed to provide satisfaction. The clothing is not about quality or durability. Instead it is about surprise, affordable fashion, and the delight of the "quick kill"—an outfit to wear tonight. H&M has grown at a 17 percent compound rate for the past eighteen years because the company understands remarkably well what women want.

H&M started out as a dowdy dress shop. Today it has more than 1,500 stores and a presence in more than twenty-five countries. It is one of a few global retailers and executes fast, affordable fashion across markets. It is one of the favorite brands most frequently mentioned in our worldwide survey. Women love it for value, currency, responsiveness, visual excitement, breadth of coverage, and the thrill of the shopping experience.

H&M's first store was called Hennes and opened in Stockholm in 1947. The line offered only dresses with a distinct view on classic style and good value. Expansion was very slow. In 1979, the company, by now called H&M, had grown to serve Norway, Denmark, the United Kingdom, and Switzerland. Sweden still accounted for 53 percent of sales in 1987.

During the 1980s, the chain added Germany and the Netherlands to its mix. During the 1990s, it added Belgium, Austria, Luxembourg, Finland, and France. It came to the United States with great fanfare but mixed initial commercial results in 2000, the same year it added Spain. During the past eight years, H&M has added Italy, Portugal, the Czech Republic, Poland, Slovenia, Canada, Hungary, Ireland, China, Greece, and Slovakia. Today it is at the top of the heap in retail, with gross margins of 63 percent, EBIT (earnings before interest and taxes) margins of 23 percent, and a multiple of 22—a higher margin and multiple than the world fashion leader Inditex, owner of Zara. H&M sources 70 percent of its goods from Asia. In the H&M business model, goods are largely forced out onto the stores with an expectation of rapid in-store stockout and limited opportunity for reorders. Net earnings growth has been in the teens or higher every year since 2001.

The company's employees are 80 percent women, and 76 percent of its store and country managers are women. Half of the twelve-person board is female.

Katie, a 26-year-old in the United Kingdom, told us that H&M is her "absolute favorite brand. It represents an easy approach to dressing with choice in terms of color, style, price, and accessibility."

Anna, from the home market, Stockholm, says, "H&M allows me to have something new whenever I want it. I don't ever feel I'm breaking the budget. I can have a new outfit any time I want. I can shop quickly, see what's new, buy what fits, and it brings a freshness to my life."

Other women we talked with acclaimed H&M for "designer style clothing at much cheaper prices"; "trendy clothes and accessories on the cheap"; and being "stylish without breaking the bank."

This is a model that can be applied in other businesses. How does H&M provide style, fashion, and low prices?

H&M is a "vertical architect"—it doesn't own any factories; it partners with designers to create looks; and it can bring a product from design to in-store hanger in just twenty days, second only to its famous Spanish competitor Zara, which boasts a fourteen-day turnaround. H&M supports and optimizes logistics. Distribution centers in each sales country moves the stock to stores. Its twenty-office network in Asia and Europe closely monitors production. It buys from 800 independent factories.

H&M has continuously advanced its fashion-price umbrella and expanded with its consumers, adding organic cotton items as well as children's clothing to provide moms with one-stop shopping. In 2004, H&M began its collaboration with fashion designers, starting with Karl Lagerfeld. The original collection was just thirty pieces for both men and women. The T-shirt was priced at £9.99, the sequined tuxedo jacket at £79.99, the wool coat at just £119. These prices represent a discount of up to 90 percent from other Lagerfeld lines in specialty stores. The H&M Lagerfeld collection drove comparative store sales up by 12 percent. It was a retail phenomenon, with lines forming outside stores and chaotic shopping on the day goods were received at the store. It was the sizzle on the steak. It introduced new consumers to H&M and set a precedent for other, similar expansions. In 2005, Stella McCartney launched her forty-piece line at H&M. This included jeans at $69.99, zip-up sweaters for $79.99, and a black wool coat for $199.90. Both designers generated hundreds of mentions in the press. Sales and traffic zoomed. This was followed by a fashion party by Roberto Cavalli. This Italian legend introduced twenty articles for men and twenty-five for women, including underwear and matching accessories. Most of these collaborations were launched in H&M's flagship stores, the 200 to 400 best-performing stores in the chain. But the buzz extended far beyond them. The actress Halle Berry described the Cavalli collection as "sexy, on the edge." She applauded the H&M collaboration, saying, "Now all women can wear his designs."[2] In 2007, the entire M line—designed to match Madonna's wardrobe—sold out in the Stockholm store in the first day. Next up was a beachwear line behind the Australian pop star Kylie Minogue. These events set H&M apart. Consumers came to the stores thinking, "I have to buy it now or I'll never see it again." Stock sold out in the first day or two.

H&M's growth trajectory, earnings, and valuation were not straight lines to success. In fact, the company's launches in many countries were problematic—stretching supply chains, reducing profitability, causing multiple design and fit efforts, adding complexity to a very successful model based on low cost, and necessitating a trade-off between short-term and long-term value. At one point, H&M's valuation declined dramatically. But the company persisted.

"I love the H&M brand because it is very stylish and up-to-date but totally affordable. I can find a huge variety of styles every time I go into the store. The price sometimes encourages me to try a new style. I can be stylish without breaking the bank," says 23-year-old Mary in the United States.

Women from all segments and across life stages in our survey say they shop at H&M:

- Single women: 56 percent
- Married without kids: 33 percent
- Married with kids: 8 percent
- Divorced: 3 percent
- Lower-income women: 11 percent
- Lower-middle-income women: 17 percent
- Middle-class: 42 percent

- Upper-middle: 25 percent
- Upper-income and elite-income women: 3 percent

In 2007, this very hungry retailer launched many new products: footwear for men and women, lingerie, organic cotton, and a skincare line for men. In 2008, H&M home was introduced on the Internet and in the catalog in the Nordic countries. And H&M continues to grow in such countries as

Lessons from H&M

The H&M concept is reproducible in many other categories: bring value and fashion together, focus relentlessly on cost, use global expansion across a tight definition as an enabler. H&M uses throwaway value to capture the emotions of its consumers. Market openings like the one seized by H&M exist in multiple categories. Food, finance, and healthcare all have middle-market gaps waiting for a cost-conscious, fashionable female offering.

Over the years, H&M created a winning business model:

1. Define a clear concept (low cost, high fashion).
2. Refine it in the home market.
3. Export to a major market.
4. Build the financial performance model and refine from low-cost, high-margin, rapid expansion.
5. Consistently add high-profile fashion excitement.
6. Always know that in the creation of a "fireworks display," there is need to continuously awe the audience and bring the user up.
7. Expand and conquer the next concentric group of demand.
8. Be courageous in the face of adverse short-term results.
9. Create a high-pitched emotive retail face—with energy, fun, and experimentation.
10. Create and embrace chaos.
11. Establish urgency: buy it now or never see it again.

And this model can be replicated across categories and geographic regions:

1. Knock off the trade-up product—the design, color, style, provocation.
2. Get the cost position right—sourcing and high-throughput retail.
3. Prove the concept in a single market.
4. Rapidly bring it to other consumers in other markets.
5. Cherry-pick the most attractive adjacent geography.
6. Repeat.

Germany, which now contributes 24 percent of total sales, more than four times the company's footprint in Sweden before it embarked on expansion. The U.S. market position is within sight of the original Swedish market. The year-ending market value in 2007 topped $40 billion. H&M is the largest public global apparel retailer, topping the market valuation of Inditex (Zara's parent) by $8 billion. It also delivers nearly $500 million extra operating profit on a slightly lower turnover. EBIT margins are 23 percent.

WOMEN SELDOM *NEED* CLOTHING; THEY HAVE TO *WANT* IT

None of the women we talked to during the course of our research actually *needed* new clothing. They have plenty of garments, for work and for play, in their closets and dresser drawers. Most could probably get away with shopping once or twice a year—as Nicole Green does—just to replenish the basics.

As a result, women have come to view clothing as an optional category. They find the process of shopping for clothes frustrating, even threatening, for all the reasons we have discussed. Finding something that fits and looks good seems completely unpredictable. Hours in the stores can yield nothing. And few stores offer service that is actually helpful.

That's why women have turned their shopping attention to fashion accessories, especially jewelry, leather goods, and shoes. You don't have to worry about your weight when you try on a handbag.

To sell more sweaters and jeans, retailers will have to listen carefully and hear about what women want in their closets that they don't currently have: excitement, energy, fashion. Retailers need to look to technology—in materials, fabrication methods, hardware, cut, and color—to add new technical features that will provide functional benefits (better fit, greater comfort, color stability, longer wear) and thus contribute to emotional satisfaction.

8.

Categories of Greatest Dissatisfaction

Financial Services and Healthcare

Women are dissatisfied with available products and services in a few categories, financial services and healthcare in particular. There are important inflection points in a woman's life when money is in motion and when she most needs help and is open to change. Key opportunities: providing women with information, respect, and rewards. Investment and life insurance are open space for the female consumer. These categories will become hotbeds of competition for both new and old dollars. Be there first.

I n many categories, women are well served by companies that can deliver products and services to meet their wants and needs, and we've described several of them in this book. But a handful of categories lag behind or, worse, are indifferent or even hostile to women's needs, including travel, cars, consumer electronics, and education.

The categories that women around the world reported being least satisfied with are also two of the most important today: financial services and healthcare. These are services that are vital to the growth of developing nations and fundamental to the continued success of developed nations. For individuals, too, healthcare and financial services serve as benchmarks of success, security, and hope for the future.

Women, as we have discussed, are in most households the primary managers of finances, caretakers of spouses and children, and decision makers in all domestic matters. It stands to reason, then, that the financial services and healthcare industries would target women as their main customers, and would put significant energy and resources into discovering and delivering what women want. But this is not so. On the contrary, both industries are male-dominated and maintain outdated business and marketing practices that still assume men to be their target consumers. This misconception is detrimental for all involved: it has made women distrustful and frustrated with both industries, and this of course is bad news for providers of financial services and healthcare.

But there is hope for all. The women we spoke to are quite clear about their problems with financial services and healthcare, as well as about what they'd really like to see.

THE CATEGORY MOST BEGGING FOR TRANSFORMATION: FINANCIAL SERVICES

Financial services win the prize as the category least sympathetic to women—and the one that offers the greatest opportunity for companies that could change this mind-set. Financial services have a vast and growing pool of female-directed revenue, even with the setbacks of the economic downturn of 2008. The worldwide revenue pool of the financial services industry is expected to grow at a rate of nearly 6 percent over the years 2005–2010, to about $1.6 trillion. Women represent the greatest opportunity for growth within this segment, for all the reasons we have discussed in this book: they control nearly half the wealth in this country, the great majority are wage earners in their own right, they are pressed for time, and, in the great majority of households in the United States, women are the ones who manage the finances. They also identify this task as one of their most serious challenges. Forty-seven percent of the women in our survey, in fact, said that managing household finances is the top challenge they face in their daily lives. Most say they don't save as much money as they would like and are uncertain if they will have enough money when they retire.

Yet despite the huge importance of finances in most women's lives, despite the fact that women's income and economic power continue to grow, and despite the fact that women need and welcome financial advice, they are continually let down by and exasperated with the level and quality of advice and service they get from financial companies.

She doesn't save as much as she wants

Even upper-class women are unsure that they are adequately preparing for retirement

Lower economic class	
Most frequent responses	%
Sometimes I cannot pay my monthly bills.	41.3
I try to save but not as much as I'd like.	36.8
I spend all of the money I make each month.	34.4
I'll start to save money in the future, not now.	15.2
I consistently save money for the future.	9.0

Lower middle class	
Most frequent responses	%
I try to save but not as much as I'd like.	48.1
I spend all of the money I make each month.	29.4
Sometimes I cannot pay my monthly bills.	25.4
I'll start to save money in the future, not now.	15.8
I consistently save money for the future.	14.4

Middle class	
Most frequent responses	%
I try to save but not as much as I'd like.	45.6
I consistently save money for the future.	25.3
I think I will be able to save enough money for my retirement.	18.5
I spend all of the money I make each month.	17.1
I'll start to save money in the future, not now.	12.6

Upper middle class and above	
Most frequent responses	%
I consistently save money for the future.	37.1
I try to save but not as much as I'd like.	31.6
I think I will be able to save enough money for my retirement.	27.0
I have no financial concerns at this point.	22.2
I'll start to save money in the future, not now.	8.1

Source: Question Q77 of survey; Lower economic class N = 943; lower middle class N = 2,456; middle class N = 5,290; upper middle class and above N = 3,058.

Dorothy Hastings: Financial Knowledge Born from Tragedy

It is during times of transition or crisis that most women avail themselves of financial services beyond ordinary bank accounts and 401(k) plans. Unfortunately, however, these are also the times when women are most pressed for time, most strained physically and emotionally, and most vulnerable to damage from bad advice or duplicity. Even the most intelligent and successful women can find themselves in hot water financially, and all too often these situations force them into an intimate understanding of financial services, without the benefit of a pleasant or satisfactory experience.

Take, for example, the story of Dorothy Hastings. Both Dorothy and Daniel Hastings had built successful careers at a respected publishing company, based in Connecticut, over a period of twenty-five years. In 2004, Dorothy was offered a one-year teaching fellowship in Oregon. Daniel decided to take an unpaid leave so he and their three children, ages 10, 15, and 19, could be with her. Just as the year in Oregon was coming to an end, Daniel, at age 52, suffered a massive heart attack and died.

Dorothy returned to Connecticut with her kids and found her affairs in disarray. Daniel had handled all the family finances. "I'm not particularly proud of it, but it's probably not atypical," said Dorothy. "We were both working full-time and raising a large family. Our division of labor resulted in my husband handling the finances. He paid the bills, he handled loans, he handled investments, the banking accounts. I really didn't have much to do with it at all, except to criticize him from afar. When he died very suddenly, I was completely in the dark. I was thrust into financial chaos."

At first Dorothy was stunned and almost unable to take any action. "I sat in my sunroom—which I called my debtor's prison—as the bills began to come in. Daniel had a lot of bank loans that I really didn't know anything about. He was constantly refinancing our mortgages. I had no idea what our mortgage situation was. Because we had been away for the year, we had been under a lot of financial stress. There were a lot of bills backed up right on the brink. I really just had to watch what was coming in the mail, and answer phone calls, and try to piece together a very complex situation."

Daniel had left a will, and Dorothy hired a lawyer to see her through probate because "I was very concerned about my vulnerability." Dorothy and Daniel's employer provided her with a financial counselor, a man whom she describes as "extremely helpful and caring—very honest and nice. I could not say that about a number of other people I had to deal with." However, she wishes she had been better able to pay attention to his advice. "I was more or less delirious. I wasn't able to focus on what he was telling me. I should have had someone there with me but I didn't. I'm sure there were things he told me that would have been useful, but I wasn't in the mental state to be able to home in on that information and make the kinds of decisions I needed to make." Now she advises any woman who is newly widowed or divorced to "have a trusted friend who really is willing to be at your side through the whole thing. I had to do it alone, and it was hard."

Armed with the book *Personal Finance for Dummies*, Dorothy then turned her attention to figuring out the complicated finances that Daniel had left behind. "I am very buttoned-down. I want things very simple and clear, and I would rather live well within my means. He was a juggler—a Cat in the Hat. His father was a commercial banker, and my father was a savings and loan guy. It's a different style and approach to money."

Initially, she says, "I was hell-bent on simplifying and streamlining my whole financial situation. I felt it was so sprawling and I was so not on top of it; I wanted to solidify the foundation and amputate all the ancillary stuff out there." Along with a primary residence, the family owned two vacation condos. She sold one "probably at a price that was too low, but I wanted to get rid of it." She also sold an expensive car that Daniel had purchased, a motorcycle, and a trailer. She cut up most of the credit cards. She put her home and the other condo in her own name, and refinanced mortgages for both with the help of a mortgage broker.

The biggest problem turned out to be life insurance. When the couple went to Oregon, Dorothy retained her health benefits, and Daniel went onto her plan (in previous years, Dorothy had been on Daniel's plan). Daniel waived most of his health benefits during the year that he went on leave, but Dorothy does not recall that he waived his supplemental life insurance. She expected a payout of his insurance to be four times his salary, giving her $320,000—"which would have made a huge difference to me."

Dorothy remembers two executives from her publishing company coming to tell her the news that she was going to receive not $320,000, but only $80,000, plus Daniel's pension of $500 per month. The insurance company claimed that Daniel had waived the supplemental benefits by telephone. "My heart just went scalding hot—I just felt my whole life collapse—if it could collapse any more than it already had. At that moment, this huge, scary, dark pit of snakes appeared—which was my financial situation. I felt I did not have the money to right the ship. I was devastated."

As Dorothy tried to fight the insurance settlement, she said the basic customer service from the company that her publisher used for benefits was "unbelievably insulting and patronizing. I would have to call an 800 number. I would have to wait for the menu and then dial this and that every time I wanted to talk to somebody. They wouldn't know who I was, and they weren't on top of the information. The insurance company sent me form letter after form letter—I got one three years after Daniel died saying, 'We have just received news of your husband's death.'"

Dorothy has now made it a point to make sure she understands her own benefits package, even though in the past this was never something she spent much time worrying about. She doesn't know whether she was badly treated by the insurance company because she is a woman, but she speculates, "I think if I had been one of the guys, the publisher would have probably just fixed it."

These days, Dorothy feels "highly educated" about matters of personal finance. "I am now very attuned to things that most of my female friends are not. I read the *New York Times* business section first. I read the *Wall Street Journal* every day. I'm very attuned to what's happening in the stock market. I'm very concerned about my retirement situation. I'm concerned about getting my kids through college. A lot of basic financial stuff is always on my mind—it's now part of my job."

Dorothy's financial portrait is now vastly simplified and she understands it all: a 401(k) in a Vanguard targeted fund, one credit card, no car loan, and little consumer debt. "I'm very busy and I just want to simplify my financial situation. It's probably gender-related. I'm a woman on my own raising a family, with a demanding job."

Dorothy advises other women to stay involved in their finances and not give up control to a spouse. "A division of labor at home where the husbands handle the money is a bad situation to get yourself into. Even though life is very complicated, and you have to divide things up, if the two of you can work the finances as a partnership, rather than one person handling it, I think it serves you well over time."

THE FAILINGS OF FINANCIAL SERVICES

Dorothy was able to adjust to her new role as household finance manager, and she was lucky to have help from a lawyer, a financial adviser, and other counselors who treated her with respect and helped her to navigate her complex financial questions and concerns. Many other women are not so lucky.

What do women want from financial services products that they are not getting now? A recognition from the industry that women view money and wealth very differently from men. Their goal is not to accumulate money. Their interest is not in playing with money—they are not always looking for new investment vehicles or tinkering with portfolios. Women do not have a great interest in money itself. They value money only as a way to care for themselves and their families, improve their lives, and—very important—ensure security. So they do not need financial products and services that offer access to complex money manipulation methods. They want advisers and services that recognize their need for short-term simplicity and long-term stability. They want solutions that help them with their most frustrating task: managing the household finances from day to day and month to month.

In particular, we have identified four service categories that financial firms could improve in order to capture more of women's business:

Household administration. Helping women keep track of family finances easily and securely and enabling them to save time spent in making calculations, writing checks, and mailing payments.

Financial education. Providing opportunities for women to learn more about budgeting, saving, and long-term financial planning.

Financial advice and long-term planning. Providing financial advisers who truly understand women's needs, who can help women with financial planning, and who treat women as equals and with respect.

Children's solutions. Effectively protecting children during financial troubles. Giving children access to funds in emergencies and teaching them about finances.

In general, women are not getting these services and solutions now. Our survey respondents were scathing in their comments about their dealings with financial services and institutions. They have experienced disrespect, poor advice, contradictory policies, and a seemingly endless obstacle course of red tape and one-size-fits-all forms that have left them exhausted and annoyed.

Here are some of the comments from our interviewees:

"First and foremost, many financial planners talk down to me. I ask a lot of questions, because I want to understand their investment strategies."

—JANICE, 46, PRESSURE COOKER

"I hate being stereotyped because of my gender and age, and I don't appreciate being talked to like an infant."

—MARIANA, 28, MANAGING ON HER OWN

"I would change how many financial service reps talk down to women as if we cannot understand more than just the basics when it comes to financial discussions. Being in the financial industry myself, I find these attitudes highly insulting."

—KAREN, 51, EMPTY NESTER

"As a single woman, I often feel that financial services institutions aren't looking for my business. They want people who are preparing for kids. While I'd love to have kids, I don't want another reminder that kids aren't in my near-term future."

—LIZ, 29, MANAGING ON HER OWN

"Advisers are almost afraid to let the woman make the decision. They tend to defer to the male, no matter who is asking the questions or doing the investing."

—CECILIA, 61, EMPTY NESTER

Although women have their quarrels with basic banking services, credit card terms, and some lending practices, the greatest opportunity for improvement lies in financial advice and investment services. The main dissatisfactions with these are that advisers and agents treat women poorly, do not understand women's needs, and do not have women's best interests in mind. Women say they want better information sources and educational materials to help them make decisions. Women also tell us they feel that rates, fees, and interest are unreasonable, and are sometimes hidden or unclear.

A key group within the Fast Tracker archetype consists of women who are most eager to find better advice. These women tend to be middle- to upper-class, well-educated, with a net worth of between $500,000 and $1 million. Yet a significant amount of that wealth—an average of 20 percent—is in their checking or savings accounts.

These women know very well that they could and should do more with their money but have not found a way that satisfies them. They say

Life events that put money in motion create opportunity

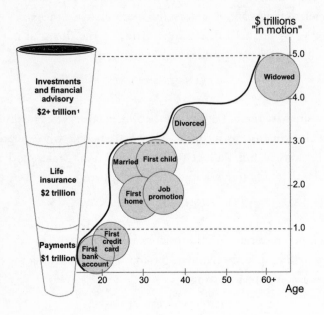

$ trillions "in motion"

Investments and financial advisory
$2+ trillion[1]

Life insurance
$2 trillion

Payments
$1 trillion

Widowed

Divorced

Married First child

First home Job promotion

First credit card

First bank account

20   30   40   50   60+

Age

1. Total market size forecast for U.S. women's wealth ~$14 trillion. Estimated money "in motion" through divorce and loss of spouse is $2 trillion.

that the financial advisers they have worked with are not proactive enough, do not provide enough information about their processes, and generally assume that their clients do not want to pay higher fees for greater access to information and their adviser's time. Our research shows that these assumptions are incorrect. Women want to have more engagement with their advisers, would rather spend time with them live than doing research online by themselves, and are quite willing to trade up for an adviser to whom they can delegate important investment decisions.

As we saw with Dorothy Hastings, there are certain periods in their

At $100K she invests more in real estate; stock becomes a greater share of her portfolio at the $1MM level

Type	<$50K	$50K– $100K	$100K– $500K	$500K –$1MM	$1MM– $5MM	$5MM+
% checking	30	17	8	10	4	8
% savings	27	23	17	11	8	9
% retirement fund	19	24	30	23	17	31
% stock	4	6	7	8	17	13
% mutual funds	6	9	8	14	14	6
% bonds	1	2	1	2	5	8
% real estate	6	9	22	28	24	14
% life insurance	6	5	4	3	3	7
% other	1	4	1	0	2	11

> **Opportunity to help her diversify, especially below $1MM**

lives when women are most in need of financial help, usually concerning life events that cause a change in their status.

For a majority of women, these include opening her first bank account, getting a first credit card, getting a first job, getting married, buying a home, giving birth, getting a job promotion, and being divorced or widowed. For a smaller number of women, there are important "liquidity events," such as selling a business or coming into an inheritance, that also put her in the market for new or better financial assistance.

At these times, a tremendous amount of money is set "in motion"—dislodged from one resting place or financial instrument and available to be transferred to another. These are obviously periods of greatest opportunity for financial services companies. If you can successfully serve a woman while she's "on the rise"—increasing her wealth or making an important investment decision—she'll probably become a loyal customer and will prefer to stay with you as she moves into higher brackets. Even if her income and net worth do not increase significantly, she is likely to remain a loyal and profitable customer of the company that helped her through a significant life event.

A woman's attitude and behavior toward money and money management also change with age, wealth, and archetype. Younger women tend to keep most of their money in traditional bank accounts. Pressure Cooker women and women who are Making Ends Meet have very high dissatisfaction with all financial services, primarily because they are under greater financial pressures than women in other segments. In those segments, women under the age of 50 are likely to prefer to do their banking online whenever possible, primarily because they feel that their financial advisers

Sheila Penrose: The Financial Services Industry Needs More Women

The financial services industry (like the beauty industry, and perhaps most industries) is dominated by male executives, as well as male financial services advisers and product developers.

Sheila Penrose, however, is one woman who has risen to the top in financial services. She spent nearly twenty-five years with Northern Trust Corporation and was the first woman named to its management committee. From 1994 to 2000, she served as president of Northern Trust's Corporate and Institutional Services, a unit with $1 billion in annual sales and client assets of $1.5 trillion, operating in more than eighty markets worldwide. Under Penrose's leadership, the business was transformed from a product-focused organization to one organized around client segments, and net income grew 17 percent annually. She represented Northern Trust with the investor community, oversaw several acquisitions, and drove the bank's global expansion.

In 2000, Penrose retired from Northern Trust and founded the Penrose Group, a provider of strategic advisory services on financial and organizational strategies. She is chairman of the board of Jones Lang LaSalle, chairs the nominating and governance committees of two companies, and serves on two other corporate boards and five other board committees. She cofounded and chairs the Corporate Leadership Center, a partnership between major corporations and the Kellogg School of Management.

Today, despite her own success, Penrose sees that women need to keep pushing corporations, including financial services companies, to change. "There has been a genuine and sincere effort on the part of businessmen and institutions to create a more effective environment for women. And there has been real progress. There are more women serving on boards, more women in the top ranks of companies. But, really, there is not that much net advance. As the first and second waves of women are retiring, we're replacing them. But the net advance is minimal. Corporate cultures are very resilient in that way. There is just not enough that is different in 2008 from when I started out."

don't understand their needs and it takes too much time to get the service and information they need.

Older women, particularly older women who are managing on their own, are the most dissatisfied as well as the most demanding customers. These women are more dissatisfied than younger women with such basic banking services as credit cards, as well as with investment services and advice. As they age, these women typically shift their wealth from stocks and bank accounts into retirement plans and real estate. They have more wealth than women in other segments and also more time to manage it, yet, even though their wealth rises, they are less willing to pay more for better information. Still, older women represent a major opportunity.

HEALTHCARE: A LONG WAIT FOR SOLUTIONS

The women in our survey tell us, resoundingly, that they worry a great deal about their health and the health of their families. In fact, women value health second only to love. Yet they are very dissatisfied with the state of their healthcare—most particularly the care they receive in hospitals and from their physicians.

Not surprisingly, time pressure is at the heart of women's dissatisfaction with healthcare. Women are frustrated by the amount of time they spend waiting to see a doctor or to get tests done or lab work completed, and by the total time they devote to the process. They are also dissatisfied with the whole business of making appointments—scheduling is difficult, doctors are overbooked, and often patients have to make multiple appointments for services that they think could be taken care of in one visit.

After the frustrations of wasted time dealing with appointments and follow-ups, health insurance is, perhaps unsurprisingly, the greatest area of dissatisfaction for women in the United States and other countries without universal healthcare. Availability, coverage, and cost are issues that cause almost constant worry. In the United States, the number of women with health insurance varies hugely from state to state, from 92 percent in Massachusetts to 72 percent in Louisiana and Texas.[1] And those with health insurance pay a great deal more for the privilege than their male counterparts do.

Women generally pay between 30 and 50 percent more per year for health insurance than men of the same age. Insurance companies claim that this is because women between ages 19 and 55 avail themselves of more healthcare services: they are more likely to get regular physical exams, go to specialists, and take prescription medications. These women are in their childbearing and child-rearing years, insurers say, so they should be willing to pay more for services that keep their bodies healthy. But women who don't have children pay just as much for their insurance coverage, and in fact most insurance companies charge a great deal more for maternity-related services.

"I've delayed having a baby because my insurance policy does not cover maternity care. If I have a baby, I'll have to pay at least $8,000 out of pocket," says Crystal D. Kilpatrick, a 33-year-old real estate agent in Austin, Texas.

Representative Lloyd Doggett, Democrat of Texas, asked, "How can insurers in the individual market claim to meet the needs of women if maternity coverage is so difficult to get, so inadequate and expensive?"[2]

Healthcare is not an easy or a straightforward problem, but women are bearing the brunt of the cost and the frustration. Still, there are companies that go above and beyond to serve women's needs in health-related products and services, and their effort pays off in the loyalty they win from their female consumers.

JOHNSON & JOHNSON: DOMINANCE OF THE MEDICINE CABINET

Johnson & Johnson, although not a provider of healthcare services, is a company that bucks the healthcare trend by delivering products that meet women's needs and that respect women's time.

Founded in 1886 to provide surgical and wound care products, J&J has transformed itself into a global healthcare leader with a portfolio that spans pharmaceuticals, over-the-counter consumer items, medical devices, and diagnostic products. Its consumer business achieves sales of $15 billion annually, of which over-the-counter products account for $5 billion, skincare $3 billion, baby care $2 billion, oral care $2 billion, and women's health about $1.8 billion.

J&J has been particularly successful at assembling a powerful core of brands for women, most of which are leaders in their fields. Take, for example, J&J's $1 billion oral contraceptives business. The Ortho division developed the first prescription contraceptive jelly, the first diaphragm, and the first test for detecting cervical cancer. Although J&J did not invent the contraceptive or the category, it aggressively marketed both—Ortho was one of the first birth control pills to be advertised on television—and quickly emerged as a leader in the category.

Oral contraceptives first came on the market in 1960, when the U.S. Food and Drug Administration (FDA) approved them for general use. J&J launched its first Ortho pill three years later. During the next ten years, J&J continued to innovate and improve its offering, by introducing lower-dose pills and introducing the first progestin-only pill created especially for nursing mothers. In the 1980s, J&J developed the first multiphasic pills, which delivered progestin in differing levels. In 1997, J&J launched Ortho Tri-Cyclen, a medicine that also had FDA approval for the treatment of acne—providing the user with two benefits. In 2002, J&J introduced Ortho Evra, a birth control patch; and Ortho Tri-Cyclen Lo, a lower-hormone pill that lowers the incidence of some common side effects. The Ortho division has made an important contribution to women's independence and ability to choose the window for pregnancy.

But J&J offers women a great deal more than contraceptives. Through the years, it has pioneered dozens of products that help make the lives of women and their families healthier, easier, and better—including dental floss, first aid kits, baby powder, sanitary napkins, and disposable contact lenses. The company has grown organically and also made a number of acquisitions. In 1959, J&J purchased McNeil Labs to gain access to Tylenol; it bought LifeScan in 1986 for its diagnostics and devices; and in the 1990s J&J brought a broad range of skincare products into the fold through acquisition of Clean & Clear, Neutrogena, RoC, and Aveeno. In 2005, J&J made the largest acquisition and biggest bet in its history, with the purchase of the well-known and trusted Pfizer consumer brands—Listerine, Lubriderm, Visine, Neosporin, and Benadryl—for $16.6 billion, more than four times annual sales and twenty times earnings before interest and taxes (EBIT).

Women in our survey often cited J&J brands as their favorites. Neutrogena and Aveeno were the more obvious picks, but women's penchant for J&J products isn't limited to skincare; Listerine, Splenda, and Stayfree were also frequently mentioned. Our survey results are consistent with the market position of J&J brands, which are number one or two globally across a wide range of categories, including baby care, eye care, pain, digestive health, and sanitary protection. The company holds leading positions in the United States, Canada, the United Kingdom, France, Italy, Russia, Brazil, India, China, Mexico, and many other countries.

With this remarkable portfolio of brands, J&J has achieved "medicine cabinet dominance." During our research, we regularly asked to take a peek inside the medicine cabinets of the women we interviewed, and in almost every one of them we found a bottle of Tylenol or Benadryl, a box of Band-Aids, a tube of Neosporin, a J&J skincare product, or a product from its baby line.

Johnson & Johnson Brands at a Glance

FEMALE-FOCUSED BRANDS

Neutrogena: A line of skincare, haircare, and cosmetics featuring clean, no-frills products without heavy perfumes and drying agents. The product lines run the gamut from teenage health and beauty (antiacne treatments, fun eyeliner shades) to mature personal care (antiaging cream, color-protecting shampoos).

Monistat: A product to treat yeast infection, and the treatment that most American women recognize and trust. The product features an easy-to-use applicator and comes in three dosage options: one-day, three-day, and seven-day.

o.b.: A line of tampons designed by a female gynecologist, o.b. differs from other brands in several distinctive ways: these tampons are far smaller than usual, they don't require a plastic or cardboard applicator, and they are made from a material that expands to custom-fit a woman's body.

e.p.t.: The e.p.t., or error-proof test, is a 99 percent accurate home pregnancy test. It offers step-by-step instructions, an easy-to-use and easy-to-read test stick, and results within two to three minutes of testing.

Ortho McNeil: A family of birth control products, including the oral contraceptive Ortho Tri-Cyclen and the revolutionary and much-disputed contraceptive patch, Ortho Evra.

FAMILY-ORIENTED BRANDS

Johnson's: A line of skincare designed to maintain moisture and softness in adult skin.

Tylenol: A leading medication for headache, fever, and pain relief. The line of over-the-counter medications has expanded to offer cold, sinus, and flu relief.

Acuvue: The first-ever brand of disposable contact lenses, and still one of the leading contact brands.

Band-Aid: The leading name in disposable bandages. Band-Aid offers an impressive variety of products, including antibacterial and pain relief bandages that make first aid easy and convenient for moms.

Sudafed: A nasal decongestant used to treat cold symptoms and allergies. Sudafed is popular for its comparative lack of side effects.

Zyrtec: A fast-acting allergy medication. Zyrtec is advertised as "time in a bottle," and promises up to two hours of time that would otherwise be lost to suffering.

Nicorette: An aid to help smokers quit that contains nicotine as an active ingredient. Originally available as a patch, Nicorette is now also available as a gum in a variety of flavors.

Bringing Science to the Art of Healthy Living

Johnson & Johnson achieves success by "bringing science to the art of healthy living." Its focus on science and technology has enabled the company to generate a significant number of patents, which it has been able to commercialize into its winning product portfolio. But J&J focuses equally on consumer research and insights to shape its products. The company spends more than $500 million annually on research and development within its consumer groups—that figure represents 4 percent of sales, double the 1 to 2 percent that most consumer products companies devote to R&D. Globally, J&J spends nearly $8 billion on R&D every year and, although much of the money goes to research in the pharmaceutical and device businesses, the company leverages partnerships with and technology findings from those and other businesses to bring scientific benefits to its consumer franchise.

J&J pursued this strategy—combining science and technology with deep insight into consumers—to help mothers cope better with their babies' sleeping habits. In interviews with parents, J&J learned a great deal about how babies sleep and, more important, how they don't. It found that babies wake up continually during the night and that this causes their mothers serious distress. In search of solutions for improving babies' sleep cycles, J&J conducted a clinical study in partnership with a leading pediatric sleep expert at the Children's Hospital of Philadelphia. Together, they developed a three-step routine designed to help babies sleep better, consisting of bath, massage, and quiet time. J&J publicized its findings and launched a line of Johnson's "Bedtime" products to complement the routine, many of them containing natural calming essences, scents that help the baby fall asleep. But what makes the "Bedtime" line so compelling and believable is not the ingredients, but rather the medical partnership and the behavioral routine, which enable J&J to market this portfolio as "clinically proven to promote better sleep for babies." It is something mothers trust, believe in, and will purchase.

This combination of science and insight enables J&J to make compelling claims about its products across the portfolio and helps generate buy-in from members of the medical community. In healthcare categories, the marketing approach with the greatest power is professional endorsement—and J&J has developed endorsements for many of its products: dermatologists endorse Neutrogena and Aveeno; dentists support Listerine; doctors advocate for Tylenol, Neosporin, KY, and Monistat; maternity professionals endorse the baby line.

The strategy has fueled J&J's growth. The company's sales have consistently grown in double digits and the company has an operating margin approaching 30 percent. Over the past decade, the pharma business has grown at a 12.5 percent CAGR; Devices/Diagnostics has grown 10 percent; Consumer has grown 8.4 percent. And J&J's success is more than just rising sales and healthy margins. The company delivers on its promises, and that has translated into genuine market value. Over the past ten years J&J has seen its market capitalization grow by more than $100 billion. Its stock has grown at a CAGR of 7 percent, outpacing the healthcare peer group average of about 3 percent.

An Unusual Focus on the Consumer

Johnson & Johnson's success with consumer brands is unusual in healthcare, where so many other companies have divested themselves of their consumer brands and businesses. J&J, by contrast, has continued to acquire leading brands, many of them focused on women. It refines these products to better suit women's needs, develops them further, invests more in them, reinvents them, and develops them even more. As it does, it builds brand value, increases consumers' loyalty, and creates market value.

This is exactly how J&J has transformed its skincare business. J&J has built its entire skincare line through acquisition—Clean & Clear in 1991, RoC in 1993, Neutrogena in 1994, and Aveeno in 1999. Each provided an opportunity to reach different segments of women, at different stages of life, and with varying purchasing power. Clean & Clear targets teens; Neutrogena and Aveeno offer natural benefits; RoC is aimed at women with higher incomes and those who will trade up for skincare products—and that is probably a majority of women. In our survey, 56 percent of respondents said they trade up for better facial skincare.

Johnson & Johnson has developed each of these skincare brands through line extensions, category adjacencies, improvements, and refinements. Aveeno has grown 27 percent CAGR; Clean & Clear 24 percent, and RoC 8 percent; and Neutrogena has achieved 12 percent annual growth.

Aveeno's success in particular demonstrates J&J's ability to respond to women and refine products for them. Aveeno was developed in 1945 in conjunction with the Mayo Clinic as an oatmeal bath treatment to relieve itching. It was efficacious and soothing, but not exactly thought of as a beauty care line. But J&J thought differently about the opportunity. In 1999, it acquired Aveeno and tapped into the growing demand for natural beauty products. J&J effectively leveraged Aveeno's trusted "natural, soothing relief" brand equity and through a series of innovations extended the brand into category adjacencies—baby care, body wash, facial care, lip care, and sun care. Women will trade up for each of these Aveeno products, and that willingness enables J&J to realize a price premium and build its share of the category. In effect, J&J has created an Aveeno "master brand" that can be improved and extended almost indefinitely across new categories. This strategy enabled Aveeno to grow at a 27 percent CAGR between 1999 and 2007—a higher growth rate than any other consumer brand, in any category.

Aveeno is a "brand without borders": women across demographics cite it as a favorite. Twenty-three-year-old women love Aveeno, as do women age 60. Most women—especially Fast Tracker, Pressure Cooker, and Struggling for Stability women—say they love Aveeno.

And Aveeno is not the only superstar in J&J's skincare portfolio. Women across all ages and income classes also love Neutrogena, a line of skin, sun, hair, and cosmetics products that manages to be both healthy and trendy, and has sufficient clinical worth to earn recommendations from dermatologists. Sharon, a 37-year-old Relationship-Focused woman in the United States, tells us that she uses Neutrogena skincare products simply "because they work." Melissa, 42, a Struggling for Stability woman in the United States, also cites Neutrogena as her favorite brand, and uses several different products. Molly, a 28-year-old Fast Tracker from Australia, loves Neutrogena because "they produce outstanding skincare products at an affordable price and it just works really well for me." Three categories of women, all of whom love Neutrogena.

J&J has achieved similar success in a wide variety of other categories by creating effective and convenient products that help women deal with the triple challenge of time. Zyrtec, for example, is an allergy medication to which J&J acquired the rights from Pfizer. Zyrtec was launched into the food, drug, and mass merchandiser (FDM) channels in January 2008, and almost immediately, consumers who had been relying on prescription drugs switched to the over-the-counter Zyrtec. In less than six months, Zyrtec generated nearly $150 million in sales and achieved a market share of more than 25 percent. The television commercial for Zyrtec is all about the importance of time. "You know that song about *time in a bottle*?" a young woman asks. She smiles. "Well, I just got time in a bottle. Just by changing my allergy medicine to Zyrtec. It's faster; it works faster and keeps working." She pauses. "You know, Zyrtec should put that on the label: ingredients—*2 hours you didn't have before!*"

Throughout its history, J&J has aggressively pursued its strategy of science in service of the consumer. It is a leader in technical innovation, expanding category definitions, pinpoint targeting, responding to specific dissatisfactions, and investing to improve the opportunity to increase margins. Women have always been at the center of J&J's efforts. By our estimate, among all companies in the world only Procter & Gamble has higher sales to women.

HOW TO RESPOND TO THE DISSATISFACTIONS

There are eight categories in which suppliers have the potential to cash in by responding to the needs of women: (1) financial services, (2) healthcare services, (3) food at home, (4) food away from home, (5) travel, (6) cars, (7) consumer electronics, and (8) home goods.

Responding in financial services requires customization of products and services to address women's needs without "insult," "denial," or "pandering." Women want respect and power. The best times to address their needs are the inflection points when money is in motion.

In healthcare, women are responsible for their own needs and also the needs of their children, husbands, and often parents. They have four primary areas of dissatisfaction: time, information access, empathy, and tangible value.

These two categories consume over 20 percent of consumer incomes around the world, but they are rife with major dissatisfactions and system failings. This is a call to action to apply the four R's and to prioritize needs and wants; assess dissatisfactions; change holistically, not incrementally; launch and refine; capture more.

In a bleak economy, women hold the cards for a new prosperity. As we have said, it is a quiet economic and social revolution driven by women's labor, income growth, share of spending, and raw ambition. There will be about $800 billion in incremental income in the United States over the next five years, and about $5 trillion in incremental income in the rest of the world. There are 1 billion working women, and their number will grow to 1.2 billion over the next five years. And the most affluent 100 million are driving the majority of wealth and social change.

PART III

Women Worldwide

The Low-Growth Economies
The Optimistic Economies
Women Want More for the World

9.

The Low-Growth Economies

Europe and Japan

The developed economies have serious problems with population re-placement, poverty, and domestic violence. The Women's World Index ranks countries in terms of economic opportunity for females. Providing paid parental leave and healthcare for women holds the potential for substantial changes in GDP. Why Sweden leads the ranking. Germany and the issue of work-family balance. French women are stressed out. Surprising dissatisfaction in Italy. Spanish women take control. We see a gradual easing of traditions in Japan.

In preparing to write this book, we conducted interviews with women all over the world, learning about their personal stories, their daily routines, and their lifelong struggles and triumphs. We conducted The Boston Consulting Group Global Inquiry into Women and Consumerism, which reached some 12,000 women in twenty-two countries, and from those responses got a clear picture of the way women all over the world think and feel: what their dreams and fears are, what their lives are like now, and how they'd like their lives to be.

Using the information from these sources as context, we set out to further analyze the data and to discover and compare the specifics of daily life for women in different geographic areas around the world. In particular, we wanted to measure gender equality in various countries, on the personal, cultural, and political levels.

The result of this research is the Women's World Index (WWI), a comprehensive index of quantitative data measuring the role and the impact of women in their respective regions. Using data from a number of sources—including the United States Census, the UN Development Programme's

Gender-Related Development Index (UNDP GDI), the UNDP Gender Empowerment Measure (UNDP GEM), and a variety of private databases and
indexes of demographic data—the Women's World Index examines virtually every facet of women's lives.

The Women's World Index improves on existing indexes by including
categories and supplementary research that further expand the base of
knowledge, particularly with regard to the relationship between national
economic health and gender equality.

The Index is divided into eight categories: (1) education, (2) political empowerment, (3) economic empowerment, (4) health and well-being, (5) support for families, (6) share of household burden, (7) commercial influence,
and (8) stress level. For each of the twenty-two countries we researched, we
measured women's position—at home and in society—using ten weighted
metrics, including control of spending, earned income, paid parental leave,
and life expectancy. The metrics were then averaged to give each country a
score between 1 and 100.

The Women's World Index has provided us with a lens through which
to view the many—and sometimes vastly disparate—roles that women
play, both in their own countries and compared with other countries and
cultures. The Index has also revealed some startling correlations between
a country's well-being and the well-being of its women. Using the Index, for
example, we found that by bringing paid parental leave and healthcare
for women to "best in class," the United States could probably increase its
gross domestic product (GDP) by as much as 35 percent.

The Women's World Index has a strong correlation with income for the
twenty-two countries we studied. The most important elements are access
to education, parity wage for parity work, professional degrees that open
up professional and technical positions, access to healthcare, paid parental
leave, and husbands who share the household burden. Sweden's high rank
is due to the 1.55 ratio of females to males in tertiary education, low stress,
a life expectancy of 83 years, and women's holding half of all seats in parliament and 51 percent of professional and technical positions. In contrast, in
India women have 30 percent fewer enrollments in tertiary education, suffer the world's highest maternal mortality rate, have a life expectancy of 65
years, earn 31 percent of male wages, and hold only 9 percent of seats in
parliament and 21 percent of professional and technical positions.

The Women's World Index also gives an indication of commercial op-

The BCG Women's World Index (WWI)

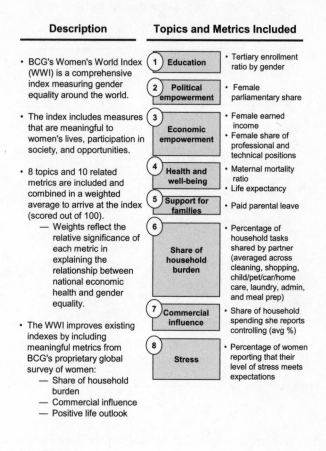

Description	Topics and Metrics Included

- BCG's Women's World Index (WWI) is a comprehensive index measuring gender equality around the world.

- The index includes measures that are meaningful to women's lives, participation in society, and opportunities.

- 8 topics and 10 related metrics are included and combined in a weighted average to arrive at the index (scored out of 100).
    — Weights reflect the relative significance of each metric in explaining the relationship between national economic health and gender equality.

- The WWI improves existing indexes by including meaningful metrics from BCG's proprietary global survey of women:
    — Share of household burden
    — Commercial influence
    — Positive life outlook

1 Education
- Tertiary enrollment ratio by gender

2 Political empowerment
- Female parliamentary share

3 Economic empowerment
- Female earned income
- Female share of professional and technical positions

4 Health and well-being
- Maternal mortality ratio
- Life expectancy

5 Support for families
- Paid parental leave

6 Share of household burden
- Percentage of household tasks shared by partner (averaged across cleaning, shopping, child/pet/car/home care, laundry, admin, and meal prep)

7 Commercial influence
- Share of household spending she reports controlling (avg %)

8 Stress
- Percentage of women reporting that their level of stress meets expectations

Source: BCG analysis.

portunities within each country, especially for businesses that cater to the specific needs of women there—a topic we'll review in this chapter.

SWEDEN AND SCANDINAVIA: SETTING THE STANDARD

Sweden tops the charts worldwide as the country that provides the most opportunity and inflicts the least discrimination on women.

BCG WWI averages 10 weighted metrics

Index incorporates 3 highly weighted metrics from proprietary BCG survey data

Metric	Weight		Resulting rankings	Score
Tertiary education enrollment ratio	15%		1. Sweden	70
			2. Denmark	69
			3. Norway	68
Maternal mortality ratio	15%		4. Finland	64
			5. Netherlands	61
Stress	14%		6. Australia	61
			7. Germany	60
Control of spending	13%		8. Spain	59
			9. United States	58
Life expectancy	12%		10. United Kingdom	57
			11. Canada	57
Share of household burden	10%		12. France	57
			13. Italy	56
Paid parental leave	10%		14. Japan	53
			15. Russia	51
Female earned income	5%		16. Mexico	43
			17. China	42
Female parliamentary share	4%		18. Brazil	40
			19. Saudi Arabia	39
			20. Turkey	39
Female share of professional and technical positions	2%		21. Egypt	32
			22. India	30

Source: BCG analysis.

Annalie Lindstrand, whom we met in Chapter 1, told us about some of the benefits of living, working, and raising a family in Sweden. Universal healthcare, paid maternal and paternal leave, guaranteed daycare and preschool for children, and free tuition at top universities are just some of the rights offered to Swedish citizens. Similar social welfare packages are available in most other northern European countries, and they are major factors in setting Scandinavia apart from the rest of Europe and the world.

One of the most significant indicators of the impact of these social benefits is the birthrate in Scandinavia—particularly Sweden—compared with the rest of the Western world. For the past decade or more, as the developed world has experienced a marked decrease in birthrate, Sweden's birthrate has plateaued rather than declined. While the birthrate is not as high as

Facts behind our proprietary gender equality index

The BCG WWI captures the relationship between economic health and gender equality

Country	WWI rank	WWI score	Ratio of F:M enroll-ment	Maternal mortality ratio	Women reporting stress level meets expec-tations	Share of house-hold spending women report control-ling	Female life expec-tancy	% of house-hold tasks shared by partner	Paid parental leave	Ratio of F:M earned income	Female parlia-mentary share	Female share of profes-sional and technical positions
Sweden	1	70	1.55	3	32.0%	64.9%	82.7	30.7%	48	0.81	47.3%	51%
Denmark	2	69	1.39	3	44.2%	71.3%	80.1	25.1%	47	0.73	36.9%	53%
Norway	3	68	1.54	7	40.2%	69.6%	82.2	28.4%	43	0.77	37.9%	50%
Finland	4	64	1.21	7	34.0%	70.5%	82.0	32.3%	15	0.71	42.0%	55%
Netherlands	5	61	1.08	6	44.1%	67.4%	81.4	32.9%	16	0.64	36.0%	50%
Australia	6	61	1.25	4	37.0%	71.8%	83.3	33.0%	0	0.70	28.3%	56%
Germany	7	60	1.00	4	47.2%	72.7%	81.8	25.6%	14	0.58	30.6%	50%
Spain	8	59	1.22	4	39.8%	56.8%	83.8	26.1%	16	0.50	30.5%	48%
United States	9	58	1.40	11	35.2%	72.8%	80.4	29.0%	0	0.63	16.3%	56%
United Kingdom	10	57	1.39	8	35.0%	66.1%	81.2	25.7%	18	0.66	19.3%	47%
Canada	11	57	1.36	7	36.3%	67.2%	82.6	29.7%	8	0.64	24.3%	56%
France	12	57	1.29	8	32.5%	66.8%	83.7	31.8%	20	0.64	13.9%	47%
Italy	13	56	1.36	3	27.3%	58.6%	83.2	17.9%	16	0.47	16.1%	46%
Japan	14	53	0.89	6	32.8%	61.7%	85.7	20.5%	8	0.45	11.1%	46%
Russia	15	51	1.36	28	31.2%	60.1%	72.1	30.1%	20	0.62	8.0%	65%
Mexico	16	43	0.99	60	34.7%	58.1%	78.0	19.4%	12	0.39	21.5%	42%
China	17	42	0.95	45	29.9%	45.3%	74.3	18.5%	13	0.64	20.3%	52%
Brazil	18	40	1.32	110	24.7%	57.6%	75.5	16.6%	17	0.58	9.3%	52%
Saudi Arabia	19	39	1.47	18	45.7%	33.0%	74.6	26.8%	8	0.16	0.0%	6%
Turkey	20	39	0.74	44	30.4%	46.1%	73.9	17.6%	8	0.35	4.4%	32%
Egypt	21	32	0.55	130	35.6%	38.0%	73.0	12.4%	7	0.23	3.8%	30%
India	22	30	0.70	450	24.3%	42.5%	65.3	22.8%	12	0.31	9.0%	21%
Metrics in order of descending weight												
Weight in WWI			15%	15%	14%	13%	12%	10%	10%	5%	4%	2%

Source: BCG analysis.

some would like, it remains among the highest in Europe, along with the birthrates in Iceland, Norway, and France.

Hillevi Engstrom, a second-term member of the Swedish parliament and chairwoman of the labor committee, talked with us about how Sweden has attained its position as perhaps the most female-friendly nation on earth. "Sweden has always had a strong women's movement with an equally strong respect for human rights. It all started in the middle of the nineteenth century, when women were given partial voting rights. From there it went on and women were finally given full and equal voting rights in 1921. Sweden has enjoyed a long time of lasting peace. The last war Sweden was involved in was in 1809, against Russia (which we lost). Moreover, Sweden was industrialized rather early and fortunate to stay out of the two world wars. These facts have laid the ground for a strong and continuous political stability, which enabled us to experience long-lasting economic growth.

"Also, various women's movements of most political ideologies have been both active and successful from the mid-1800s. Their political influence must not be underestimated and has been instrumental in changing the general view on equality as a political issue. These views have been manifested in Sweden's traditional high regard for human rights as well as individual rights, which became apparent in the political upheaval and turmoil in the 1960s.

"These factors have all contributed to make Sweden maybe the most equal country in the world—although we are far from perfect."

The activism and advocacy for women have resulted in legislation with a clear focus on the well-being of women, children, and families. "Parents are entitled to between 390 and 480 days of paid parental leave. Two months of the parental leave are legally earmarked for the fathers and cannot be transferred to the mother. If the parents are same-sex parents, the same rule applies. 'Parental pay' depends on the parent's annual income, but the ceiling is set to an approximate maximum of [the equivalent of] $38,000 per annum."

Interestingly, Sweden is encouraging men to take greater advantage of parental leave, but without great success. "In general, men are underrepresented in terms of taking advantage of parental leave. Since men earn higher salaries, moms tend to stay home far more often than men. Newly introduced legislation requires men to make use of 20 percent of the total parental leave, but enforcement of this law is obviously not working, as studies argue that 60 percent of the men fail to take any parental leave at all."

Some companies are more hospitable to women than others. "There are companies and organizations that don't take too kindly to parental leave at all and their corporate culture doesn't encourage the staff to utilize parental leave. On the other hand, other companies use parental leave as a competitive tool when it comes to attracting the best and the brightest. Hence, these firms compensate personnel privately for the financial loss that comes into effect when high earners go on parental leave."

Companies are also encouraged, although not required, to have women on their boards of directors. "State-owned companies in Sweden aim at having some 40 percent women on their boards of directors. Companies listed on the Stockholm stock exchange have a code of conduct that strives for equal gender distribution—a sort of 'comply-or-explain' policy. Today, however, the number of women on the boards has decreased."

Engstrom believes that Sweden will become even more attuned to the needs of women. "The younger generations in Sweden are more likely to refrain from thinking in traditional gender terms. Working with or under women is a natural state of professional life and they are not caught in a patriarchal system of beliefs or behavior. Hence, female opportunity will come into play and effect as the younger generations take over society in terms of politics, business, and the public debate. Having said that, some future political encouragement will probably prove necessary. History has told us that progressive politics is paramount in trying to change society at large."

She recommends that societies introduce the concepts of human rights and gender equality very early in life. "Start in kindergarten. Create understanding of the implications, pitfalls, and opportunities of a more gender-equal society. Only if boys and girls, at an early age, are given the same conditions and opportunities for personal growth, education, and career development can a society truly become more equal."

Of course, despite the social welfare systems and legal requirements that make working and having a family easier, Sweden is not a utopia. Swedish women have many of the same frustrations and concerns as women all over the world. Finding time for themselves is a major point of difficulty for 49 percent of Swedish women; 39 percent are dissatisfied with their daily stress level. The number of hours Swedish women work, both at work and at home, is comparable to the number for women in other countries surveyed. The number of Swedish women who say their husband or partner rarely or never helps with household chores is in keeping with the global average.

Swedish women have a generally positive and optimistic outlook on life and the future, but their satisfactions are somewhat less pronounced than the global average. The average Swedish woman feels loved and appreciated, but slightly less so than the overall figure—63 versus 67 percent and 43 versus 47 percent, respectively. She is also 10 percent less fulfilled than the global average, and feels 10 percent less successful in her work and personal endeavors. Also, only 23 percent of Swedish women report feeling beautiful often or always, compared with the global average of 33 percent.

The Swedish woman prioritizes other people and other things ahead of herself: her partner and kids come first; then parents, friends, money, and job; and then herself. Pets are a higher priority to her compared with the rest of world (31 percent versus 18 percent). Religion is given a much lower priority, 4 percent versus the 13 percent average.

Happiness, satisfaction, peace, and feeling appreciated are most important to Swedish women. They value love above all else (76 percent), then health and honesty. Significantly fewer women than the global average cited achievement as a source of happiness—11 percent versus 25 percent.

Iconic Swedish Brand: IKEA

IKEA, the furniture and home goods store, has become the signature Swedish brand globally, offering practicality, value, quality, and attention to design.

IKEA was founded by the Swedish entrepreneur Ingvar Kamprad in 1943, on the principle that simple cost-cutting strategies could provide good functional products at lower costs, making them more accessible without diminishing their quality. That premise has afforded the company extraordinary success. IKEA had more than 580 million visitors to its 300 stores in more than 30 countries in 2007. Its global sales for the fiscal year ending August 31, 2008, were 21 billion EUR (about $30 billion), up 7 percent from the previous year, and compared with just 4.4 billion EUR (about $6.3 billion) in 1994. Sales in Sweden accounted for 6 percent of its revenues in fiscal 2008—the fifth-largest figure by country.[1]

IKEA appeals to women across demographic categories by offering its

Women Around the World Love IKEA

Swedish women are proud of their country's famous brand and love the many advantages it offers. Many of them list IKEA as their favorite brand.

> "You do not have to spend a fortune and it looks good."
> —Maja, 46

> "Seventy-five percent of my home is furnished by IKEA and I love my home.
> Good stuff for a good price—perfect to mix with other details.
> You can get something and exchange it later without it being
> such high cost to change your home."
> —Elin, 38

Many women around the world agree:

> "There's a human element and it offers variety and selection."
> —Mei, 38, China

> "The widest selection of goods that are incredibly practical,
> appropriate, and stylish."
> —Jessie, 18, United States

> "Allows me to customize and give a personal touch to my home."
> —Sunali, 37, India

> "Offers novelty and originality, and it makes me happy when I visit stores
> because then I imagine what I could do in my house.
> This is a brand that gives me ideas and stimulates me."
> —Gabrielle, 48, Belgium

> "It is a brand that has something for everybody. . . . It is the only place where I
> go shopping with my partner and we always greatly enjoy it. The brand is
> honest and does not pretend to be what it is not. Professionally I admire it
> as a genius marketing concept with perfect implementation."
> —Marie, 27, Austria

distinctive combination of quality and affordability; the vast selection of products makes it possible for almost anyone to find something at a desired price point. IKEA is a one-stop shopping paradise for home goods, offering everything from kitchen appliances to major pieces of furniture to interior decoration to food to textiles to household odds and ends like lint rollers and live plants.

**Globally, money and chores cause
the most arguments with her spouse**

Rank	U.S.	(%)	EU5	(%)	Japan	(%)	BRIC	(%)
First	Money	40	Chores	29	Money	35	Money	38
Second	Chores	24	Money	27	Chores	21	Chores	36
Third	Sex	18	Work schedule	20	Raising children	18	Raising children	29
Fourth	Work schedule	18	Raising children	18	We never argue	17	Household purchases	25
Fifth	Raising children	15	Sex	16	Chores	17	Work schedule	25

Note: This question not asked in Middle East.
Source: Q19 of survey, U.S. N = 3,442; EU5 N = 2,350; Japan N = 557; BRIC N = 2,186.

GERMANY: WRESTLING WITH FAMILY-WORK BALANCE

Women in Germany are representative of women in many other central and western European countries; they are right in the middle of the spectrum of wealth, education, equality, and general satisfaction with their lives.

Like women everywhere, German women seek happiness through family and social connections. German women listed love, honesty, health, and security as the things they value most in life.

Seventy-eight percent of German women work outside the home, and most of them feel pressured by the multiple demands on their time and energy. Twenty-three percent say they never feel successful at work. Some attribute this feeling to gender discrimination, saying that because they are women they do not get the promotions or job responsibilities they deserve;

others say it is because they cannot devote the time and effort that it takes to excel in their field, owing to the many other demands on their time. Most German women do the lion's share of household duties—they shoulder 93 percent of household responsibilities, a figure among the highest of any country surveyed—and this means long hours of shopping, cleaning, running errands, cooking, and childcare before and after work. They also do more than the average share of traditionally male duties, such as car care and home repair.

The work-life balance is a major concern for German women. Women are still very much expected to leave the workforce after having children; those who do not can be labeled "bad mothers" and may face suspicion and discrimination from peers, employers, teachers, and school officials. This attitude, compounded by a lack of subsidized, flexible childcare options, has contributed to a rapidly declining birthrate in Germany (and in countries with similar attitudes, such as Austria, Switzerland, and Italy). Of German women polled by the European Commission across the Continent in 2006, 16.6 percent said that having no children was the ideal lifestyle.[2]

Despite the constant stress of balancing family and career, however, German women express general satisfaction with their lives. Most report feeling appreciated and recognized for their efforts by their husbands and families. Home life tops the list of priorities among the women we surveyed, and most find their homes as rewarding as they are important: pets, sex, and children were all sources of great happiness rather than anxiety. They spend twice as much time as the average global respondent on family activities and childcare. When asked about life goals and sources of happiness, virtually all survey respondents described having children and spending time with their husbands and families.

Interestingly, however, when it came to describing "dream days," far fewer women included their families in their plans; most instead devoted these time-free, budget-free days to time and activities for themselves:

- "I would meet friends, go shopping, have a great lunch and dinner."
- "I would get up, have breakfast with my friend, go shopping, for lunch have a Chinese buffet, at night go out to a club and have cocktails and dance until the morning."

- "I would get up early to really profit from my day; go shopping to buy everything I want without having to think about money; realize my friend's biggest wish; tell my opinion to people where I usually need to be quiet; make love with my fiancé."
- "I would sleep late without a bad conscience, meet friends for a long breakfast in a restaurant, fly to the Mediterranean Sea to go to the beach and swim, take a helicopter to a mountain and have dinner, then fly to a metropolis to see a musical and go out."

Iconic German Brand: Miele

One company that has served German women well is Miele, a manufacturer of high-quality domestic and commercial appliances. Miele has a long history of offering time-saving devices for the housework that German women devote so much time to. Founded by Carl Miele and Reinhard Zinkann in 1899 in Gütersloh, Germany, the company originally manufactured cream separators, and in 1901 added the Meteor butter churn to its line, "taking much of the workload off the hands of farmers' wives."[3] Its technical innovations since then include the first electric-motor washing machine (1911), the first European electric dryer (1929), the first fully automatic washing machine (1956), the first domestic tumble dryer (1958), the first washing machine program for a hand-wash cycle (1997), patented "honeycomb drums" in washers and dryers that improve gentleness and reduce creasing (2001), and touch controls on appliances (2005).

Miele charges a premium for top-of-the-line technology, dependability (its products are engineered to last for twenty years), and style. Miele continually refines its products to reflect the most innovative technologies in home appliances.

Miele is in a top competitive position in the luxury appliances market, and its growth outpaces the industry. According to the company's financial report for 2007–2008, it experienced 11 percent growth the first half of 2008, while competitors' sales were stagnant. In Germany, specifically, Miele has not only a strong reputation but a large market share, which earned it *Appliance* magazine's award for the most successful company in Germany in 2007.

Demands on a woman's time are a key challenge globally

What type of challenges do you face in your daily life?
Too many demands on my time.

Percentage of respondents

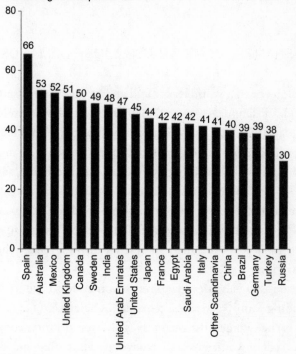

Source: Question Q30 of survey, N = 11,747.

Commercial Opportunities in Germany

- *Financial services.* German women express great dissatisfaction with the way their money is managed, especially insurance, investments, and banking; they want fast, comprehensive services that will free up their time and give them a sense of security about their assets.
- *Clothing,* especially work apparel, is a category with great

potential for growth, particularly as it is a category in which German women will trade up.

- *Telecommunications services.* To help cut costs, German women are seeking tailored products that meet most common needs, but that have no other frills. (For example, what channels does a woman really want? What bandwidth will she really use? More texting and fewer music downloads. And so forth.)

FRANCE: MORE STRESS, MORE DEMANDS

France has long been a world leader and an important trendsetter in ideas, fashion, food, and language—even though English is slowly replacing French as the language of international diplomacy. The biggest challenge for the typical Frenchwoman is finding enough time for herself. The majority work long hours (more than thirty per week) outside the home and also take charge of 93 percent of household responsibilities, among the highest shares of any country surveyed. For mothers, childcare occupies 15.7 hours of the week, versus the global average of 11.2 hours. They also share or are solely responsible for more than 90 percent of the grocery shopping and meal preparation.

All these responsibilities give Frenchwomen less time for leisure pursuits, including family activities, personal hobbies, and exercise. Only 28 percent of Frenchwomen list themselves as a top priority, compared with about 50 percent of women overall. No wonder more than half report being unhappy with their stress level. Only 7 percent say they feel powerful, and 35 percent report feeling angry most or all of the time.

Perhaps some of the stress is caused by the country's prevalent attitudes about gender roles. Female politicians—including the Socialist Party leader Martine Aubry, the presidential candidate Segolene Royal, the former president of the European parliament Simone Veil, and the minister of finance Christine Lagarde—have been positive role models, and a majority of our respondents say that a woman is an electable leader. These high-visibility women, and the value of equality trumpeted since the French Revolution, may have raised the average woman's expectations for parity between men and women. The reality seems to be disappointing. Only 22 percent believe women have achieved social and economic equality in France, one of the lowest responses among all countries surveyed.

Frenchwomen do not report high optimism about the world or their own lives. Though 59 percent believe their daily life, happiness, and financial situation will improve in five years, this is still lower than the overall average of 67 percent. Only 18 percent are optimistic about the future of their community, their nation, and the world. This is far lower than the overall average of 35 percent, and extremely low for women in a developed nation.

Given the legendary French sophistication in beauty and fashion, it surprised us to learn that only 21 percent of Frenchwomen rate themselves as very attractive. The French are also concerned about their weight, despite the claims in the best-selling book *French Women Don't Get Fat*, by Mireille Guiliano. We found that 70 percent say they weigh more than they want to.

Despite all these negatives, there is some good news from France. Most respondents feel loved and appreciated often or all the time. Most say that in reaching their goals, support from those around them is more important than their own hard work. So is a romantic relationship, with 67 percent reporting that sex is a major source of happiness. Pets, which are often seen on public buses and in cafés in cities and towns around France, are also a source of happiness. Sometimes simple things lead to happiness, too, says a 21-year-old: "A smile, beautiful countryside, love everywhere, small things that are not obvious but bring the spark back to daily life."

Frenchwomen may not feel powerful, but they do control 67 percent of household finances: more than $530 billion of annual discretionary consumer spending. As Frenchwomen's collective annual income rises past $500 billion in the next few years, they will become an even more powerful force in the national economy.

France has more social services than many other developed nations, so Frenchwomen feel more secure than women in some other countries. France, in fact, has a high rate of fertility partly due to high tax incentives and a good system of childcare that includes children as young as 3 months.

Still, money can be a source of stress instead of a motivator. Compared with women in other countries, Frenchwomen tend to make shorter-term investments, largely in savings and money market accounts. Although 21 percent say they have no financial concerns, only 10 percent feel they will be able to save enough for retirement. "I'd like more money to be able to say yes instead of no when I am asked for something," says Jeanne, 56, who is a member of the Managing on Her Own archetype.

Like women in most economies, Frenchwomen complain that financial services do not meet their needs. They are also dissatisfied with work clothes, and they will trade up to get a better product. Three of their five favorite brands—Adidas, Nike, and Puma—are related to sportswear. Given the world-famous dining options in their country, it's no surprise that women are also willing to pay a premium for food, restaurants, and wine. Another favorite brand, Danone, is best-known internationally for its yogurt, but it also packages many fresh dairy products and owns Evian and Volvic, two brands of bottled water.

Above all, Frenchwomen are trying to satisfy a diverse set of needs that drive their happiness. They want to build a family and close relationships with friends, maintain a successful career, and achieve financial security. On a personal level, they want to achieve physical and emotional wellness, and pursue travel and leisure activities. When Helene, 48, a Pressure Cooker mother, was asked what she would like to achieve, she summed up the balancing act that many of her countrywomen face: "To devote more time and energy, including necessary travel, to a meaningful job. To have the time to stand back and think about my role as a mother so as to contribute in a better way toward the development of my children, rather than reacting and just getting through from day to day. To reach a lasting peaceful equilibrium with my husband."

Commercial Opportunities in France

- *Work clothes that work.* Frenchwomen say they are dissatisfied with work clothes, and will trade up for better products that fit their busy lifestyle. A line of high-quality, sophisticated, forward-thinking work clothes that focus on the brand's philosophy and high performance.
- *Kid-friendly services.* Frenchwomen have tremendous responsibilities for the home and with children, and could use help with that time crunch. Businesses could create child-friendlier stores and leisure pursuits, and make it easier for women to multitask with

children in tow by offering play areas for kids at stores, interesting displays or visuals with kids in mind, and easier layouts to expedite errands. Develop a French version of CineMá (the Mexican movie theaters with showings for moms with babies).

- *Family meals made better.* Frenchwomen value cooking and eating as a family, but these responsibilities are a time burden. Businesses could create more healthy options for dieting women; create kid-friendly options for kids and healthy options for adults; offer meal kits, so meal prep can become a family activity; and provide optional wine pairings for special or everyday meals.

ITALY: SURPRISING DISSATISFACTION

Italian women are among the most generally dissatisfied of women in all the countries we surveyed. They put in long hours both at work and at home, and struggle with maintaining household finances and staying ahead of the curve at work. Fifty percent list their job as one of their top five priorities, compared with 39 percent globally. A key concern for these women is the sacrifice they must make at home in order to take on leadership roles at work. More than half of the respondents are unhappy with their daily stress level, and 70 percent say they rarely or never feel powerful. Fifty-four percent say they have trouble finding enough "time for me."

Italian women also report lower positive self-perception and self-importance, compared with the global average. Only 18 percent consider themselves very attractive, and 56 percent say they weigh too much. Only 38 percent consider themselves very emotionally healthy, one of the lowest rates among global respondents. In a striking divergence from virtually every other group of women surveyed, the average Italian respondent believes that luck and others' support are more important than her own hard work in achieving her goals.

The disenchantment among Italian women extends not only to their personal circumstances but also to their view of their country and the world. The average woman is broadly dissatisfied with Italy's politics and economy: a mere 7 percent say these are a source of happiness, whereas about 70 percent say politics and the economy make them unhappy. Only 22 percent of Italian women are optimistic about the future of their community, their country, and the world. Furthermore, only 20 percent of Italian respondents believe women have achieved equality in their country; this figure is one of the lowest of all the countries surveyed. Half of Italian women believe a woman is an electable leader—but this percentage is low relative to that in other developed markets, and few of these Italian women believe that a woman will be elected in the near future.

Italian women draw happiness and satisfaction chiefly from sex and relationships, followed by food and pets. The average Italian respondent reports satisfactions in her romantic relationships different from the global average: sex is a source of happiness for 75 percent of Italian respondents, higher than the 65 percent global average; more Italians are highly satisfied and fewer are dissatisfied with their sex life.

Italian women also find happiness in life's simple pleasures, in their families and friends:

"Little things, little gestures of people, especially in a moment when people are becoming overall more selfish. Unconditional love and support. A smile from those whom I love."

—GIULIA, 35, FAST TRACKER

"When I see that my family and friends rely on me for their lives. Having a good workout: it means I'm in good health (body and mind). Sailing."

—DONIELLA, 43, FAST TRACKER

"My pets, because they have taken only the good aspects of my character."

—LIS, 33, RELATIONSHIP-FOCUSED

"Doing something which satisfies me, changing something which is always the same in my life, being with those who make me happy and being able to travel and succeed in what I do."

—ALLEGRA, 21, MAKING ENDS MEET

According to our survey responses, Italian women control 59 percent of household spending: about $400 billion of annual discretionary consumer spending. Their financial patterns are different from those of overall

Women control the greatest share of household spending in developed economies, and the least in the Middle East

What % of your household's total consumption do you control or influence?

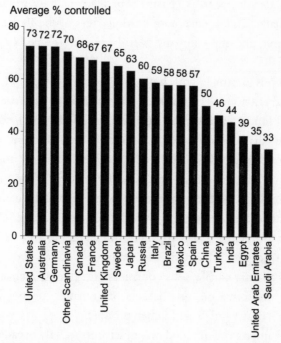

Average % controlled

Note: Estimated mean computed by assigning the midpoint of each ten-point range as the value for that response, then averaging responses.
Source: Question Q94 of survey.

respondents. Forty-three percent of Italian women, versus 56 percent of global respondents, say money is a source of happiness in their life. Only 8 percent of Italian respondents report saving money consistently, and 21 percent do not save at all. Those who do save money make fewer long-term investments than women in other developed economies. Checking accounts are the most common means of saving money. Only 6 percent feel they will be able to save enough for retirement.

Italian women's earned income is projected to grow by more than

$100 billion to more than $340 billion over the next five years, giving women more to spend.

Iconic Italian Brand: Barilla

One of the most popular brands among Italian women is Barilla, a manufacturer of pastas, pasta sauces, other pasta-based Italian entrées, and baked goods. Barilla began as a pasta shop in Parma, Italy, in 1877, founded by Pietro Barilla. Today, corporate headquarters of the Barilla Group remain in Parma, and the company is still privately owned by the Barilla family.

Barilla foods are made with high-quality ingredients, and the focus is on health and nutrition. The products are consistently well made and reliable, so it's a brand Italian women trust and feel good about feeding to their families. The Barilla brand has a long-standing reputation in Italy, and the company continues to release new and convenient products, such as whole grain pastas, and different shapes and sizes designed for use in soups and salads and for children. Women can pick and choose, mix and match, and create a tasty and nutritious equivalent of a meal made from scratch. The Web site has a section for recipes, many from gourmet chefs, as well as suggestions for wine pairings and information on traditional Italian cooking. The online store, Academia Barilla, sells gourmet pantry items such as top-of-the-line vinegar and olive oil; gift baskets of gourmet meats, cheeses, and spreads; chef's coats; and other kitchen products.

Barilla is among the top food manufacturers in Italy because of its convenience and authenticity, and it is also a leading global brand. It distributes about 1,500 products across twenty brands and sells more than 2.8 million tons of products annually. The company employs 18,000 people, and its products are exported to more than 125 countries around the world. In 2007 Barilla had sales of about $5.6 billion, with 3.4 percent growth. Still, Italian consumers account for 42 percent of its total revenue, and geographic expansion is a priority for the company. It has a potential for tremendous expansion; since entering the U.S. market in 1994 it has become the largest pasta manufacturer in the country, and the market leader.[4]

Commercial Opportunities in Italy

- *Financial services*, including banking, insurance and investments, topped the list of categories in which women are most dissatisfied, and women are also looking to save money in these areas.
- *Work clothes* do not meet their needs; 50 percent are willing to trade up for better clothing.
- *Electronics*. They are dissatisfied with several personal electronics products and services, and prefer to trade down in these categories.
- *Healthcare*. Hospitals are a significant area of dissatisfaction among Italian women, and also one where they trade up.
- *Personal care*. Italian women will pay a premium for better-quality products in several personal care categories: facial skincare, cosmetics, haircare, and perfume.

SPAIN: WOMEN IN CONTROL

Women in Spain typify the global trends in challenges and satisfactions. The results of the survey in Spain were remarkably close to the global average on nearly every topic. Forty-nine percent of Spanish women are dissatisfied with their daily stress level, as are 49 percent of women worldwide. Sixty-seven percent of Spanish women feel loved, compared with 66 percent overall. They feel similar levels of appreciation, fulfillment, loneliness, and worry over money.

There are two significant differences between Spanish women and the global average: demands on time, and control. More Spanish women cite demands on their time as the most serious challenge in their lives than do women in any other country; 66 percent, compared with 45 percent overall. At the same time, 69 percent of Spanish women cite control over their affairs as one of the most important factors in managing their lives, compared with only 59 percent of women worldwide. This indicates that women in Spain are willing to put in the long hours at work and at home, and manage the daily stresses and frustrations of money, self-image, relationships, and childcare—as long as they are in charge.

This attitude seems to have benefited Spanish women: they are responsible for only 76 percent of household activities, the lowest figure among developed countries, and 22 percent of those duties are entirely shared with their partners. They also feel at least as loved, appreciated, and recognized for their efforts as women in general around the world.

Love and family are priorities in Spain, with 84 percent of women valuing love above all else. Spanish women put their families ahead of themselves on their list of priorities: 79 percent prioritize parents, compared with the global average of 63 percent; and 51 percent put their siblings ahead of themselves, compared with 37 percent overall.

In general, Spanish women are happy and satisfied with their lives. Like women everywhere, they feel a need for more time, both to accomplish their daily tasks and to relax and do things for themselves. They value products and services that can help them maximize the time they do have, and they are willing to trade up for goods that deliver quality and value for themselves and their families.

Iconic Spanish Brand: Zara

Zara, the clothing retailer, is the flagship chain store of the Spanish Inditex Group. Zara has become world-famous, and incredibly successful, by creating on-trend clothing at accessible prices and bringing them from the runway to the hanger faster than any other company in the industry. Zara operates in seventy-three countries, with more than 1,500 stores at premier locations in major cities, which is up significantly from its presence in twenty-nine countries, with 449 stores, in 2000.

Zara has essentially changed the rules of the fashion game. The industry standard lead time—the time it takes from the initial design of a new article of clothing to the moment it gets hung on a rack or stacked on a shelf—is about nine months. At Zara, the process can take as little as fourteen days.

Zara is not driven particularly by the haute couture runway shows; nor does the company concentrate all activity on the traditional fashion "seasons"—fall-winter and spring-summer. Rather, Zara seeks to stay close to the market, watching for what's selling best and what new trends are emerging, and responding quickly.

It does this by creating and maintaining a close connection between the store managers and a team of more than 200 designers who work at the headquarters in La Coruña, Spain. When a store manager notices that a particular style is moving briskly, for example, she can order more units, using a customized handheld device. The order is placed immediately and sent to one of Zara's factories, most of which are in Spain. Factory deliveries are made twice each week, resulting in about eleven inventory turns per year, two to three times the industry average. Any store manager may also make a suggestion for a modification to an existing style or propose an entirely new article or design. The designers at headquarters collect and evaluate the suggestions as they arrive, produce designs on their computers, and, when these designs are finalized, send them over the company intranet to a factory.

The result is that Zara designs and produces as many as 10,000 new items every year. Although its manufacturing costs run some 20 percent higher than its competitors', Zara rarely needs to write off unsalable inventory.

Not only has Zara focused on women's needs in fashion; Inditex is virtually a women-operated company. The group employed 79,517 professionals of 140 nationalities at the end of 2007, and 80 percent of them were women.[5]

Commercial Opportunities in Spain

Spanish women say they are overwhelmed by demands on their time (66 percent versus 45 percent for the rest of the world). They would welcome suppliers that could help them save more, provide variety and ease of consumption in food, and provide them with a health checkup. They are very open to new providers in banking, car and life insurance, and investments. Travel abroad is a significant area of interest.

JAPAN: BOUND BY TRADITIONAL GENDER ROLES

With its low birthrate (1.34 births per woman in 2007)[6] and its middle-class standard of living, Japan might seem like an easy place for women to thrive, but traditional gender roles are strongly entrenched, and a rice paper ceiling can prevent women from reaching top positions in the corporate world.[7] A lack of good childcare in Japan is also likely a factor in the relatively low percentage of women in the workforce.

The Japanese have a strong tendency to describe themselves as middle-class. "All Japanese are middle-class" is a mentality that has remained fairly well entrenched for more than thirty years; it is reinforced by the culture, which encourages conformity. That makes middle-class "normal," and everyone wants to be seen this way. Those who could be classified as upper-class still want to seem humble. Those in the lower class are reluctant to identify themselves as such, because it would put them in a minority. Yet this is changing as the income gap between rich and poor widens and the number of Japanese who cannot make a living even though they have a job increases. The lower class is becoming more conspicuous. The book *Low Class Society*, published in 2005, sold 800,000 copies.

Behind the veneer of normalcy, Japanese women experience insecurity about health and well-being. Our survey found that they cite good health as the factor most important to the life they would like to achieve, making Japan the only country where health ranks in the top five wants. "I'd like to lead a healthy and safe life," one respondent told us. Another said, "I'd like to stay healthy, keep enjoying hobbies, and maintain friendships." Financial security ranks a close second. Having a happy family is in the middle of the list, somewhat lower than in most other countries in our survey. Career falls to the bottom of the list, despite women's concern for their finances. Their biggest fear is to confront something that could destroy the stability in their lives, especially disease, injury, or the death of someone close.

Japanese women also worry more than women in other countries about unexpected tragedy in their lives, such as an accident or a natural disaster like an earthquake. In general, they are pessimistic compared with others in our survey. Only 29 percent of Japanese women believe that their personal lives will be better five years from now—the lowest figure in our survey. Even fewer—only 7 percent—thought that the world around them would be better five years from now, also a low for the survey. The self-esteem of Japanese women is also low—only 7 percent rated themselves as physically attractive, and 69 percent say they are heavier than their ideal weight. Just 23 percent, the lowest percentage in the survey, describe themselves as emotionally healthy.

Perhaps because of the low birthrate, Japanese women seem to dote on their pets as never before. There are pet-centered oxygen bars, gourmet restaurants, social networking sites, and yoga classes.[8]

During a dream day with an unlimited budget, "normal" Japanese women indulge their hidden desires for luxurious activities. The majority would take time for themselves in activities such as going to a spa, a salon, or an aesthetic clinic and getting a massage. "I'd buy what I want," said 28 percent of the respondents. Food came in a close second, with 25 percent saying they would eat luxurious foods. Other picks (in descending order of importance): traveling, spending time with family, and spending time with friends.

Even though spending time with family is not at the top of the list for a dream day, women still cite their families as their primary source of happiness. Good health, friends, and community were next, followed by romantic relationships. Career was at the bottom of the list.

Perhaps Japanese women have made work a low priority because they lack good professional opportunities. They say it is difficult for them to find jobs that give a sense of achievement or satisfaction. There is still strong gender discrimination. Japan's "gender empowerment measure" was 54 among ninety-three countries in 2007. The proportion of female legislators, senior officials, and managers in Japan is low: 10 percent, as compared with 25 to 40

Yukiko Nagashima: Rejecting the "Christmas Cake" Theory

Yukiko Nagashima is president of Recruit Staffing, one of Japan's major temporary employment agencies. She says that the environment for women in general in Japan has changed since the 1980s.

"For example, the marriage age has increased. There used to be the 'Christmas cake' theory, which meant that a woman was past her 'use-by date' after the age of 25, just as a Christmas cake is worthless after December 25. I got married when I was 27!"

But in business, change has been slower to come. "The working environment is worse in Japan than in other developed countries and should be improved. I think that we should not only accomplish numerical goals but also improve the process. Say we set a goal to increase the women on management boards to half, and we do it; people will say that a woman got the position not because she is capable, but because she is a woman. That is not good for women. I think that men and women should be given equal opportunity in business, and that women should be promoted though the same process as men. A woman who is not prepared will face difficulty if she becomes a management executive.

"I don't see any advantage in treating men and women differently in knowledge work. As far as I have experienced, there is no work that women cannot do. The only area where women have a disadvantage in business is that some of them have to devote time to raising children. We don't have to do anything but provide child support. It makes economic sense to treat men and women equally. That's it."

percent in most developed countries. The estimated earned annual income of women is $17,802, only 48.3 percent of that of men. As many as 39.9 percent of Japanese women agree with the statement "Women should concentrate on the household while men work." Men and women of the younger generation, however, have a more positive attitude about working women: 56 percent of those in their twenties responded favorably to the idea, as compared with 37 percent of those over 70.

Iconic Japanese Brand: Uniqlo

Japanese women tell us they like Uniqlo because it brings them affordable, good-quality casual clothes that work for almost any woman. Uniqlo appeals to younger, urban women who are looking for trendy casual clothes at very low prices, but also to those who want reliable, casual basics at great prices in a variety of colors and materials.

The brand is worth $5.4 billion. It reported ¥586 billion of sales (about $6.1 billion) for the fiscal year ending August 31, 2008, up from ¥339 billion in 2004—with a very strong CAGR of about 15 percent for the years 2004–2008. It has done fast retailing, with the flagship brand Uniqlo accounting for approximately 90 percent of sales. The first store opened in 1984 and underwent a significant expansion in 1998 as a result of a highly successful fleece line and the opening of the first urban store in Tokyo's trendy Harajuku area. Now there are more than 750 stores in Japan, plus international expansion to six other countries on three continents. Uniqlo maintains a global R&D network with locations in Tokyo, New York, Milan, and Paris, which tries to "ensure that we are the first to pick up on trends."[9]

Uniqlo's research covers several areas to meet customers' needs: what the customers want; what the top trends for the season are; and what the best process is, from material production through store sales, to deliver the highest-quality product at the lowest possible price. The company responds with reliable casual basics at low prices that make them available to as many people as possible. Recent success with skinny jeans in all international markets shows how Uniqlo is beginning to respond with cutting-edge fashions that the brand makes available to a wide array of shoppers. Uniqlo continues to refine its product offerings to keep up with trends and its expanding consumer base.

A variety of Japanese women told us the clothes work for them. "They are simple and easy to wear," says Akiko, 22, a Fast Tracker. "I like them because they are cheap," says Mayumi, 44, a Pressure Cooker woman. "The clothes are relatively inexpensive, there is good variety, and they can be worn to work and out at night," says Lauren, an American who is 29 and is in the Struggling for Stability archetype.

Commercial Opportunities in Japan

- *Healthcare.* Given the typical Japanese woman's concern over health and well-being, a company that delivers high-quality healthcare in Japan has a ready clientele. Japanese women say they will pay a premium for better healthcare products and services and would embrace an upscale holistic health and wellness center as well as a Zagat-style guide to doctors and hospitals.
- *Home decor and remodeling.* Home decor and remodeling projects rank third on the list of categories in which Japanese women are most dissatisfied. Approximately 40 percent of Japanese women are willing to trade up both for a home or an apartment itself as well as for home decor. Japanese women say they are overextended with home responsibilities and receive less outside help in comparison with respondents from other countries, particularly because 74 percent of men rarely or never help around the house. Opportunities exist in full-service design and decor consultancy (including installation) or an upscale version of IKEA for those who prefer do-it-yourself.
- *Food prep and shopping.* Japanese women spend significantly more time than the worldwide average on both cooking and grocery shopping, and the majority of women take responsibility for both tasks. There is a need for a grocery service that offers price incentives, a continually expanding and shifting array of foods and cuisines, and the tailoring of foods and meals to diet and weight-management plans. Mobile technology could be used to facilitate planning and shopping for meals.

Nagata Mitsuko: Unique Individual Typical of Her Culture

Nagata Mitsuko helps us see some of the complexities of women both as participants in their societies and as commercial targets.

Nagata Mitsuko, 29, lives by herself in Tokyo. She has a BA in French literature from the University of Tokyo and earns her living by writing advertising and media copy for a number of graphics design and digital production companies in the city. Nagata feels pressure to get married—especially from her parents—and knows it will intensify when she turns thirty. Many of Nagata's friends who are her age have signed up for online dating services, some of which arrange meetings with Western men. Nagata, however, is happy with her work and likes living alone. "I'll know when the time is right to get married," she says. "It's just not that time yet." Nagata works hard, saves money, and finds fulfillment in the life she has created for herself. If she's worried about her future, she doesn't show it.

Women Leaders in Selected Countries

The status of women as business and political leaders varies widely from country to country, and women wield influence in some countries where one might not expect them to.

- *Spain*. Although women make up just 4.1 percent of corporate boards (the average in Europe is 11 percent), the Spanish government has more female than male ministers. Carme Chacón Piqueras, Spain's first woman defense minister, made news when she inspected troops while she was eight months pregnant.[10]
- *India*. Since the 1990s, India has required women to serve on a minimum of one-third of village councils. Objective standards indicate that women govern these villages better than their male counterparts.[11]
- *Rwanda*. In some developing countries, women have taken on new roles with surprising alacrity. In Rwanda, for example, the parliament, which sets aside twenty-four of eighty seats for women, was the first parliament in the world with a female majority—in 2008, women held forty-four seats. According to the executive director of Unifem, Inés Alberdi, the Rwandan genocide most likely prompted many women to become more politically involved.[12]

- *Cuba.* In the National Assembly of People's Power, 36 percent of the parliamentarians are women.
- *Kyrgyzstan* ranks the lowest of 189 countries surveyed by the Inter-Parliamentary Union (IPU) about women's participation in policy: it has no female lawmakers. But in March 2007, a woman, Aichurek Eshimova, was named head of Kyrgyzstan's central election commission.
- *Belarus.* Women compose approximately 30 percent of its upper and lower houses. Belarus, therefore, has higher levels of female representation than countries such as Poland, Canada, and the United Kingdom.
- *United States.* Women hold 16.3 percent of seats in the House of Representatives and 16 percent of seats in the Senate.[13]

SELECTED SITTING FEMALE LEADERS, 2008

- *Mary McAleese*, president of Ireland. Elected November 1997. She succeeded Mary Robinson, making Ireland the first country in history to have two female presidents in a row.
- *Maria Gloria Macapagal Arroyo*, president of the Philippines. Elected January 2001. She is the second woman president of the Philippines. Her father, Diosdado Macapagal, also served as president.
- *Michaelle Jean*, governor-general of Canada. Elected September 2005.
- *Angela Merkel*, federal chancellor of Germany. Elected November 2005.
- *Michele Bachelet Jeria*, president of Chile. Elected March 2006.
- *Prathiba Patil*, president of India. Elected July 2007.[14]

If Nagata lived in New York, Göteborg, Paris, Shanghai, or São Paulo, she might be seen as just another young, single working woman among thousands and thousands of others, with plenty of time to get married—or not—and with the freedom and financial strength to do pretty much as she pleases. In Tokyo, however, Nagata feels herself to be something of an anomaly. Japanese women in their early twenties often live alone or with their parents, work full-time, and spend their money socializing with friends, buying apparel and accessories, and traveling abroad. But they are also always preparing for the marriage they hope and expect to enter before the age of 30—looking for the right partner and tucking away some of their cash to supplement the future husband's salary when they set up a life together. Not only are Japanese women expected to marry by the age of 30; it is assumed that they will stop working once they do. And as a result, few

Japanese women—only 12 percent of our respondents, the lowest figure of any country we surveyed—feel they have achieved full social and economic equality with men. So Nagata may be less able to simply enjoy her single, self-sufficient years than are young women in other parts of the world.

What's more—whether or not she shows it—Nagata *is* concerned about the future, both for herself and for the world. In fact, women in Japan are surprisingly gloomy about what may lie ahead for them. Less than 30 percent are optimistic about their personal future, and only 7 percent are sanguine about the outlook for their community, their country, and the world in the next five years—the lowest levels of any country we surveyed.

In many other respects, however, Nagata is very similar to women in Japan and in countries around the world. Family is important to her; she very much wants to be loved; she's focused on her health, attractiveness, and emotional well-being. She seeks financial security and is trying to balance the demands and expectations of work and family.

Nagata is very much an individual, with her degree in literature, her successful and self-built career, her independence, and her self-assurance. Yet she is typical of women in her young Fast Tracker segment—well-educated, professional, competent, self-sufficient. Finally, she is also very much a creature of her culture, strongly affected by Japan's view of women and general pessimistic outlook.

THE CHALLENGES OF THE LOW-GROWTH ECONOMIES

The fourteen top-ranking countries in the Women's World Index are developed economies, and in these countries women fare well in the ten important factors we considered. These women participate fully in the educational system, have low maternal mortality rates, have long life expectancies, earn substantial incomes, and hold influential positions in business and government.

Yet achievement and gender parity have not brought universal satisfaction to women in these countries. Perhaps because women have gained so much, they are in a position to want and expect more. Even so, we heard a strain of concern and pessimism throughout the developed economies: first, about women's ability to achieve full gender parity in their own cultures; and, second, about the possibility that global society will change and improve significantly in ways that are important to women. Add to this pessimism the issue of population replacement. In many developed societies, the birthrate is falling and populations are having difficulties replacing themselves, in part, no doubt, because of the complexity of managing a family and work at the same time. The issue of low growth, and even no growth in some economies in some years, is very challenging to the economies and to the companies that operate within them. Demand for consumer goods and services remains flat or falls. The supply of talent shrinks.

In a survey conducted by the European Commission across the Continent in 2006, women said they wanted an average of 2.36 children, yet no country in Europe has a birthrate above 1.9. Interestingly, Hans-Peter Kohler, a professor of sociology at the University of Pennsylvania, explains that it's stay-at-home moms who are having fewer children. "High fertility was associated with high female labor force participation . . . and the lowest fertility levels in Europe since the mid-1990s are often found in countries with the lowest female labor force participation."[15]

Although many European countries, including Norway and Italy, offer their citizens monetary compensation for having babies, such systems seem only marginally effective. More successful are policies like those of France, where programs include tax breaks, travel discounts, and museum passes for families.

In some societies, such as the United States, working mothers do not get the kind of support—in the form of healthcare, childcare, and paid leave— that other countries, such as Sweden, afford their female citizens. In certain countries, such as Germany, there is still some cultural stigma associated with women who work and raise kids. In any country, women find that the two endeavors—creating and nurturing a family and building and maintaining a career—simply cannot hold positions of equal status in their lives.

Nicole Green tries mightily to be a superwoman who can do it all, but ultimately puts family ahead of work; she is the go-to parent when there is a pressing need at home. Nagata Mitsuko, at 29, steadfastly puts her career first in a country that expects her to be married and on the way to motherhood by now. Annalie Lindstrand looks forward to a life that seems to provide a fine accommodation for working mothers—generous paid leave for her and her husband, a guaranteed position to return to, and a reserved spot in childcare for her children. But Annalie is not there yet. She has yet to find herself in the kitchen at the end of the day, juggling the often conflicting demands of children, spouse, employer, and self. She has not yet felt the stress of having to do and do and do and do for others. Even with the support of her husband and her society, Annalie will no doubt find herself lacking time for herself and, like women around the world, putting her needs low on the list of daily priorities.

As Nicole Green put it, "Somebody's got to have the children."

And companies can help women far more than they do, in ways ranging from creating products that restore time to women and make their lives more convenient and wonderful, to building companies that value women as employees and support them as they start and maintain families.

The opportunities are boundless.

10.

The Optimistic Economies

BRIC, Mexico, and the Middle East

The developing economies face high birthrates, fast population growth, increasing demand for goods and services, and too few jobs, but are still quite optimistic about the future. China believes in itself. India sees still more growth. Women in the Middle East have less stress and less control. Cultural stereotypes have a basis in attitudes, controls, access to education, and ambition. Women in the developing world want high-quality branded goods. They aspire to a better life and are willing to sacrifice the "now" for their children's future.

Although developing societies face many troublesome issues—including high birthrates, rapidly growing populations, high demand for goods and services, and too few jobs—women in these cultures generally expressed a more positive and optimistic attitude than those in Europe and Japan.

Females are disproportionately poor in the developing economies. Women who subsist on less than $1 a day account for 60 percent of the working poor worldwide. High illiteracy rates and a lack of education greatly contribute to poverty: of the world's 876 million adults who cannot read, 75 percent are female; and approximately two-thirds of children lacking primary educations are also female.[1]

However, according to the Inter-Parliamentary Union (IPU), an organization that tracks the number of female lawmakers around the world, developing countries are taking more steps than developed countries to promote gender equity in parliaments and similar governing bodies.[2] In

Women in BRIC countries are most optimistic about their community, their country, and the world

Five years from now, how will the world, your country, and your community have changed?

Average % will be better

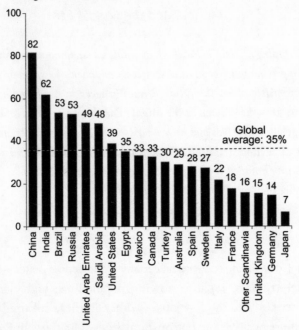

Source: Question Q32 of survey; Australia N = 480; Brazil N = 576; Canada N = 410; China N = 488; Egypt N = 187; France N = 533; Germany N = 613; India N = 539; Italy N = 321; Japan N = 557; Mexico N = 348; Russia N = 583; Saudi Arabia N = 202; Spain N = 346; Sweden N = 351; Other Scandinavia N = 193; UAE N = 199; UK N = 537; U.S. N = 3,445.

India, there has been a requirement since the 1990s that women serve on at least one-third of village councils. An economist, Esther Duflo of MIT, studied these villages and found that, on average, women are more effective than men at running them. Women take fewer bribes and focus more resources on critical infrastructure such as wells.[3] Rwanda is the first country to have a female majority in parliament: women hold forty-four of the eighty seats, although only twenty-four are specifically reserved for females.[4] In comparison, women hold 16.3 percent of seats in the U.S. House of Representatives and 16 percent of the seats in the Senate.

The presence of more women in positions of authority is a positive sign, but women in the developing economies are still struggling to gain the rights and privileges that many in the developed world take for granted.

CHINA

Ming Gao: Realizing the "New American Dream" in China

Ming Gao is not one of the struggling ones. When Ming was growing up, her goal was to become a Chinese "superwoman"—successful, professional, sophisticated, attractive, and self-fulfilled.

Now, looking at the polished, metropolitan, smartly dressed financial services professional that Ming has become, few would disagree that she has realized her goal. She embodies the new generation of the professional elite in mainland China. She speaks fluent English, holds two degrees from respected Western educational institutions, and earns a global-level salary. She chose to return to her home country to pursue a career, lead her life, and maintain traditional Chinese values.

Ming says she has lived a Chinese version of the American dream. "To me, the concept of the American dream is about relying on your own efforts and hard work to achieve something. Step by step, to walk out into the world. I respect that type of spirit and like the feeling of satisfaction."

Ming was born in 1979 in Beijing, spent her childhood there, and attended the public schools. When she was fifteen, she moved to Hong Kong with her parents. Living in one of the world's great commercial cities, Ming became fascinated by business and finance. Thanks to her parents' support, she was able to spend her senior year at a boarding school in the United States. She then entered the University of Michigan, where she earned her bachelor's degree in business administration.

After graduation, Ming decided to return to China. Yes, she wanted to be closer to her family, but she also realized that China—with its rapid growth and dynamic business environment—could offer her many exciting opportunities. Just a decade ago, it was still relatively rare for young Chinese to go abroad to be educated and then return to China to live and work. Today, however, tens of thousands follow that path.

When Ming first came back, she worked in a top accounting firm for three years. She then joined one of the world's foremost private equity firms, a dream job even for the international elite, and has made a success for herself. Today, at the age of 29, she earns close to 1.7 million RMB ($250,000), lives in an attractive 1,800-square-foot apartment in Shanghai, drives a new Lexus, and is in a happy relationship with her boyfriend. Ming has the best of both worlds. She has realized the American dream back home. "The things I like the most, the environment I like to live in, is still in China. And the older I get, the more I like China."

So the sky would seem to be the limit for Ming. She could take on greater responsibility, earn more money, acquire a second home, travel abroad, continue her learning, get involved in philanthropy, pursue whatever leisure activities might interest her. Instead, she put on the brakes.

Ming did not hit a glass ceiling. "I haven't noticed any inequalities at work, although in the longer term there might be, since there's not a single female managing director that I know of. No, it was a personal choice for me to get involved in private equity, and I shouldn't expect the firm to do special things for me."

The simple fact is that Ming is burned out.

Even without a husband or children, Ming has been hit by the same challenges to her time as women in other countries face. Her work is highly demanding and her life is filled with deadlines, frequent late-night calls, weekend overtime, and perpetual sleep deprivation. Her job has pushed Ming to her physical limits and left her with no time for herself. "My physical and mental health have suffered. I just wasn't in a good state in private equity. The job was not sustainable in the long term."

Ming told her company that she needed some time off, a leave of absence. She needed to rejuvenate herself and reflect on what she really wants in life. "I felt I was being sucked into the vortex, pulled in by my ambition and vanity. Of course, I'm not blaming private equity. I enjoyed my work. I learned a lot. But eventually we have to go back to the fundamental question: what do you really want?"

Chinese Women: Optimistic and Resolute on Destiny

Unlike Ming, the majority of Chinese women express great optimism and enthusiasm about the future, both in their personal lives and with regard to their communities, their country, and the world. Eighty percent of women in China—this figure tops our survey—believe that their careers, families, and personal happiness will improve in the next ten years; more than 80 percent also believe that China's future, as a country and as a global player, is bright.

This optimism has many wellsprings. Thanks in part to China's one-child policy, girls of Ming Gao's generation enjoyed unprecedented support for and access to education. Parents invested all their efforts in the development of their only child, regardless of gender. Ming is fully aware of this and appreciates all that she has received. "I'm very lucky and thankful that my parents have provided me with the opportunities, a higher starting point. My education and jobs have helped me see a lot more, a lot quicker."

Ming's parents and others of their generation believe that education is the best and probably the only way to lead people toward a brighter future. Members of this generation witnessed and bore the burdens of one of the most turbulent periods of Chinese history: the Cultural Revolution. Their belief systems and consumption habits in turn were formed by their experience of being forced to perform hard labor on farms and in factories. Only those with the foresight and diligence to catch up on academics in their spare time, often poring over borrowed textbooks, eventually became the ones who were able to take full advantage of opportunities for themselves and their children, after the dust had settled and China's doors were reopened.

As a result, Ming and women like her feel a tremendous obligation to perform well and meet their parents' expectations. "As a child you want to fulfill this responsibility, because your parents sacrificed so much for your education. You want to achieve a good position with a good salary."

Even with this sense of obligation to the past and optimism for the future, most Chinese women are not particularly happy about their lives now. Survey respondents feel less loved, less satisfied, and less appreciated than the global average. They also report having a lower self-image and a lower sense of emotional health.

Chinese women work slightly more than the global average, while shouldering 77 percent of household responsibilities (a figure similar to the global average), but only 26 percent report feeling appreciated for their efforts (compared with 45 percent overall). More Chinese husbands help women with household chores than husbands in most other countries, but women are unsatisfied with the level of help they receive: the assignment of chores is the number one argument the average Chinese woman has with her husband.

To make matters more complicated, the Chinese concept of the "core family" includes both spouses' parents. Though the grandparents can provide substantial support with childcare in the early years, they themselves need to be taken care of in old age. The lack of developed pension and retirement plans and of social safety nets for the elderly, exacerbated by the one-child policy, means that Chinese couples have to shoulder the burden of providing for four parents by themselves. As a result, 35 percent of Chinese women in our survey cited "caring for aging parents" as one of their top three challenges; the worldwide average was 15 percent.

Qin Liu, the 31-year-old Pressure Cooker woman we discussed in an earlier chapter, is acutely aware of the problem. "In a few years, both my husband's parents and my parents will become very old and need to be taken care of. It will be a very heavy burden for us, because we are both only children and don't have any brothers and sisters to share the burden with."

But the problem of parents also provides a partial solution. Many couples have parents living close by, and the grandparents are often heavily involved in the rearing of a couple's child. Qin's mother moved in with the family and helps with cooking and childcare. Many families also engage outside help. The Greens found themselves spending nearly a third of their household income on childcare and household help; by contrast, maid services and daycare are relatively cheap in China.

Yang Mian Mian: We Can Always Achieve More

Like Ming Gao, Yang Mian Mian has achieved great success in China by combining the Eastern model with the Western model. She is one of the rare female leaders of a large industrial company—president of the Haier Group, a Chinese manufacturer of appliances known as the "General Electric of China."[5]

Unlike Ming, Yang thrives on her work. She started her professional life as a teacher, transferred into a technical field, and was appointed to run the factory when it was in bankruptcy. "In my childhood, I never imagined I would run a company of this size. I just wanted to be a technician," she told us. Yang graduated from what is now Shandong University in eastern China in 1963; she joined the Qingdao Refrigerator General Factory, which later became known as Haier, in 1984. With her technical training, she learned how to sort out problems, and she applied these skills when she had the chance to become a manager. Yang saw a career opportunity at Haier. "It was the right place, the right time, and I was the right woman."

The manufacturer was almost bankrupt and had few prospects for growth. "When the factory was set up, we didn't have technology to create an upmarket product. I visited other factories, including some in Germany. We set up higher standards and made a better product. We won the respect of colleagues. We brought home their technology and innovated." Haier merged with other companies and began to grow. It is now the world's fourth-largest white goods maker, with 240 subsidiary companies and more than 50,000 employees throughout the world. From 2006 to 2008, *Forbes* magazine named Yang one of the 100 Most Powerful Women in the world; she is the only Chinese woman who has won the title three years in a row.

In China, Yang says, there is "some bias" against women. She was able to counter the bias by "setting a higher standard than the normal work standard." When she reached that standard, "all the people gave me respect." Yang argues that Chinese women have equal access to education and, bias or no bias, can rise to important positions in both industry and government. What's more, Yang thinks women make better managers than men. "They have better learning skills. They can learn more technology. Women can take more variables. They can take difficulty better than men can. Women can do better in bad conditions. They will think how to survive." Still, there is room for improvement. "Chinese women need to put more emphasis on practice. They should be more open-minded to bigger issues of strategy and to respecting the knowledge of others. They can learn more by respecting other cultures."

Yang also says that being a woman has helped her build the Haier business. "Being a woman in home appliances helps a lot. I am the designer and manufacturer and also the user. I know what the end users are thinking and what they want." One of her early challenges was designing a freezer that was comfortable for women to use. "When we started with freezers, all of them were big and designed for access by big-framed people. Most women are shorter than men. I had to climb into the freezer and it was not comfortable." By dividing the freezer into two parts—a top with shallow shelves and a bottom with a drawer—Haier was able to make its product more appealing to women. "The change is small. However, it was a big success and it took everyone by surprise."

Yang wants to keep improving her company's products and to acquire new companies in the future. "It is 25 percent female in top management today. We can achieve more. And we will."

Iconic Chinese Brand: Li Ning

Li Ning is a well-known and respected Chinese gymnast turned entrepreneur. His company, founded in 1990, has its headquarters in Hong Kong and is one of the leading sports brand enterprises in the People's Republic of China. His products include footwear, apparel, and accessories for sports and leisure.

Li is an inspiration to the Chinese people. He earned the title "prince of gymnastics" after winning six of seven medals awarded at the Sixth World Cup in 1982. He also won six medals at the 1984 Olympics. In 2000, Li was the first Chinese person to be inducted into the International Gymnastics Hall of Fame. Li's fame contributed to the success of his sporting-goods empire. He endorses a number of athletes and teams, in China and elsewhere. According to an interview with the *Wall Street Journal*, Li feels he is "representing Chinese people, and Chinese sport."[6]

Li Ning recognizes pride in the Chinese culture and the desire of Chinese women to feel proud of their country. A great number of women in China chose Li Ning as their favorite brand not only for the clothing but also out of respect for the brand's leader. Li Ning responds to women by offering a sporting clothes brand for leisure that is both comfortable and stylish, in addition to its sporting clothes for sports and training.

Li Ning has unparalleled product research, development, and design. Li Ning has R&D centers in China and the United States, and it has collaborated with Michelin and developed innovative fabrics and antishock footwear technologies to improve its technical sporting gear. Li Ning continues to refine its products by taking advantage of consumers' growing interest in sportswear, an interest that was inspired during the Beijing Olympics. The company also focuses on unique consumer segment dynamics in China to better compete against international competitors. It had $637 million in revenues in 2007 and 40 percent CAGR over the prior three years ($275 million in 2004, at current exchange rate).

What Chinese Women Say They Want

"I'd like to have a stable income and work that makes me happy; my own business would be the best—my own brand, which is well-known. A loving husband, a good person who earns as much as me, the more the better. To have all family members healthy and happy. Also a big dream: world peace."

"A leisurely and comfortable life working eight hours a day so that I can develop my own hobbies. My dreams: to find a good part-time job; learn to dance; become a writer."

"To have a more reasonable annual leave system; to manage my workload to be more evenly distributed; a more stable and worry-free job. My dreams: an independent discretionary space; some spare money; not have to face solitude when I am alone or sick."

"Become the focus of the world, enjoy the jealous staring of everyone, be liked by numerous outstanding people, possess unmatched self-confidence, become successful in my career; be together with my significant other and enjoy the best food in the best environment."

"On my dream day, I'd just let myself relax."

Commercial Opportunities in China

China has a population of 1.3 billion and the purchasing power of its rising middle class is increasing (despite the current economic crisis), so one might expect that Chinese women would have adopted Western attitudes and behaviors regarding shopping—and, in particular, would have discovered the many joys of trading up to premium goods.

But, strongly influenced by their parents' spending behavior and without the luxury of many pennies, Chinese women have typically not developed the habit of shopping for its own sake. Yes, women like Ming Gao—who do have substantial incomes—like to go shopping for handbags, shoes, and clothes regardless of whether they actually need these items, but Ming's discretionary spending is low relative to her income.

Perhaps because memories of their parents' hardships are still fresh in their minds, Chinese women will quickly adjust their casual spending to

A woman's responsibility for chores varies globally

Who is responsible for the following
activities in your household?

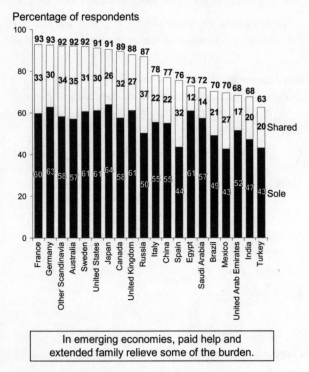

Percentage of respondents

In emerging economies, paid help and
extended family relieve some of the burden.

1. Average of responsibilities for cleaning, cooking, laundry, grocery shopping, and childcare.
Source: Question Q17 of survey.

their income and situation—they are not likely to take on debt or distort
their spending for unnecessary purchases. As Ming puts it: "You just adjust
your lifestyle according to how much you earn. The desire for money is
insatiable. We have to control it wisely." This self-restraint allows Ming to
invest almost 30 percent of her income in stocks and divide the rest into
savings and a cash reserve.

Companies can better understand and serve Chinese women by focusing on these attitudes and on their dissatisfactions. They are willing to
trade up for goods and services that free up time for themselves, help them

to provide for their families (parents, children, and spouse), and make them feel appreciated and beautiful—all, of course, in a convenient, cost-effective way. The biggest opportunities are:

- *Lingerie.* Forty-five percent of Chinese women are dissatisfied with their lingerie, and 71 percent say they would pay more for better options. They are looking for comfort, style, and versatility.
- *Beauty care products.* Chinese women are more concerned about aging gracefully than most, and they are currently dissatisfied with facial skincare products, cosmetics, and haircare products and in the market for better options. There is currently a rift between low-end and high-end cosmetics, leaving room for middle players.
- *Food*, particularly versatile grocery items that can be used for basic meals or more advanced gourmet recipes; 81 percent of Chinese women say they will trade up for food, much more than the overall proportion (65 percent).

INDIA: GROWTH AND SOCIAL CHANGE

Since the early 1990s, India's economy has experienced a dramatic growth rate, attracting more foreign investment and an information technology boom. Perhaps as a result, Indian women are among the most optimistic of those we surveyed regarding women's political, social, economic, and professional future. We found that 81 percent believe their personal life will be better five years from now. When Indian women look outside their own lives, their optimism declines, but 62 percent still predict a better future for their community, their country, and the world.

As is consistent with emerging economies, accumulating goods that can visibly display wealth and having a successful career are serious themes for Indian women, and these ranked ahead of wanting a happy family. Possessions—especially houses and cars—are important to the average Indian woman. She mentions her career more frequently than anything else, and also cites her own hard work as the major contributor to her current and future success. In other emerging countries, mentions of a career rank second or third. Fear of failure was spoken of more often in India and Mexico, two countries where a successful career is an important part of the life women would like to achieve.

Indian women also place a higher value than global respondents in general on knowledge and achievement. Jobs are a source of happiness for 79 percent of Indian respondents, compared with 56 percent of women overall. Money, which is one of the five top priorities for 56 percent of Indian respondents, ranks higher than children among our sample.

These priorities became clear when our Indian respondents were asked to describe their hopes and dreams in their own words. "I would like to reach the top level in my career, and to see my children be at the top. I would also like to see peace and happiness all around the universe," says Devi, 44, a Fulfilled Empty Nester. Divya, 24, a Fast Tracker, is even more ambitious. "I would like to become a successful businesswoman with my photo on the cover of leading business magazines around the world. I want to become a billionaire, so that I can build my own bungalow with a swimming pool and farmhouse, and so that I can cure my grandmother's diseases and send my parents on a world tour. The third dream is to become a mother."

Overall the average Indian woman is quite satisfied, and most aspects of her life, including her happiness and her partner, meet or exceed her expectations. Husbands in India contribute to women's happiness more than the average survey respondents' spouses, and 78 percent of Indian women say they often or always feel loved. Perhaps this leads to their positive self-perception, which is higher than that of other women in our survey. Nearly half of Indian women describe themselves as "very attractive," and 61 percent say they are "very emotionally healthy."

This optimism carries over into the realm of politics, where Indian women feel that women are achieving well and are destined to achieve even more. Though individual women in our survey talk about gender discrimination, 61 percent of Indian respondents believe that women have achieved equality in their country; this proportion is high compared with that of others surveyed. Indira Gandhi became prime minister in 1966 and left a positive legacy of leadership—89 percent of Indian women believe a woman is an electable leader in their country, a very high percentage relative to other developing markets. Eighty-six percent believe women will achieve more economically and professionally in ten years—the highest figure of any country surveyed—and 77 percent believe that women will achieve more politically and socially in ten years.

Still, there are stresses. The Indian woman is trying to satisfy a diverse set of needs that determine her happiness. She wants to find romantic love, build a happy family, and have close relationships with friends. At the same time, she wants to maintain a successful career, achieve physical and emotional wellness, and pursue travel and leisure activities. Chandani, 55, a Fulfilled Empty Nester, exemplifies just how many different things can contribute to happiness: "Being with my family, being recognized and appreciated for the work I do, being busy, having a few hours of leisure in a week, traveling, reading a good book, and being surrounded by my family again."

Fulfilling so many different needs presents challenges and entails trade-offs. Typically, Indian women work long hours, while at the same time performing a significant portion of the household chores. Overall, 27 percent shop for food every day, versus 13 percent globally; 43 percent shop for household items at least once a week, versus 24 percent globally. This could be because India has many vegetarians who need to shop frequently for fresh vegetables and cook more often than people who follow a different diet and can take advantage of prepared foods. It could also be because of the predominance of residential street markets in Indian cities rather than our one-stop, once-a-week destination supermarkets.

The typical Indian woman performs twenty-nine hours a week of at-home chores, compared with the overall survey average of nineteen hours a week. However, her spouse is more helpful than the overall average in raising kids (75 percent are involved) and managing the household. Although 28 percent of Indian men rarely or never help their wives around the house, the global average of men who rarely or never do chores is 39 percent. Indian women can also rely on paid help to relieve part of the burden; this is typical of developing economies we surveyed.

Demands on a woman's time and conflicting priorities are major sources of dissatisfaction. Women have difficulty achieving a work-life balance, and 30 percent of Indian women are dissatisfied with the level of stress in their lives, though this figure is low compared with 49 percent of women globally.

According to survey responses, Indian women control 44 percent of household spending: more than $150 billion of annual discretionary consumer spending. As Indian women's collective annual income rises past $260 billion in the next few years, they will become an even more powerful force within the national economy, but their financial behaviors are different from those of the respondents globally. More Indian women save consistently and feel prepared for retirement. They tend more toward longer-term investments such as life insurance and mutual funds, although only 15 percent of Indian respondents have a retirement fund.

The Srinivasans: Two Generations of Love, Learning, Caring, Connection, and Change

Jyoti and Sharika Srinivasan, a mother and daughter, are typical of Indian women in that they think in the long term, as keepers of their family flame. To understand them is to understand how many Indian women think about the changing relationship of work and family in their country.

Jyoti Srinivasan was born in Madras and attended college at Hyderabad, where she earned a degree in English literature and economics. She married at age 19 and soon gave birth to a son and then to a daughter, Sharika. Jyoti's husband, R. Srinivasan, a businessman, was elected to the Indian parliament as one of its youngest members. As soon as she could make arrangements, Jyoti returned to the university for a postgraduate degree in political science and, after that, another degree in library and information sciences. She also studied French and German.

The importance of education was one of the values that Jyoti emphasized to her daughter, Sharika , who is now 31 years old, married, and living in Mumbai with her husband and infant son. Sharika and Jyoti are extremely close, and talk about three times a day.

At her mother's urging, Sharika attended the Stella Maris women's college in Madras. Immediately after graduation, she attended Madras Loyola for an MBA, and later she studied for a year at Northwestern University in the United States.

Along with education, Jyoti valued work, and she has spent her career in communications. She ran a distribution agency for a popular publication, the *Hindu*, and is now managing partner of Inclinks, which handles newsletters and other corporate communications for companies.

Sharika was deeply influenced by her mother's active career. "My mother was the critical influence in my life. She works full-time. She encouraged me to pursue a career." Following her mother's advice, Sharika went to work as soon as she finished her schooling. Her first job was in sales at CPG Britannia, where she was the only woman in the department. "My boss treated me with kid gloves." Sharika then took a position in marketing and brand management at a multinational company. Over the past ten years, she has watched more women enter business. "There are far more women in the workplace now," she told us. "I am treated regularly. In my current job, seven other women work with me."

Unlike her mother, who married quite young, Sharika put off marriage until she was 24. She met her husband, who was a management trainee and in sales, without her family's help—a break from tradition, as many marriages in India are still arranged. "He had similar interests," Sharika said. "We were on the same wavelength."

Sharika and her husband do not follow the traditional Indian gender roles in their marriage. "My husband is not typical at all. It's still usual in India that the woman is a servant to her prince husband. The father leaves the running of the house to the mother. His only role is to provide money to do it. We chose to do it differently. We agreed on a financial system, for example. We make about the same amount of money. We split the cost of the house. I pay for my own clothes. We keep a common account where we save a set percent of income—about 50 to 60 percent."

Most Indian women do not continue working after having children. But after taking a five-month maternity leave to have her first child, Sharika returned to her job full-time. Only a small number of married women work, and the number of women with children who work is even smaller. Since daycare is practically nonexistent in India, Sharika and her husband hire nannies and household helpers.

Sharika is ambitious for herself, and even if she and her husband decide to have more children, she plans to continue her career and climb "much higher up." And she wants more Indian women to think as she does, beyond home and family. "Indian women were raised to believe they need to stay at home with their children. They work from age 21 to 23, then drop out of the workforce once they have children. They need a support system!"

She believes that women could play a crucial role in the Indian economy if they participate. "Conditions for India are improving, but I meet a lot of women who don't know that things are better than they were fifteen years ago. It will make the country develop if women go to work." She observes that Indian women are beginning to have access to jobs with higher compensation. "The pay disparity is disappearing in corporate India."

Commercial Opportunities in India

- *Education and financial services.* Education, career, and financial success are the top priorities among Indian women. Companies could create business-oriented educational, career, and financial counseling services geared toward developing professional women.
- *Haircare and cosmetics.* Indian women are careful about their appearance and also value local and native ingredients. There are opportunities to create premium haircare and skincare cosmetics, an Indian version of Brazil's Natura.
- *Groceries and food preparation.* In India, grocery shopping is considered the most important household responsibility. Opportunities exist for creating larger household appliances, such as refrigerators that could hold more food and thus reduce the number of shopping trips required, and that are extremely efficient, to help counteract the high cost of utilities in India.

RUSSIA: MONEY AND SELF-ESTEEM

Russia has experienced a renaissance over the past two decades. The end of the Soviet Union led to a booming economy, unprecedented opportunities in education and travel, and mass access to goods and services that had previously been reserved for the elite. A lot of hard work and repositioning of values and priorities has gone into this revival, and women have put in their fair share—and they are also reaping their share of the rewards.

Even though the economic crisis of 2008 caused a harsh wind to blow across the country, Russian women reported levels of satisfaction significantly higher than average in many personal aspects of their lives, as well as more sources of happiness. The average middle-class Russian woman is satisfied with her level of peace, appreciation, and control; she feels beautiful, healthy, and reasonably well-off. Sex and money appeared on 84 percent of Russian women's lists of top sources of happiness; a further 77 percent cite shopping; and 78 percent reported a positive outlook on the future—versus only 58 percent of women worldwide.

Many Russian women don't quite fit into any single archetype; they are

Women are optimistic about their financial situation

Five years from now, will your financial situation
be better, the same, or worse?

Average % will be better

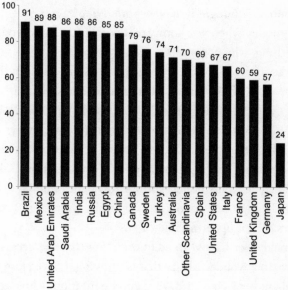

Source: Question Q32 of survey.

more likely to straddle one or more archetypes or move from one to another with greater rapidity than women in other countries. Russians generally place a high value on wealth and consumption—58 percent of Russian
women list these as a priority, compared with 15 percent globally. They want
to enjoy their newfound wealth, and this presents tremendous opportunities for more brands—both global and national—to establish themselves
and thrive in Russia.

Nina Kovaleva: Focused but Uncertain

When you first meet Nina Kovaleva, it's difficult to place her in a segment—she has characteristics of the woman Striving for Achievement as well as one who is Relationship-Focused. Nina is 31 years old, tall, fit, fashionably dressed, and unmarried. She is a confident working woman, successful, bold in her assertions, eager to talk about her travels, luxury goods, and independent lifestyle. She wears a squarish watch with a diamond-encrusted case—"Raymond Weil," she says; "I bought it in Geneva"—and carries a Louis Vuitton handbag. "I bought it in New York. I like bags. I have five others. It cost a lot of money when you compare it with a Russian brand, but if I can afford something, why not get it?"

Nina lives in the heart of Moscow, just 300 meters from the Kremlin. "It's the equivalent of living near Fifth Avenue in Manhattan," she says. Although she owns a $63,000 Jaguar, which she bought (with the help of a bank loan) to celebrate her twenty-ninth birthday, Nina always walks to her office, which is just ten minutes away. She works as assistant general director for an investment holding company and earns a monthly salary of more than 140,000 rubles, plus bonuses, the equivalent of about $4,500, which places her in the top 1 percent of young working women in Russia. Even so, she considers herself upper-middle-class.

What makes her happy? In addition to jewelry and accessories, many things. "I live in a wonderful city that is growing. I have close friends who I can see whenever I want. I have a good education. I love to travel. I'm blessed with a great family."

Nina has a boyfriend, Sergei, who is ten years older than she is. He owns a company that makes wrought-iron goods, such as railings and outdoor furniture. They have been together for five years. They talk every day and see each other two or three times a week. Nina hopes they will marry. "I believe that a woman's main purpose in life is to have children," she says. "Of course, it all depends. Sergei hasn't offered to marry me yet."

So although Nina is happy with her life of the moment, there is an undercurrent of discontent, stress, and worry, mostly because of the issue of timing. Now 31, Nina would like to have her children by the age of 35. "So when the child reaches 20 years old, I'll be only 55. I will still be good-looking. I'll have time to spend with a child. And I will have the physical ability to travel and enjoy life." That leaves just four years for Sergei (or someone else) to make his proposal, for the couple to get married and find a place to settle together, and for Nina to get pregnant. Doable, but getting tight.

Plus, although Nina says she is well-educated, she did not finish college. She has only a year to go, and she would love to find the time to finish her degree. But where would that fit?

And yes, Nina lives in a nice apartment in town, but she is not quite the independent, self-sufficient woman she appears to be. Her mother actually owns the flat and lives there, too, along with Nina's sister and brother. Her mother takes care of the rent and buys all the food for the household. This means that Nina can spend most of her money on travel, jewelry, clothing, dining out with friends, going to museums, and entertainment.

Nina is outspoken about gender roles, and her views differ sharply from those of women in the United States. "In our nature, Russian women never wanted to be equal to men," she says. "Yes, we can work a lot. Yes, we can make more money. But we are not saying out loud that we want to be equal with men. We love when men open doors for us, take the chairs, and hug us. But if you want a man to treat you like an equal, then you cannot also say, 'Oh, you know, I am a woman.' So yes, a Russian woman can be tough and strong. Especially when she has children and a family to take care of. But we can work and do all that, and still be capable of looking good, taking care of ourselves, and really enjoying men's company in ways that make us feel like a woman."

Iconic Russian Brand? Campbell's Seeks to Succeed in a Country That Loves Soup

As much as Russian women want glamorous global brands, they, like Nina, also have a very traditional streak and feel deeply about other, far more humble goods—like soup.

Russia is, in fact, a bastion of soup culture; it is among the highest per capita soup consumption markets in the world. Yet until 2007, Campbell's soup could not be found on the shelves of Russia's shops. When this company decided to enter the Russian market, it at first failed to recognize the deep significance of soup in Russian culture. Russian women pride themselves on their skill at making soup, and family recipes are passed down from generation to generation.

"Your grandmother's signature recipe is the one you still make today," says Larry McWilliams, president of Campbell's International. "I watched as they cut the vegetables, sliced the meat, tied themselves to their burners. With gas output through the line surging up and down, Russian women literally stand by the pot to make sure it simmers at the right boil. They have a word, *dousha*, which literally means soul and gets associated with soup and its importance to the family. It's a very emotional and significant word."

Campbell's soon realized that the canned condensed soups so popular in other countries for their uniformity and convenience would not pass muster in Russia. "There is still a stigma to convenient products," McWilliams explained. So Campbell's created a new line of products with the Russian woman in mind: a "starter" soup, a base on which the cook can build, enhancing and customizing it for her own family.

"We cut more than half the preparation time," said McWilliams. "We believe Russia and other developing markets will get to fully prepared products ultimately but not right away. The starters allow *dousha* without shame. We've learned the hard way that product choice is not a logical process; it's at least 65 percent emotional."[7]

Commercial Opportunities in Russia

- *Healthcare.* Only 59 percent of Russian women are satisfied with their healthcare options, the second-lowest percentage among the countries we surveyed. Russian women want better service across the spectrum of health and medical services—hospitals, physicians, dentists, and optional medical.
- *Weight loss.* Although 51 percent of Russian women say they feel very attractive and only 5 percent feel unattractive, 61 percent say they are overweight.
- *Beauty and cosmetic products.* Beauty is very important to Russian women; the average Russian woman spends two hours more per week on personal grooming than the average woman globally, and personal care is the category that she prioritizes above all others.
- *Clothing and shoes.* Fashion is a priority to Russian women, who make an effort to look their best at all times. Luxury brands in particular are in high demand.

BRAZIL: BIG ECONOMY, INTENSE EMOTIONS

For many tourists, Brazil is best known as the site of the pre-Lenten carnival street party, or as a beach resort with a perpetual samba soundtrack and round after round of caipirinhas. Brazil is also an economic powerhouse. It is Latin America's largest market and also ranks as the world's tenth-largest market measured in GDP. Swept up in this robust economy, Brazilian women tend to be more optimistic than women in the rest of our survey. An impressive 91 percent believe they will be better off financially in five years. The outlook for daily personal and family life five years from now is also positive for 86 percent, compared with 67 percent globally. Slightly more than half are optimistic about the future in their community and the world. They also predict a bright future for women in Brazil. More than 80 percent believe that over the next ten years, women will make economic, professional, and educational gains. This was the highest percentage in the survey, tied with India. More Brazilians than the global average expressed the belief that women will achieve more in politics.

In their personal lives, Brazilian women place strong emphasis on education to help them achieve their goals, with 87 percent citing it as a key to success, versus the global average of 64 percent. When asked to describe the life they would like to achieve, many women mentioned college. "I'd like to go to college to finish my education, find a job, have a fixed salary, and buy a house in a beautiful place," one woman told us. Another said, "I'd like to earn enough money working with my handicraft, have money to buy whatever I want, have my own house and car, learn how to drive, go to college, and be happy."

Many Brazilian women cite accumulating possessions as an important goal in life. Having a successful career comes in a distant second. They frequently mention cars and homes in their narratives about what they want. They like smaller purchases, too. "I'd like to buy clothes and perfumes every day," said one.

In the marketplace, Brazilian women are much more inclined than women in other parts of the world to trade up for products that make them feel and look good—food, haircare products, fragrances, cosmetics, and clothing. Perhaps the Brazilian Gisele Bundchen, one of the highest-paid supermodels in the world, sets the tone. Also, the Brazilian climate lets women be outdoors a great deal, with more of the skin and hair exposed than women in colder climates, who can hide their flaws under hats or

Annual household expenditure
Top categories in key countries

Category	United States	France	Japan	China[1]	United Kingdom	Germany	India[1]	Brazil
Food, beverages, and tobacco	$6,921	$8,848	$10,450	$1,860	$6,067	$4,338	$629	$1,684
Apparel and footwear	1,888	3,843	2,222	533	2,607	1,383	98	447
Housing, furnishings, equipment, and utilities	15,294	11,629	16,935	783	12,086	12,228	229	2,781
Healthcare	2,759	1,770	2,522	359	758	1,257	92	682
Transportation and communications	9,583	9,556	8,468	697	7,962	5,752	N/A	1,441[2]
Recreation and education	3,243	6,017	7,987	681	6,256	3,709	95[3]	509
Other	8,710	8,897	11,469	210	11,660	2,766	376	290
TOTAL	$48,398	$50,560	$60,053	$5,123	$47,396	$31,433	$1,519	$7,834

1. Figures representative of urban residents only. 2. Figure represents transportation only.
3. Figure represents education only.
Note: All figures representative of average-size household for each country; currency conversions calculated at current exchange rates, November 17, 2008.
Sources: 2006 US Bureau of Labor Statistics; 2006 INSEE (French National Institute for Statistic and Economic Studies); 2006 SNA (Statistics Bureau of Japan); 2007 China Statistical Yearbook; 2007 UK Office for National Statistics; 2006 Statisches Bundesamt Deutschland; 2006 Indian National Sample Survey Organization; 2003 Instituto Brasileiro de Geografia e Estatistica.

sweaters. The result: 46 percent of Brazilians in our survey report that they often feel beautiful, versus 33 percent globally, though 68 percent of the Brazilians believe they are overweight, a percentage that is fairly consistent with the global average.

The average Brazilian woman's stress level—55 percent—is higher than average, and 39 percent report feeling angry. They fear violence more than other women in our survey; this is understandable in a country where street crime in cities and tourist areas is quite common. In all categories of personal satisfaction—including happiness, appreciation, peace, stability, fulfillment, work-life balance, recognition, and control—their level of satisfaction is below the global average. Brazilian women report lower emotional health than women in other countries.

Brazilian women value love most of all, followed by health. Religion is

Does Religion Make a Difference?

Religion and spirituality are given varying levels of priority all over the world. Some women find their religion a source of comfort, support, community, and personal well-being; for others, spiritual health is a nonissue. Although levels and methods of religious participation are deeply personal and vary greatly from woman to woman and country to country, we did notice some patterns that were influenced by the strength of a country's dedication to religion:

- Hindu women allocate the highest amount of time for chores: 10 percent more than Jewish women, 7 percent more than Christian women.
- Hindu women claim to spend twice as many hours volunteering per week, nearly three hours.
- At least 40 percent of Christian, Jewish, and Hindu women claim to be above-average or gourmet cooks.
- More than 50 percent of Christian, Muslim, and Hindu women do not rank themselves in their top five priorities.
- 57 percent of Jewish women say their pets make them happy, compared with 40 percent of Christian women.
- 43 percent of Jewish women say they control 90 percent or more of household spending; 38 percent of Christian women make this same claim; only 9 percent of Hindu women make the claim.
- 11 percent of Muslim women say they control less than 10 percent of household spending.
- The majority of Muslim and Hindu women say their life satisfaction and happiness greatly exceed their expectations, compared with only 10 percent of Christian women and 7 percent of Jewish women.

more important to them than to women in most other countries, with 35 percent placing a high value on it versus the global average of 15 percent. Perhaps as a corollary in a country where spirituality is strong, 71 percent mention luck as a factor in their success, too.

Iconic Brazilian Brand: Natura

Natura's model of women selling cosmetics to other women sounds similar to the U.S. companies Avon and Mary Kay, but Natura is tailored to the needs of women in the Brazilian market. By combining high-quality beauty products, convenient shopping, and income-earning potential for women in one company, Natura has found a way to give Brazilian women what they want. Natura also offers a convenient way to shop, a trustworthy brand, and a product line women feel good about using.

Founded by Antonio Luiz da Cunha Seabra in 1969 in Cajamar, São Paulo, Natura is still completely Brazilian-owned. Its products—skincare, sun protection, perfume, cosmetics, and haircare—target a wide range of consumers. Its underlying principle of offering eco-friendly products is also broadly appealing. Sales "consultants" sell products directly to other women, creating interpersonal relationships that make it convenient for women to shop and that help foster brand loyalty.

Customers have responded enthusiastically. Between 2002 and 2006, Natura's share of the Brazilian market nearly doubled, to 22.8 percent, making it the second-largest company by sales, after Unilever, in the cosmetics and toiletries industry. The company now has $1.8 billion in annual revenue, with an impressive 25 percent CAGR from 2002 to 2007, and market capitalization of $3.8 billion as of November 2008. The number of direct sales consultants has more than doubled in the past five years, with more than 632,000 in Brazil and another 86,000 spread throughout Argentina, Chile, Peru, Mexico, Venezuela, Colombia, and France.[8]

Women from all segments of our survey tell us they like the quality of Natura products. They report that the prices are reasonable, and using the products makes them feel good about themselves. "It leaves me feeling pretty and cared for," says Iara, 30, Struggling. "I adore cosmetics and I find theirs excellent," says Valeria, 42, Pressure Cooker.

Natura *recognizes* women's desire for a wide range of high-quality, unique, affordable products. It also appeals to customers on an ideological level. Its slogan, "Bem estar bem" ("well-being and being well"), implies happiness, not just smooth skin. Its products are developed and manufactured without animal testing, reflecting the *research* that revealed women's concerns about the environment and sustainability. This message seems to resonate with customers. "Natura cares about being environmentally friendly," says Beatriz, 35, Managing on Her Own. Taking it one step further is Lilian, 60, of Mexico, also Managing on Her Own. "This is my favorite for the natural look of its beauty products, its benefits, and the satisfaction I feel when I use them. It is a differentiated brand for its respect to nature, sustainable production, and the recognition of the products nature provides for well-being, health, and personal care."

Natura also *responds* to the desire for products that work, and the desire for a trusting and honest relationship with the brand. Another Natura slogan is "Truth in cosmetics." This refers to the company's commitment to play it straight, and not to promise results that the cosmetics can't deliver, such as eliminating wrinkles or puffy eyes. Honest claims give consumers faith in the brand, building long-term trust.

Finally, Natura constantly *refines* its products, offering on average one new product every three working days, but previous lines are still available for refill through consultants, offering both variety and consistency.

As of 2007, 96 percent of Natura's sales were still in Brazil, but that is slowly changing as international expansion continues. After initially moving into other South American countries and Mexico, Natura opened a store in Paris and hired a team of consultants in France. The products are also sold in duty-free sections of Brazilian airports, cleverly introducing them to customers from around the world, especially foreign tourists. Natura is well positioned for future growth at the forefront of the sustainable products market, a growing global trend.

Commercial Opportunities in Brazil

- *A different kind of personal care.* There is opportunity for a personal products line positioned differently from current leaders like Natura and mass-produced global companies. Offering any of these products online could also be a good opportunity. Also, a line of premium skincare and haircare products that caters to Brazil's ethnically diverse population, with a variety of skin and hair colors and types.
- *Best-value alcohol.* Brazilian women are looking for better value for wine, beer, and spirits. Alcohol accounts for three of the top ten categories where they want to trade down. A line of best-value alcohol across all categories—wine, beer, spirits—could be created, with strong branding that could help sell all three types of alcohol at once.
- *High-end box store.* Brazilian women love to shop, but there is no true "luxury" market in Brazil. Shopping makes 80 percent of Brazilian women happy, and they have more leisure time to shop than women globally. They spend an average of twelve hours a

week online; this is higher than the overall average. So there is a need for a higher-end big box store, a Brazilian version of Target. Ideally, the store would take a multichannel approach, allowing women to shop online as well as at stores.

- *Banking for the future.* There is a large first-mover opportunity waiting in financial services in Brazil. Brazilian women are less likely to have any savings vehicle, in comparison with women in other countries. They are less fiscally responsible than they would like to be or could afford to be. Money and saving are a point of conflict with their spouses. Financial planning and banking services are needed in Brazil, especially services that offer online access.

MEXICO: THE MOST WORKING WOMEN

In the past twenty years, Mexico has experienced tremendous economic growth, leading to the rise of a stable middle class. Despite the current downturn, economic growth is projected to continue for many years, if at a slower pace, and average incomes and consumer spending are both expected to increase in consequence. It is perhaps no wonder, then, that Mexican women are among the happiest and most optimistic of those we surveyed.

More Mexican women work than the women of any other country surveyed—94 percent, compared with the global average of 78 percent—and Mexican women also work slightly more hours per week than the global average. They report the same demands on their time and the same frustration with their stress level as women in other countries. Yet despite all this, Mexican women report greater levels of satisfaction in nearly every aspect of their lives: they feel more than usually loved, fulfilled, satisfied, appreciated, acknowledged, successful, important, powerful, and beautiful. They are most satisfied with feeling appreciated (81 percent), happiness (76 percent), satisfaction (71 percent), and peace (71 percent). Sex (79 percent), the outlook for the future (79 percent), and their jobs (76 percent) provide the greatest happiness—and these rank much higher than the global average.

This may be in part because, although Mexican women work long hours and have busy schedules, they also have more help at home than women in most other countries. Husbands in Mexico shoulder more chores and childcare than the global average, and women also maintain strong networks of family and friends to help ease the stress of the daily balancing act. Also of note is the fact that Mexican women prioritize themselves and their own needs higher than any other group surveyed—77 percent listed themselves first, compared with 52 percent globally; next are their parents, partner, job, and kids.

Mexican women have bright hopes for the future, as well. Seventy-nine percent see the future as a source of happiness, compared with 58 percent globally. Eighty-four percent believe that their daily life, happiness, and financial situation will get better—one of the highest percentages among the countries surveyed. Eighty-four percent believe that over the next ten years women will achieve more, economically, professionally, and educationally. Eighty-one percent believe that women will achieve more in politics over the next ten years.

Blanca Treviño: Mexico as a Supplier of Minds, Not Just Low-Cost Labor

In Mexico, where machismo and traditional roles for women are the norm, Blanca Treviño is in the vanguard as CEO of Softtek, an IT company known as a tech mover and shaker. Since taking the top position in 2000, Treviño has been credited with more than tripling the company's revenues, according to *Fortune* magazine, which in 2007 also named Treviño a "Rising Star" among the 50 Most Powerful Women in Global Business. Softtek generates a significant number of new jobs, and now employs about 6,000 associates in thirty offices. Women make up 40 to 45 percent of this workforce. Softtek is also a pioneer in "nearshoring" (a term the company trademarked), which means delivering services to a country that is nearby or adjacent, and using the proximity as an advantage.

Treviño received a degree in computer science at the Instituto Technológico de Estudios Superiores de Monterrey, one of Mexico's leading universities. She was initially hesitant to major in computer science, but her family was supportive. "I told my dad that I was scared and thought I would underperform. But my dad said that he would prefer a dumb daughter to a daughter who was afraid."

When she was still a student, Treviño started working with Grupo

Alfa; she stayed there for seven years, until the company experienced a financial crisis in the 1980s. She and others began building what became Softtek. "We built it from nothing. From the beginning, it was not tied to the rules. We were open to embrace diversity," says Treviño.

Treviño met her husband at Monterrey Tech, as it is commonly called in Mexico; they have two daughters, ages 15 and 19. She credits her extended family with helping her balance working and raising children. "We have a broader family with my mother and sisters. When my daughters were born they helped me." Treviño travels for forty to forty-five weeks of the year, but she tries to keep a flexible schedule, and works from home when she can.

Though women are a tiny minority among CEOs in Mexico, Treviño sees her gender as a management asset. "I run the company differently from how a man would run it. I believe that when you face a difficult situation, you keep the team together and give them confidence. More emotional skills are required. When you are a woman, you don't give orders. You are more inclusive."

Treviño also likes to be a mentor to other women, and she is open to hiring women, especially as women in Latin American go to work to help stabilize the family income during times of economic crisis.

"I am more conscious of the help I have received as a woman and want to give it back. A company that grows as much as we do gives me the chance to give opportunities. I like to challenge women, to tell them to set high goals."

Iconic Mexican Brand: Cinemex's CineMá

The Mexican movie theater company Cinemex addresses a huge group of women in an ingeniously specific and astute way: the theaters offer CineMá, shows and rooms for mothers with young children.

Offered Thursday and Saturday mornings, CineMá showings include features such as lowered sound levels, warmer temperatures, and lights that remain on, at 50 percent brightness, so mothers can attend to their babies, plus amenities including changing stations, bottle heaters, wipes, diapers, and other baby products. Valet parking for baby strollers is also available. CineMá showings cost the same as a regular adult ticket—babies are free. The movies are popular and recent releases, movies that young parents want to see but would be unable to see at another theater because of the hostility toward crying babies and squirming children. CineMá leverages the strengths that Cinemex is known for as well: nice, comfortable, high-end movie theaters and market-leading customer loyalty programs.

CineMá allows time-crunched mothers of young children to multitask while they relax. The many thoughtful amenities actually make it possible for moms to enjoy a movie in a premium theater facility while still properly caring for their babies. According to the CineMá Web site, parents can rest assured that it's OK if their babies cry during the movie, because at this screening, unlike a usual showing, "all the audience members are in the same situation." Moms are also welcome to walk fussy babies around the lobby or theater hallways during CineMá showings.

Commercial Opportunities in Mexico

Mexican women look for products and services that will save them time and offer them quality, security, and value. The average Mexican woman would be willing to pay more for better-quality, healthier food and better grocery store options. Seventy-four percent say they will trade up for food, and 70 percent perceive themselves as overweight. They also want fast, convenient options that will fit into their lifestyle. This commercial opportunity would include:

- A store such as Whole Foods, selling organic, natural, healthy foods
- A focus on local tastes and cultural factors
- Extensive and convenient online shopping

Another opportunity to serve Mexican women is in beauty. Women in Mexico value their appearance; they spend more time than the global average on personal hygiene and grooming.

- Open an affordable but high-quality holistic spa
- Offer a one-stop beauty destination

- Focus on cosmetics, haircare, and medi-spa treatments specific to Mexican women

THE MIDDLE EAST: LESS STRESS, LESS CONTROL

Women in the Middle East have different roles and priorities from their peers elsewhere, but those who responded to our survey also demonstrated that they have the same basic needs, wants, and frustrations in daily life.

The average Middle Eastern woman works fewer hours at her job, but takes on more of the household burden than women in other developing countries. Political stability and religion rank foremost among her priorities, more so than was true of any other country or segment of women we surveyed. Middle Eastern women are happy with most areas of their lives and are less stressed than the average woman globally, but they want more control over their finances, careers, and future.

Women in the United Arab Emirates (UAE) struggle with trying to succeed in their careers while keeping up with their responsibilities at home; they feel they must continually make sacrifices in both areas. They also express a much greater sense of trying to succeed in a man's world. The average household in the UAE is more than twice the size of the global average—6.3 people versus 3.0 overall—and the woman of the house is younger than average. Only 33 percent work full-time, and 26 percent are not employed but are looking for work; those that do work are predominantly in clerical positions. Women in the UAE list stability, happiness, and peace as most important in their lives. They prioritize others ahead of themselves.

They have very little control over household finances, budgeting, and management of household affairs. In the UAE, women control less than 40 percent of household spending. Most worry about saving money; 23 percent spend all the money they make each month, and only 10 percent believe they will have enough saved for retirement. But they are willing to pay a premium for the best goods and services available in those items they are responsible for purchasing. In particular, they are willing to trade up for personal care and healthcare, both for themselves and for their families.

Saudi H&M: For Women Only

The first H&M store in Saudi Arabia, opened in the fall of 2008, is a women-only shopping destination. Staffed entirely by women, the store offers only women's clothing and is located in a family mall, the Mall of Arabia in Jidda. The store is a "beauty" facility that offers lingerie, accessories, and beauty products.

Saudi Arabia already has a number of women-only malls and stores, operated solely by women for women, whereas family malls are open to both sexes and are staffed largely by men. The H&M will provide women with a sanctuary in the mixed malls while still allowing them the convenience of shopping either as a family or for their husbands; the store is adjacent to a full-size H&M "fashion" store that sells both men's and women's clothes.

H&M also is working to build franchise operations in Oman, Bahrain, and Egypt. There are already H&M stores in Dubai and Kuwait.[9]

Commercial Opportunities in the Middle East

Commercial opportunities exist for companies to better meet Middle Eastern women's needs, which are often different from the needs of women in other parts of the world. Women in the Middle East agree with the overall sample on only three of the top fifteen dissatisfactions: work clothes, physicians, and lodging. They feel that retailers and fitness and beauty companies do not understand them, and they want help in the area where they spend most of their time—cleaning the home.

In Egypt, our survey sample tended to be younger and more often single. Egyptian women spend more time than the global average on the Internet and watching television, and, concurrently, they spend less time socializing. Egyptian women prioritize satisfaction, peace, and stability as most important in their lives; reducing stress and gaining recognition are less often priorities.

Women in Saudi Arabia are pessimistic about financial security. Twenty-seven percent spend all the money they make each month (versus 19 percent globally), and only 5 percent think they'll be able to save enough money for retirement (versus 18 percent globally). Only 14 percent consistently save for the future.

Commercial opportunities exist in Saudi Arabia for businesses that

Egyptian Women: In Their Own Words

"Leading a successful career; having a lovely family; having a very good relationship with my husband; raising healthy and successful children; being closer to my family; having many friends; somehow, being famous for doing something good and helpful for my society, to help in eliminating all social diseases from my country (unemployment, violence, poverty, etc.); being closer to Allah; having more time for reading and for new hobbies; understanding who I really am."

"I would like to have useful work for me and for my family, even if it is charity work. I wish to marry a successful man who appreciates marital life. I wish to travel around the world. I would like to be useful to the community. I would like to be introduced to the women in my community."

"I would like to have an understanding, mature husband; to have a healthy, clean, simple, and perfect house. I would like to be the most beautiful woman."

"I dream of becoming a successful businesswoman. To have a very big house for the future. To have a great position in the future."

"I need help in my housework to save time to take care of myself and spend more time with my husband. I would like to have a small business to be independent."

"I would like to start a small organization to help educate women in third world countries, help orphans by educating them and building schools and shelters for them. Open a small restaurant or coffee shop or designer store. Marry a smart and open-minded, ambitious man who will help me with my dream goals."

can cater to Saudi women's limited spending power. Saudi women agree with the global sample on only three of their top fifteen areas of dissatisfaction: physicians, hospitals, and banking. Their top categories of dissatisfaction are health clubs and trainers, hair products, home decor and remodeling, oral care services, and dress clothing. They have high trade-up tendencies and will pay more for healthcare, the home, personal care, and food. They will trade down in toys, entertainment, and exercise-related categories.

A WORLD OF INDIVIDUALS

Qin Liu wants to climb the corporate ladder as high as she can go, while taking the best care she can of her daughter and husband.

Ming Gao, highly educated and very successful, feels burned out at age 29 and isn't sure what she wants to do next.

Sharika Srinivasan shares household duties, including paying bills, with her husband and plans to keep working even if they have a second child.

Nina Kovaleva has a good job but still thinks of her future in terms of her relationship with her boyfriend—when and whether they will marry and have kids.

Nicole Green expects that her life will get a little easier as the kids get older, but wishes the world would be more accommodating to working mothers.

Annalie Lindstrand will probably have two children, a nice house, a better bike, a horse, and a long, happy life.

As different as they are, all of these women—Chinese, Indian, Russian, American, Swedish—deal with the fundamental challenges of being a (working) woman in today's society: juggling priorities, carving out time for themselves, working in male-oriented organizations and societies, and putting up with goods and services that don't meet their needs.

11.

Women Want More for the World

All women want to give back and help others. "Giving circles" have great power to create change. Social policy must accelerate progress and drive prosperity for women and for all. There are five key needs for greater global prosperity and a better world for women: broad availability of daycare, paid child leave, flexible career tracks, access to education, and healthcare. Improving women's lot is an important lever on the growth of national wealth.

HELPING OTHERS

Women want more. Yes, they want goods and services that give them more time, greater connection, and more personal satisfaction. But women also want to have a higher purpose, fulfillment, and inspiration, and they want to think that the brands and companies they buy from are doing good for the world in some way.

Many of the 12,000 women who participated in our survey give money and time to make the world a better place. Increasingly, female corporate executives, public officials, business owners, and stay-at-home moms are entering the world of philanthropy, many of them focusing on charities or organizations that help women and children.

Women care about the world around them; they care about the people they love as well as people they've never met. Companies who understand this passion for giving and can harness it in a way that is both useful to the world and impressive to their female consumers, will gain women's attention and their loyalty.

In our interviews and surveys with women around the world, we were surprised by the variety of ways and means they go about helping other people. Regardless of education, income, and personal circumstances, women from every segment expressed the desire to help those less fortunate than themselves. When asked about their dream days and life goals, nearly half our respondents included some kind of charity or philanthropy in their ideal life:

- "I'd pay my own bills, then help people who deserve it by paying their bills."
- "I'd help others as much as possible, and do volunteer work after retirement."
- "My dream day is to arise with the sun, donate to the Red Cross and Salvation Army, then donate food items to the Alliance church to help feed the poor."

Lower-income women tend to want to help in their own communities and make modest donations to local charities or organize and raise funds for local causes. As their incomes increase, their philanthropic giving increases as well, and they generally focus their gifts on causes that have an immediate and visible impact on their communities; they like to see where their money is going. The greater a woman's wealth, the greater the scope of her philanthropic activity is likely to be.

Whether it's a personal donation to small local charities or corporate philanthropy, women, across the board, are a little more generous than men. "Women for the most part are not interested in [renown]," said Holly Duncan, president of the Women in Philanthropy program at Morton Plant Mease Hospital in Dunedin. "They're much more focused on the impact, particularly the impact on people."[1]

Women view charity as a moral obligation, but they are as careful in their choice of causes as they are in all their decisions about shopping and spending. Women are more likely to contribute to a charity or organization that works toward a goal they hold personally dear, especially when it benefits women and families. And they tend to give the most to education, religion, and health-related causes.

Josette Sheeran: Solving Worldwide Hunger

"People call this my Mary Poppins bag," says Josette Sheeran, the energetic executive director of the UN World Food Programme (WFP), as she reaches into her handbag and brings out a bright red mug. "This is a food ration mug like the ones we've distributed to more than 20 million children last year. For many children it is the only food they receive each day, and many times children will eat only half so they can bring the rest home for their brothers and sisters too young to get a cup of their own at school. One cup costs 25 cents. Just 25 cents a day to feed a child."

Sheeran reaches into her bag several more times during the course of our meeting to show a variety of nutritional inventions that have been designed by WFP to increase its toolbox to help ensure that each food assistance dollar maximizes its nutritional impact. In sequence, she pulls out the mug, a large white bag, iodized rock salt, meals ready to eat, and a variety of nutritional inventions.

WFP, officially established in 1963, is the frontline United Nations agency mandated to combat hunger, which now impacts 1 billion people worldwide. It has a dual mission: to save lives through food assistance in emergencies and to work with developing nations to build food security and safety nets through targeted nutritional interventions such as school feeding and food-for-work programs.

Well-regarded for its operational focus and lean operating budget, in which more than 90 percent of every donated dollar goes to feed the hungry, WFP is the world's largest humanitarian organization, a sprawling organization with over 10,000 employees that last year provided aid to more than 100 million people in nearly eighty countries. Because WFP has such an extensive "deep field" reach, it also has responsibility for logistics within the United Nations system as a whole during emergencies, helping to distribute critical life-saving supplies for other UN agencies or nongovernmental organizations.

As executive director, Sheeran is a hands-on leader who travels the globe supervising one of the most complicated and ambitious food distribution systems in the world. Sheeran is also a passionate advocate for her cause and has testified before the European parliament, the British parliament, the U.S. Congress, and leaders of state in Japan and many Middle Eastern countries to raise awareness about hunger and to give a voice to the voiceless. She is also a remarkably successful fund-raiser, a necessary part of her job since WFP is totally donor-funded, bringing in funds from governments large and small as well as from foundations such as the Gates and Howard Buffett foundations and from corporate donations. In 2008, WFP under Sheeran's leadership raised over $5 billion, nearly double the amount in years past. "Hunger is destabilizing for the world," Sheeran says. "It drives people to arms and war. Children under 2 who receive inadequate nutrition are crippled for life. Inadequate nutrition reduces the income potential of the child by more than half. If you get the child food, you change a life."

The year 2008 was a particularly difficult one for the world's hungry, with what Sheeran called the "three Fs"—the food, fuel, and financial crises. "We experienced a perfect storm—rapidly rising food and fuel prices, compounded by the financial crisis that hit late in the year. These factors constituted an unprecedented threat to the world's poorest, women and children primarily, and required an extraordinary response."

The World Food Programme puts a strong emphasis on helping women and families, as 80 percent of its beneficiaries are women and children. "Women in particular are key to change," says the WFP mission statement. "Providing food to women puts it in the hands of those who use it for the benefit of the entire household, especially the children. WFP assistance will aim to strengthen their coping ability and resilience." Under Sheeran's leadership, there has been a particular emphasis on ending child hunger and malnutrition, which kills 3.5 million children worldwide every year.

Sheeran argues that food assistance, while necessary to save lives, especially in natural disasters or man-made conflicts, does not bring about change; self-sufficiency must be the goal. As an example, she talks about the WFP initiative in Africa to produce iodized salt. "We have about 7,000 women who are now producing iodized salt as part of a WFP development program," she says. "This is a win-win-win project because through it we create a local source of iodized salt that we need for our food rations, we provide long-term work for women, and by teaching these women how to put iodine in salt, we help eliminate iodine-deficient disease." Worldwide, about 2 billion people get too little iodine in their diet. "We helped them secure credit for the equipment needed to produce the salt and we helped them contract for the sale. We have gone from saving lives to creating a sustainable circle of hope."

Why is iodized salt such an important commodity? Studies show that iodine deficiency is the leading preventable cause of mental retardation; even a moderate deficiency, especially in pregnant women and infants, can lower intelligence by ten to fifteen IQ points. Just a bit of iodized salt in the diet improves the entire potential of a nation.

Sheeran has a remarkable résumé and just the experience needed for the WFP job. Prior to being named the eleventh executive director of the United Nations World Food Programme by UN Secretary-General Kofi Annan in 2007, Sheeran had served as U.S. undersecretary for economic, business, and agricultural affairs in the State Department, where she was active in aid and development work in China, India, Pakistan, Afghanistan, and Lebanon. She was also deputy U.S. trade representative, where she worked to help developing nations in Africa and Asia to compete in the global marketplace. Sheeran has also had a successful career as a journalist.

"Helping nations end hunger is an achievable goal," Sheeran says. "We have done this before. Just a few generations ago my family suffered through famines in Ireland. Just 18 years ago, China was WFP's largest program. Today we don't feed one person there. We need $6 billion this year to fund our programs. This is a significant amount, no doubt, but compare that to the size of the financial bail-out packages!"

GLOBAL ORGANIZATIONS TACKLE SYSTEMIC PROBLEMS

The World Food Programme is hailed as one of the most effective humanitarian organizations within or outside of the United Nations system. Because WFP is part of the United Nations, its leaders have access to resources, social and political networks, talent, and other benefits on which smaller, less established organizations cannot depend. Yet even without such resources, some women's organizations have risen to global prominence and are of a caliber equal to UNICEF, Amnesty International, and WFP. These charities use the same principles and strategies as the corporate and government organizations, but they have the added advantage of appealing specifically to women in order to help other women. This allows them to spread a very personal, heartfelt message, and many women leap forward to help in any way they can.

The Global Fund for Women, for example, is an international network of women (and some men) who advocate and defend women's rights. They raise money to create grants, which they award to women's groups around the world, supporting organizations of all sizes that seek to raise the status of women in their societies. Founded in 1987 in San Francisco, this fund has awarded more than $65 million to 3,679 women's organizations in 167 countries. The organization receives more than 3,000 applications for aid each year. Some are e-mailed on standard forms; others arrive scribbled in pencil on scrap paper. All are given equal consideration.

Kavita N. Ramdas, president and CEO of the Global Fund, believes that the women who apply for help know best what they need and that the organization should not make assumptions about what is best for them. "We see these women who, even though they are in the middle of all this war and turmoil, are constantly imagining a different world for their children," Ramdas said. "That's what the world needs most today—a new imagination about what we can become."[2]

Zainab Salbi: Personal Philanthropy Takes On Personal Causes

Another type of women's philanthropy—one that perhaps best demonstrates the extraordinary capacity of women to turn hardship into opportunity, and to unite through a passion for helping others—is personal causes. These philanthropies are often grassroots-type organizations that are built by a woman or groups of women with a particular, personal goal in mind. The organizations run the gamut from the very small and amateurish to good-sized and well organized to large-scale entities whose success and impact are nothing short of phenomenal.

One personal cause organization that falls into the latter category is Women for Women International (WfWi), founded and led by Zainab Salbi. Zainab's story is so inspiring that we wanted to repeat it the way she told us. It's a story of emotion, commitment, and practical, earnest solutions to a global crisis.

Zainab Salbi was born into an upper-middle-class family in Baghdad, Iraq, in 1969. In 1979, Saddam Hussein came to power in Iraq, and a few years later he drafted Zainab's father, a commercial airline pilot, to work as his personal pilot. The Salbis' family life began to intertwine with that of Saddam and his family. Zainab often visited Saddam's palaces and played with his daughters. Her mother was wary and tried to protect Zainab. "Learn to erase your memories," she instructed her daughter. "Saddam can read eyes." When Zainab was 19, Saddam began to make subtle—and not-so-subtle—advances on her. Zainab's mother now feared for her daughter's well-being, and although she had taught her daughter to be independent and self-reliant, she arranged a marriage for Zainab with an Iraqi exile, living in Chicago.

"My mother wanted to get me out of Iraq," Zainab told us. "I was forced to marry a man thirteen years older than me." The marriage did not save her. "My new husband was verbally and physically abusive. He raped me. He demanded that I stay at home and said, 'You are to deliver babies.'" Zainab was forbidden to attend college and was shut off from contact with her family. Her husband demanded that she perform a set of what he called "wifely duties"—which meant she was to slavishly cook, clean, shop, budget, and provide services on demand. In 1990, Saddam invaded Kuwait and the first Gulf War began. Zainab was cut off from her family in Iraq. She found that she could no longer tolerate her marriage. "I could not let him continue to treat me that way. My mother taught me never to tolerate abuse," she said. Zainab escaped from her husband with only a few dollars in her wallet, two suitcases of clothing, and a small Persian rug. "But I could not go back to Iraq. And my family could not leave Iraq. We were at war," she said. "I vowed to start life again."

Zainab's situation was complicated because she was living in the United States on a short-term visa. So, when she left her husband, she appealed to the U.S. Immigration and Naturalization Service and was granted a temporary work visa, which enabled her to work at a series of low-wage retail jobs. Her break came when she got a job as a translator at the Arab League in Washington, D.C. There she met a young man who was sympathetic to her plight, and, after she divorced her first husband, the two eventually married.

About six months after their marriage, Zainab read an article in *Time* magazine exploring the issue of the rapes and "rape camps" in Bosnia. The reporters described how Bosnian Serb soldiers used systematic rape as a strategy to destroy the ethnic identity of Bosnia's Muslim women. Rapes took place in some eighty cities and villages throughout Bosnia. Serb soldiers often raped women in public or forced Muslims and Catholics to rape their own family members. Victims ranged in age from 13 to 60, but there were reports of repeated rapes of girls as young as 6 or 7.[3] The men of the village were killed or dragged off to prison camps and the women were herded from their homes and taken to improvised rape camps, usually in cafés or high schools, where they were detained. There they were raped repeatedly with the intent of impregnating them. No one knows how many Bosnian rape victims there are, though estimates range from 30,000 to 50,000 women, most of them Muslim.[4]

Zainab had an immediate and visceral reaction to what she saw. "I had an obligation and duty to do something about it. I could not just sit and watch. I grew up in Iraq and saw injustice and was not able to do anything about it," she said. "I knew what rape meant. I knew what it meant and what it felt like. I had a duty to do something about injustice."

Zainab had saved about $2,000 and used it to travel, with her husband, to Bosnia to see what she could do to help the victims. Soon after they arrived, they met a woman who had been held in a rape camp for eight months. The woman had been released within one month of delivering her baby, who died shortly after being born. Zainab learned that there were thousands of women who had suffered similarly who were now living in refugee camps with signs above their tents that read "rape victim."

Zainab vowed she would make helping these women her mission in life. She left her job at the Arab League. Her husband quit his job, too. "We became poor quickly," she remembers. "We talked at temples, mosques, churches. We spent 100 percent of every penny on the organization. I had to ask myself, how do I pay for postage? I was blessed; checks came to pay the rent."

Soon four women had joined Zainab in the cause, and then the number steadily grew. "Four grew to 400. Four hundred grew to 4,000," she said. "By chance I had an appearance on *Oprah* where she allowed me to tell the story. It led to $2 million in donations. The charity now has an operating budget of $28 million and operates in ten countries."

In the first three years of operation, Salbi and her colleagues were able to help 400 women. "That was stage one of our existence," she said. "Inexperience. Passion. Learning. Errors. Luck. But we created a template that worked. War shows the best and worst acts of humanity. War ended in Bosnia. People wanted to rebuild their homes. How do we re-create economic opportunity?"

Then an angel appeared. Peter Buffett, Warren Buffett's son, learned about Salbi's work. "He came to visit and said, 'How can I help you to take this to the next stage?'" Peter and his wife, Jennifer, the president of the Novo foundation, helped Salbi and her team enter phase two of her organization—building a more stable infrastructure.

Today, Women for Women International is in stage three of its development. It has an established organization, a moderate infrastructure, a worldwide reputation, and a clearly defined and expansive vision. WfWi now has 600 staff members, and they are working with 153,000 women. About 55 percent of the budget comes from donors making contributions of less than $5,000. Ninety percent of donations come from people who give $500 or less.

The women sponsored by Women for Women International take on all kinds of jobs to help make themselves self-sufficient. They bring vegetables to market; fish; collect scrap metal; weave fabric; make shoes; raise crops; haul rocks; and design, sew, and market clothes. They also meet with other women to take part in business education programs, to learn to read and write, and to learn about women's rights. The programs are part job creation and part networking—helping women form bonds with other women who have similar histories.

"At first the women tend to act like victims," Zainab said. "So we work to move them from feeling like victims to seeing themselves as survivors and then to become active citizens. We group women in circles of twenty. They meet together for a year. We help create vocational skills. We teach them about specific subjects like economics. We help them build their self-esteem. We get them to understand their rights and encourage them to stand up for them boldly. We teach them that the husband does not have the right to slap them.

"A century ago," Zainab said, "90 percent of war casualties were male soldiers. Today 90 percent of war casualties are civilians. Up to 75 percent of those victims are women and children. In Bosnia, Herzegovina, Rwanda, Sudan, and Congo, war has led to epidemics of rape and mutilation of women. Rape is used to achieve political goals and destroys the social fabric. Raped women become an object of shame."

Zainab says that when a war is over, the bulk of rebuilding falls on the shoulders of women. "Women are the ones who are in charge of life. We tell their stories in order to help prevent other women from facing the same crimes." WfWi works with them to rebuild economies, school systems, and the civil system. "The end of a war provides a chance to reshape the social order and bring new hope. We help women by giving them a way to earn cash incomes. Money translates into dignity, influence, and ultimately power."

Zainab Salbi has built an organization that takes models of success for women from the developed world and expands them into the troubled spots of the world: "Stronger women build stronger nations. We are laying the foundation for women most at risk."

THE SOCIAL AND PHILANTHROPIC POWER OF GIVING CIRCLES

One of the important ancillary benefits of women's traditional roles in philanthropy—as working volunteers, soup ladlers, bake sale coordinators, personal caregivers, and more—has always been the social aspect. Women banded together for a cause, and through their shared interest found friends and kindred spirits, formed lasting relationships, and sustained groups.

Organizations like Women for Women International and the Global Fund for Women do foster a sense of community, but there is no single philanthropic organization that offers as great a sense of social connection—and fun—as a "giving circle." These charities consist of groups of women— often a number of friends who invite their colleagues and acquaintances— who get together on a regular basis to socialize, give to the organization of their choice, and, almost always, share food and drink.

Giving circles enable women who may have limited time or financial resources to engage in philanthropy and make a difference, and these circles are popping up all over the country. There are at least 220 circles in forty states, according to a study reported in February 2007 by New Ventures in Philanthropy, a research organization based in Washington, D.C. The organizations' gifts may range from $100 to $20,000 annually, though several big circles have donated hundreds of thousands of dollars in a year. Members often volunteer their time as well, and encourage their children to participate, too. Since 2000, according to the organization, giving circles have donated more than $44 million to a variety of causes.[5]

This new grassroots philanthropy comes as traditional charities feel the pain of an ailing economy, said Daniel Borochoff, president of the

American Institute of Philanthropy in Chicago. "With the economy trending down, that means there's going to be less money for charity at a time when needs are greater," he said. "Giving circles can meet some of those needs."[6]

Lynne O'Shea Nellemann: It's Very Lonely If You're the One and Only

Women can leverage the power and pleasure of the social network in many ways. Lynne Nellemann, past president of the Illinois affiliate of the International Women's Forum (IWF), has succeeded by following the advice her father gave her in fourth grade. "He said to me: multiply yourself through others. Make others leaders. Sponsor others. Multiply your thought through others. That's how you will feel not alone."

Lynne's first job was as one of the first women in brand management at Procter & Gamble, handling the brand Ivory Liquid. "I was in the Big Daddy of all divisions—packaged soap and detergent. You learned fast to make your memos the best they could be and only present ideas that would build market share. You had to be tremendously creative. It was very high risk with very fast feedback. I worked eighty hours a week." In Lynne's four years there, three other women assumed management roles in the division. "Consumer packaged goods companies are an excellent place for women to be."

She then went to work for the advertising agency Foote, Cone & Belding in Chicago. "Many of our clients were heavy-duty financial institutions, and their executives were all men. I wanted to be on the most 'male' accounts and become one of FCB's first female vice presidents." She did so and spent a decade in client services in the advertising industry and then moved to International Harvester (IH) as its first female vice president and the first female corporate officer in a Fortune 50 company. (International Harvester was the twenty-seventh-largest industrial company at the time.)

"This was a company that made agricultural equipment, trucks, and heavy construction equipment. You rarely find women in the culture of such companies. I was surprised by the height of the divisional officers. These men all seemed to be over six foot two. I found the corporate culture quite adversarial for women and minorities." Then came a major strike, which required dealings with the United Auto Workers. "They would have nothing to do with me." After four years at IH, Lynne moved on to Gannett Media as vice president. She helped move the company's start-up newspaper *USA Today* into the black through the creation of a new marketing division, GannettWork. "I had seven years of welcome and gender equality there."

Today, Lynne is a management consultant, heads the women's leadership program at Dominican University, and serves on several corporate and nonprofit boards. She was appointed by Congress as a federal "glass ceiling" commissioner, and then selected by the commission as its Republican cochair—on direct report to two U.S. secretaries of labor—in both the Clinton and the Bush administrations. She has held faculty positions at the Kellogg Graduate School of Management; the S.I. Newhouse School of Public Communications at Syracuse University; the Graduate School of Business for the University of Chicago; and the Kellstadt Graduate School at DePaul University.

The goal of her work with the International Women's Forum is to "bring along women so they can master organizational leadership, often as an alternative to getting an MBA. People skills are an area where women excel. We're now focusing on countries in the Middle East—including Saudi Arabia, Egypt, UAE, and Afghanistan. We're working, too, in developing countries to raise the importance of women in their families and villages and to show men how it economically benefits them."

Lynne has five main points that she stresses as she mentors women throughout the world for leadership positions.

1. *Climb mountains.* Learn that you don't progress through equal steps. Sometimes you can climb straight up. Sometimes you have to go down to advance. Sometimes you can find a pass that makes the journey easier. You advance at various paces. You must adjust to what you find.
2. *Multiply yourself through others.* She repeats the advice her father gave her so long ago. Help others become leaders, sponsor them, and extol the capabilities of those who report to you. There is a collective wisdom that comes through when you focus on working with and promoting others.

3. *Be very symbolic.* Don't let possessions and material things define you. You don't need the accoutrements of position. Meg Whitman, chairperson of eBay, took a middle office. Connect with your company's consumers. Connect with employees. Make a symbolic connection with others so you can easily be remembered as the person who did *X*—whatever *X* is.

4. *Do nonprofit leadership.* Find ways to bring your organization to nonprofit leadership. Think of philanthropic activity not as a perk but as a passion. In today's world, one needs to learn the interdependencies of corporate and community roles and to add value at every step of the way.

5. *Keep up your energy level and sharpen your presentation skills.* Get to the bottom line immediately. Be simple. Think about what you have to say and what it means to the organization. Make yourself memorable. Become known as a leader whose effectiveness exceeds expectations.

THIS THEY BELIEVE

Josette Sheeran believes we can end world hunger. Zainab Salbi believes we can create peace and harmony worldwide. Lynne O'Shea Nellemann believes that we can create a whole generation of female leaders through networking and mentoring.

Three women, among millions, who are changing the world.

Women—as consumers—want every organization, every brand, every product, and every service to somehow be involved in that great endeavor.

Conclusion

Women Ascendant

A Future of Parity, Power, and Influence

The female economy will contribute to leading the world out of economic crisis. The commercial opportunity to serve women remains enormous. Organizations that enable women to participate are more successful. Even as women are better served, their fundamental satisfactions and dissatisfactions are unlikely to change. Women want a better handle on time, more connection, and fulfillment in their lives. Suppliers that focus on the dissatisfactions of women in their categories will generate growth and value.

We write in the midst of a severe economic downturn. This worldwide crisis will certainly have an effect on the rise of women—as individuals, wage earners, relationship partners, mothers, influencers, leaders, philanthropists. It may well be that the economic crisis will *hasten* women's ascendancy, as old structures crumble and new sources of energy become necessary. Certainly, the continued march of women into the workforce is inevitable. And when the dust from the economic crisis settles and we begin to see the shape of an economy and world order that lie on the far side of the current turmoil, women will emerge in an even more important position than they now occupy. It may even be that women will be the force that pulls us through the crisis and will be instrumental in rethinking and remaking the world that lies ahead.

What might the female economy look like?

In some ways it will follow the same trends that have been developing over the past five decades.

Even more women will be members of the workforce, in both developed and developing societies. The number of working women has been increasing at about 2.2 percent per annum. We had expected an addition of about 90 million women to the workforce by 2013, but that number may be higher than anticipated as more women seek work out of necessity. And we have seen that men are exiting the workforce in greater numbers than in the past, as large companies seek to reduce the size of their workforce or restructure it. By February 2008, 82 percent of the layoffs that came about as a result of the economic downturn had been men, and the number of women in the workforce was poised to surpass that of men.[1]

Even though women have yet to achieve wage parity with men, they will continue to increase the amount of wealth they control. The $20 trillion of spending power that women now possess will climb. The rise to $28 trillion will take five years or more, but the amount will still rise significantly.

Women's earnings will continue to increase. Their current $12 trillion in earnings worldwide could increase to as much as $18 trillion in the same period. The gap between males' and females' earnings should continue to close. Women currently earn $0.54 for every $1 earned by men, but over the next five years the ratio of female to male income is expected to increase by $0.05 to reach $0.59. Also over the next five years, the global average income earned by females is expected to increase by $3,300. This growth in relative wages will be likely to continue as education drives growth in women's income.

We are certain women will continue their love affair with education. Today, 57 percent of students in college or higher education in the United States are women, 55 percent of students in Europe are women, and 47 percent of students in the rest of the world are women. We expect that the educational trend will continue. Well-educated women will want and expect their daughters to be well-educated and encourage them to advance their education as much as possible. The affordability of college is likely to become an even more important issue than it is today, and pressures on personal incomes, college endowments, and financial assistance funds may exacerbate the problem. But these pressures will pertain to everyone, male and female, and we do not expect women's educational aspirations to abate at all.

A critical issue for women is access to childcare. Our Women's World Index shows that the economics of affordable daycare are not controversial. Universal access to daycare will allow more women to progress in their careers during their critical working years—their late twenties to early thirties. Women who continue to work while they are starting and building families will increase their lifetime incomes, advance their careers more rapidly, and dramatically increase their control of wealth.

We may see a dramatic increase in women's entrepreneurial activity. Already women own 40 percent of firms in the United States, generate $1.7 trillion in annual sales, and employ about 13 million people. Women-owned businesses are growing at twice the rate of all U.S. firms—faster than male-owned businesses—and this rate may increase.

THE COMMERCIAL OPPORTUNITY REMAINS

No matter how the economy evolves, and what roles women play in its transformation, the commercial opportunity will continue to grow because women's dissatisfactions remain and run very deep.

Women will still be dealing with the triple challenge of time—work-family balance, conflicting demands, and too little time for themselves—and it will probably become even more acute as greater financial pressure is felt across all segments and as there is less money available to outsource household tasks. Accordingly, women will be all the more eager to purchase products and services that help them leverage their time and make the most of every minute of their day. The new time-based competition is about reducing total time for product consumption—from decision to buy to preparation for use, to use, to after-use.

Our survey shows that financial pressures lead to negative emotional states. Money does, in fact, buy happiness. Women feel sad more frequently when they are worried about money, feel less important, are less satisfied with their appearance, and feel in less robust emotional health. So they will be looking for goods that help relieve those stresses—both directly, through financial services and other such helps; and indirectly, through goods that make them feel more attractive and healthy.

The economic crisis will also no doubt open up a new range of commercial opportunities. Women in particular seek to buy products and services from companies that do good for the world, particularly for other women. Brands that—directly or indirectly—are seen to promote physical and emotional health and well-being, protect and preserve the environment, provide education and care for those in need, and encourage love and connection will benefit, especially in difficult times.

Women will probably become less and less willing to settle for products that ignore or fail to fully meet their needs, or that address needs only cynically or superficially. Women may love pink forever, but not when companies try to present the favorite color as a technical or functional benefit. Women will increasingly assess companies and brands in terms of values and of commitment to a community that they care about. And women will increasingly resist being stereotyped, segmented by age or income, lumped together as "all women," or, worse, undifferentiated from men.

THE ORGANIZATIONAL IMPERATIVE

The rise of the female economy offers huge commercial opportunities—in terms of creating and selling products and services for women, like the ones we have identified in financial services—but it also presents a great challenge and opportunity to business organizations: to create environments where women can thrive, contribute their best, fundamentally influence the organization, and rise to leadership.

There is evidence that, even as women slowly gain more positions at the top of the world's largest companies, they are increasingly seeking other types of organizations in which to work. They are starting their own companies, working for smaller firms or not-for-profits, and creating different forms of commercial entities—circles, associations, and networks.

Increasingly, too, women are refusing to accept the separation of their professional and personal lives—or refusing to make the "choice" between one and the other—that has characterized corporate life for decades. They do not believe that "business is business" and that decisions can be made in a business context that are disconnected from other parts of their lives or the world.

For the foreseeable future, women will continue to face the issue of how to manage a career and childbearing. Just at the point when the young female doctor, who has spent ten years preparing, reaches her professional goal, she also finds herself running out of time to start a family. The young woman who wants to attend business school finds it difficult to see how and when she can fit in having children.

As a result, women are often forced to make one or more of what seem to be artificial choices: to place their work "above" their family; to place family "above" work and accept that their career path may be negatively affected; to try to be superwomen who excel at both work and family life (and often take on too much stress or burn out as a result); or to construct some kind of workable sequence—taking time out of, or reducing involvement in, the career to focus on family or concentrating their involvement in the career at the "expense" of family engagement for a certain length of time.

All of our research shows that an expanding role for women in a company improves it. Greater gender diversity introduces more varied skills and experiences to the workforce, and nurturing and developing women will build the base of high potential leaders. Currently, however, the business environment in the United States is one of the least hospitable, among the developed countries, for women.

Lynne O'Shea Nellemann, of the International Women's Forum, offers this advice. "To the guys in the corner offices, I say: give women the toughest assignments. Don't give them the easiest ones. Bring them into the important meetings. Invite them to the annual meetings. Rotate them through investor relations so they can see interest and needs. Put them on the weekly or monthly call with the analysts. Show the women that you value their femininity." She argues, particularly, that women are advantaged in creating products and services for women, because "women understand the motives and needs of other women."

There are many steps that companies can consider taking to improve the situation, including the following.

Nontraditional job rotations and cross-discipline opportunities. H&M is one company that believes job rotation is a good way for colleagues to develop and can help the company grow. In an H&M store, job rotation may mean that a person's duties vary from customer service, the cash desk, fitting rooms, and unpacking to display and follow-up of advertising and campaigns. When H&M opens stores in new markets, job rotation may involve colleagues from established H&M countries supporting a store manager and store colleagues on-site for the intensive period that precedes the opening. In other companies, job rotation may involve more dramatic shifts—from marketing to distribution, for example, or from finance to operations.

Flexible hours and work arrangements. Principal Financial is known as one of the most female-friendly financial services companies—or, for that matter, one of the most female-friendly companies of any type—in the United States. Women hold 50 percent of its 1,700 most senior positions, and five of fourteen directors are female—that's 35 percent, in comparison with the insurance industry average of just 16 percent. The company has been actively recruiting women for four decades. As early as 1966, Principal was advertising job openings for "mothers of schoolchildren" and offering part-time hours and summers off. Principal introduced flexible work schedules in 1974.

Principal went even further with these policies as it prepared for its initial public offering (IPO) in 2001. It needed to hire many new employees, and its HR managers determined that employees who stayed with the company for three years were less likely to leave after that point. So it developed programs that would support its people throughout what the HR executive James DeVries calls the "whole career life cycle." Standard maternal leave at Principal is twelve weeks after the birth of the child. Women can return to work on a part-time basis and gradually reassume full-time responsibilities. Principal has invested $8 million in a subsidized early-childhood learning center. Twenty percent of enrollment at the center is reserved for infants, so new mothers can take advantage of the facilities. DeVries says those measures cost the company very little. "It's a virtuous cycle," DeVries told *Fortune*. "Just about every metric you review around employee productivity has increased: Our sales results are higher than they have ever been, our investment performance is great, our stock price has tripled."[2]

Paid parental leave and healthcare. As we learned in the story of Annalie Lindstrand, Swedish companies lead the way in providing generous paid parental leave and access to healthcare. Our research shows that companies in the United States and other developed countries could follow suit without jeopardizing performance. However, companies in developing countries often face special difficulties. One of these is a lack of adequate infrastructure—healthcare services may not be available, or they may not be accessible owing to poor roads or lack of transportation.[3]

Access to childcare and services. Companies such as eBay cite their access to childcare as an important attraction for female employees, but childcare services are rarely a stand-alone solution for working mothers. In Singapore, according to a study by Working Mothers' Forum, a support group, mothers say that a far more important element than organized childcare is a dad who plays a hands-on role in parenting and taking on tasks related to managing the kids and their schedules. In this study, one in three Singaporean mothers felt that their society did not understand the needs of working mothers. This finding relates directly to an even more fundamental problem in Singapore: the fertility rate there is 1.29 per woman, far below the 2.1 rate that is necessary for any population to replace itself.[4]

Mentoring and modeling. Boris Groysberg, an assistant professor at Harvard Business School, conducted a study of 1,000 women stock analysts and found that most of those who become stars at their companies had mentors. "In fact," he writes, "the most conspicuous difference between star and non-star women in equity research is access to a supportive mentor."

However, women can have a difficult time finding a mentor and getting the most out of the relationship. "The female analysts in the study reported that even when they were mentored," Groysberg says, "they tended to be treated as more probationary than their male counterparts. Consequently, they missed out on one of the most valuable services a mentor provides: access to a network of relationships.

"What's more, men who do mentor women can't offer much in the way of psychosocial support—how to deal with sexism, for instance, or how to balance a career and family—whereas female mentors, when available, may not be in a position to facilitate their protégés' integration into the firm culture."[5] So, mentoring works extremely well when it works—but there are many challenges involved.

Philanthropic programs. As we discussed in Chapter 11, women want to work for companies that give back, do good for the world, and support women. Goldman Sachs operates a global initiative called 10,000 Women, whose goal is to improve the quality and capacity of business and management education around the world. Women have been a key factor in achieving this goal: the program has attracted tremendous employee interest and participation, particularly among female employees, and there is a waiting list of employees who want to serve as mentors in the program. The program has been a strong success in increasing the number of underserved women receiving business and management education. Over a period of five years, Goldman Sachs—in partnership with sixteen academic institutions throughout the world—intends to help 10,000 women receive a business and management education.

The decision to focus the program's investments on women entrepreneurs was born out of research conducted by Goldman Sachs, the World Bank, and others, which found that investments in women deliver strong social and economic returns.

The 10,000 Women initiative will expand the female entrepreneurial and managerial pool in developing and emerging economies. Women will be empowered to build their businesses and communities through increased access to training, technology, and professional networks. And a larger network of women will be created within business communities, creating role models for younger women and facilitating their entry into the business environment in the future. There is also a multiplying effect; the education that women receive enables them to educate and provide employment within their own communities.

"Women are the catalysts of change of our time," said Melanne Verveer, cofounder and chair of Vital Voices Global Partnership, a nongovernmental organization (NGO) that identifies, trains, and empowers emerging women leaders and social entrepreneurs around the globe. "We know from a growing body of research that investments in women's education and training pay significant dividends for society. Without women's full participation, no country can prosper, but in order to tap their potential, women need the tools for effective leadership. There is no better investment for our world."[6]

The 10,000 Women initiative is a particularly striking example of an institutional philanthropic project. It makes Goldman Sachs an important player in supporting women worldwide while increasing its attractiveness to women as an employer and a place to make a career.

Nicole Green on What Companies Can Do

Nicole Green, our Fast Tracker mother with way too much to do, has been dealing with male-oriented organizations for years—first in graduate school and then in her work life.

"A lot of the women in my department at graduate school were having kids. That's actually a great time to start a family, because life is flexible at that point. But others in the department tend to see pregnant women and women with babies as not being serious, because they have to back off a little bit to look after their kids. Some of them may decide to take eight years to get through the graduate program instead of five. Does that make them less committed?"

As to work, Nicole makes more money than her husband does and puts in as many hours—even if some of her tasks are accomplished at home. However, if there's a conflict between the job and family duty, Nicole is almost always the one who will make the accommodation. "Whenever there's a quick shift that has to happen because one of the kids is sick, the default position is that I will be the one to stay home unless he is free and I am absolutely swamped. I'm the mom. I'm the one who's supposed to be there."

Male coworkers can compound the problem. "The male members of my department often schedule meetings at 7:30 in the morning, which drives the mothers of young kids absolutely crazy. What makes you think I can be at the office by 7:30 in the morning? School opens at 8:20. There is absolutely nothing I can do about it. Knowing a lot of other working moms, I know I'm extremely lucky to have the kind of flexibility I have. But it seems you have to work your ass off to earn enough flexibility to be able to do what you need to do."

What more could companies do?

The Silicon Ceiling

A study conducted by the Anita Borg Institute and the Michelle R. Clayman Institute for Gender Research at Stanford University showed that women in technical professions bump hard into the glass ceiling when they reach the middle levels in their companies.

According to *Climbing the Technical Ladder: Obstacles and Solutions for Mid-Level Women in Technology*, published in 2008, very few women reach top technical positions in high-tech firms, such as technology fellow or vice president of engineering. The report says that men are 2.7 times more likely than women to be in a high-level position, and that women are an increasingly smaller proportion of the workforce at every level of the technology corporate ladder. As a result, 29 percent of women polled by the researchers say they plan to leave their mid-level positions at high-tech companies within twelve months and pursue alternative options.

The study cites many barriers that get in the way of women's advancement in tech companies, including these:

- Technical women in management positions are perceived as less technically competent than their male counterparts. This perception creates an environment in which women are viewed (and can view themselves) as "not fitting in" with the company culture.
- Mid-level women are more likely than men to believe that extended workdays are a requirement for success. This belief may lead to a perception

continued

among women that those who cannot regularly stay late are less likely to advance.

- Although both men and women value family, men are nearly four times more likely than women to have a partner who assumes the primary responsibility for the household and children. The report shows that to achieve career goals, 34 percent of mid-level technical women have deliberately delayed having children.
- Women are more likely than men to suffer poor health due to excessive work-related stress, and more than 68 percent report limiting their amount of sleep to achieve their career goals.

The study also makes recommendations for companies that want to retain and advance technical women, including these:

- Investing in professional development is the most profitable step high-tech companies can take to advance technical women and retain all technical talent. Companies should create opportunities for all technical employees, at all levels, to participate in technical, leadership, and management development activities on company time.
- Since mid-level technical men are much more likely than women to benefit from partners who do not work full-time and who take care of household responsibilities, companies need to offer flexibility in work schedules. Flexible scheduling is essential for retaining mid-level women, who often face unique work-life challenges.
- A diverse leadership team is essential to foster a culture that values diversity. One way companies can demonstrate their commitment to diversity is to increase the female representation on their board of directors and other leadership entities.[7]

"Companies need to acknowledge that there are parents who work for them and that sometimes crises happen. My company has set up systems that make it possible for people to work at home when they need to. The IT people set up a secure network. We all carry our secure ID cards where the number changes every thirty seconds so that you can log in and you can be connected to the company network. We all have pagers and various communications devices that make it a lot more possible for us to work wherever we are. That's very different from the healthcare organization where I worked before. It was extremely male-oriented, and you were frowned upon if you tried to leave work early. It was not family-friendly at all."

WORKING WOMEN HELPING OTHER WORKING WOMEN

Although improvements in specific categories, changes in organizational structures, and new social policies are all necessary to improve conditions for women, perhaps the most powerful and fundamental force for change is women helping other women. Working together to overcome obstacles and challenges, enabling others to participate fully, sharing ideas and practices, modeling, mentoring, and leading are all essential practices for success.

Carol Evans: Advocating for Working Mothers

Carol Evans's way of helping is to advocate for working mothers.

Evans, CEO of Working Mother Media, never expected to become a CEO when she dropped out of college at age 18 to travel around the country. She returned to school at age 23, paying her own way and reading English literature chronologically from *Beowulf* to Beckett. After graduation, she started a book publishing company and published five collections of short stories before she ran out of money. She took a job selling magazine advertising and found she was very successful at it. "I was the girl who said she would never, ever, get involved with business. But I really started to love the business world," she said. "I was surprised at the creativity and the kind of challenge that it offered." She moved to New York to manage advertising sales for *Working Mother* at age 27.

Evans left *Working Mother* after ten years to work with *Stagebill* for seven years, and then with *Chief Executive* magazine for six. Her experience at the latter inspired her to aim higher in her own career. "I said to myself, 'If these guys are the chief executive officers of the world, the biggest and the best, I can certainly do that.' And that's when I decided I would be a CEO."

Evans procured financing from an investment capital group to buy *Working Mother* magazine in 2001, just three weeks before 9/11. "At first our mission was just to help working mothers, but after 9/11, we expanded our mission, 'To Serve Women Boldly.' So today our mission is to help companies to shift their cultures around the issues of work-life balance, advancement of women, and diversity and inclusion."

As someone on the front lines of advocating for women in the workplace, Evans cites three key issues: flexibility, childcare, and the advancement of women. "One of the biggest issues in the United States is whether women can actually get the flexibility that we need. And flexibility, to us, means can you flex your day, your week, your year, and your whole career. If you can flex your day, great; but can you flex your career? Each kind of formula works differently for each person, and no one formula really solves all the problems, so you have to have this very expansive view of what flexibility means. So that's the first thing that we're fighting for, for women in the United States."

On a practical level, Evans says, this means that women need to take their own "heart rate" for ambition. "Do you really want to go ahead or is the stress really getting to you? I want women to be able to say, 'Let me take a step backward and stay within this field.' Or, 'Let me stay where I am and stay within this field.' Or, 'Let me work three days a week for the next three years.' I just want them to be able to take that bottom point where they have the stress and find real solutions, not fake solutions."

As for advancement, Evans sees slow progress. "I think that for all women, the slowness of advancement is still a big issue. You have a huge culture shift and a huge swiftly advancing change over the last thirty years, but all along the way, you have these really slow progress areas. Equal pay is still slow. The glass ceiling is still firmly in place."

Still, Evans does see some positive signs of change. "Ten years down the road, I think we'll have made some progress on governmental support for childcare and for paid maternity leave and paid sick leave if we have a change at the top. But it's still going to be slow going in terms of the women at the very top. I imagine we would go from ten or eleven CEOs in the Fortune 500 to twenty. Thirty would be huge."

Evans believes women in mid-level businesses are more successful than those in the top tier. "We'll be making a lot more progress in the middle because we're so competent, we're so focused on the work. Companies are supporting women there and advancement in the middle will keep getting stronger and stronger. We have to prove ourselves over and over in the middle before we get to the top."

The Federal Government Could Award More Contracts to Women

Women own almost half of the small businesses in the United States, generating almost $2 trillion in revenue. Yet in 2007, female small-business owners were awarded only 3.4 percent of annual federal contracts.

It's not for want of trying or for want of supporting regulations.

The Women's Business Ownership Act was passed in 1988, to establish programs and initiate efforts to assist the development of small businesses owned and controlled by women entrepreneurs. It also established the National Women's Business Council and provided for the collection of statistics relative to women-owned businesses.

In 2000, Congress ordered that 5 percent of federal contracts be awarded to female small-business owners each year, an amount that is estimated at $435 billion.

However, the original provision covered only four industries. (Senator Olympia J. Snowe of Maine called it a "sham.") In 2008, the number of industries was increased to thirty-one, but that is still less than a third of the 140 industries eligible for government contracts.[8]

THE WANTS WON'T CHANGE

"I would like to be happy."

Not many women in our survey stated what they want quite so simply as this American woman. More often, they describe a particular kind of happiness they aspire to—in their work, in their relationship, with their family, in a particular endeavor, regarding their finances, or in their larger role in the world.

- I would like to provide more for my kids than I'm able to right now.
- I would like to have a successful enough career that I find fulfilling, but where I can also balance spending time with my family.
- I would like to make a positive impact on the world in a meaningful way.
- I would like to find someone to love, to spend my life with.

- I would like to have a job that keeps pushing me outside my comfort zone, is intellectually demanding, requires creativity, and has little to no routine.
- I would like to eventually own, or at least work for, a business that has more than profit in mind at the end of the day.
- I would like to feel financially secure.
- I would like to have enough money to eat healthy, delicious food any time I want.

We have simplified the key wants to three intersecting desires. Women want:

- *Love and connection.* A lasting romantic relationship with a trusted partner, a healthy family, strong connections with networks of friends and colleagues, and a genuine sense of community.
- *Fulfillment.* Women want the freedom to pursue the life they choose, to feel empowered, to have the flexibility to customize a life and a career, to be free of any suppression or boundaries, and to feel encouraged to succeed by those around them.
- *Work-life balance.* Ways to mix, blend, and accommodate the many demands on a woman's time and opportunities in her life, some of which are strictly time-limited.

Accumulation of money, or earning money for its own sake, is not a goal for women. For them, money is a means to learning, loving, connecting, security, and achieving a better life for their families.

In the end, it all comes down to happiness, however one defines that. As one woman put it, "I would like to close my eyes at the end of my last day on Earth and say, 'I liked my life, I am happy, now I can leave this world.'"

Radhika Shapoorjee: Back to the Sari

Radhika Shapoorjee, president of a top public affairs and public relations consulting firm in India, provides a glimpse of how women can hope to achieve such a wish in the emerging female economy.

Shapoorjee never really expected to attain the success she now has. "I

What women want: Time, value, a better life

Love and Connection
- A lasting romantic relationship and love
- Trust, support, honesty, and commitment in a partner
- A happy, healthy family
- Connections with family, friends, colleagues, and neighbors
- A sense of community

Fulfillment
- Freedom to pursue happiness and satisfaction however they choose
- Empowerment and flexibility
- Absence of suppression
- Unlimited boundaries
- Encouragement to achieve

Money as a Marker
- Women earning and controlling more; balancing inflow and outflow
- Careful, hungry for insight on how to spend money wisely
- Expectations about value for money increasing; skeptical about claims
- Seeking security, higher savings, a better future; willing to sacrifice

Work-Life Balance
- Time-stressed and strained, looking for agents of leverage and convenience
- Worried about how to make it all happen, making trade-offs and tough decisions
- Women taking on more – juggling work, family, and home; looking for ways to "source time" or share the burden

could not have imagined twenty years ago that I would be doing this job," she says. "I was not an academic genius. I worked hard to make up for that, but still I never thought I would get to be a president."

As a young adult, she distinguished herself as a basketball player and got a scholarship to St. Stephen's College, one of the best institutions of higher learning in the country. There she excelled more in sports than in academics. "In academics, I just figured out how to do well enough to get by, and never well enough to be a class-topper. If I could do it all again, I would spend more time on my studies," she admits.

Once she graduated, Shapoorjee applied her competitive zeal to finding a job. She craved financial stability, something her family lacked when she was growing up. "My focus and aspiration were all around work—making money, doing well, moving up the ladder, and being stable. I wanted to be able to support myself."

In Shapoorjee's first job, as a salesperson for the Yellow Pages, she worked hard. "I was pushy, aggressive, and a very good salesperson. But in those days I was a follower. I didn't question what was asked of me and what the organization stood for. I didn't question anything."

After six months, Shapoorjee knew she wanted a different position but decided to continue with advertising. She cold-called a CEO and landed a job with a firm called SCB Ulka Advertising. Within nine months she was promoted to supervisor and placed in charge of a large account, working with the creative department. Things did not go well at first. "I pushed creative very hard and harassed them to deliver. I think they became afraid of me. I became known as a superbitch. But no one ever told to be more gentle, because I got the job done."

For the next nine years, Shapoorjee continued to advance. She saved money and bought an apartment. Her financial success gave her the confidence to end a romantic relationship that had not been going well. Later, she met Nosh, a colleague at Ulka. They soon married and immediately started planning for their financial future. "We bought a flat together and started a kids' education fund. I made my husband take life insurance. We only put money into real estate, safe funds, and insurance."

After Shapoorjee gave birth to her first child, their daughter Taira, she decided to change her career. "Advertising was not the right thing for raising kids, because the clients were too demanding and variable, so I moved into public relations." Since she had no background in PR, she studied hard, read the *Harvard Business Review,* and met with people in the field until she "put it all together."

She then joined Genesis, India's largest PR firm, and made her first client presentation to a life insurance provider. "It was the best presentation that Genesis had seen and the client had seen. Clients loved us, and we became a wonderful bridge between them and the media."

Shapoorjee became more expert at customizing her career. When she was pregnant with her son, Zahaan, she arranged for a sabbatical from Genesis for four years. She kept her hand in by doing some consulting work. During this time, Nosh had a steady, well-paid job, but he traveled so much that Zahaan barely recognized his father. When Nosh quit his job to spend more time with his young family, the decision tapped into all of Sapoorjee's worries about not being able to provide for her family.

"It was a traumatic time for us because I had focused on financial security and this was going to be a hit. We had to pay for the mortgage, insurance premiums, and investment plans. We had enough savings, but there was no way I wanted to eat into them. I could see that Nosh was getting stressed out. So I decided to go back to work with Genesis."

At Genesis, she was put in charge of strategy for all of India, but she clashed with her boss and left the firm for a rival, Ipan. When her boss there left in 2008, she was promoted to president.

Like working mothers the world over, Shapoorjee has trouble finding balance. "Balance? I haven't hit it. There's a lot to do and not enough time with both work and family." She tries to reserve weekends for family time. She also realizes that having a family of her own has helped her to grow as a leader. "I learned how to work together and to value how to work in collaboration. Until then, I was a loner, I thought I could do everything myself."

Even so, she often wonders what message she is delivering to her children. "I realized my role is to give my children confidence and the feeling of strength to accomplish anything. I need to keep the same elements in mind at work. I remember feeling insignificant at work, and now I want everyone at work to feel significant."

Shapoorjee struggled for such a long time to achieve financial security that she was recently tempted to take a better-paying job. "But I love this job and I'm doing well enough. And the money I'm making now is more than I had thought I ever could make. It's my calling and I don't want to give that up frivolously."

As she has gained confidence in herself as a leader, Shapoorjee has changed her dress style. "Through my thirties, I had to look and talk like a man to be accepted. At least I did in my own mind."

Recently, she arranged to have a makeover. "I realized the power of being a woman, especially in the PR and communication age. I realized women have a sense of grace, dignity, and class that is very useful and powerful in this industry."

So she went back to wearing a sari. "But a sari with a very different look. Senior, refined, and classy. It reflects confidence and elegance. And

The Female Economy in a Nutshell

Women are the <u>most powerful consumers</u> in history:
- *Education, politics, career opportunities are making them more so.*
- *Companies that understand them and cater to them will <u>win in the long term</u>.*

To do so requires responding to women's dissatisfactions, and designing products and services that address women's <u>technical, functional, and emotional</u> needs:
- *Leverage a woman's time.*
- *Address her needs.*
- *Speak to her heart.*

Every company should ask: "Are we . . ."
- *<u>Listening</u> and <u>responding</u> to a woman's second nature?*
- *Addressing her emerging needs?*
- *Thinking broadly enough about the opportunity?*

THE OPPORTUNITY

- As much as $8 trillion in incremental sales to women over the next decade.

THE TRIPLE CHALLENGE OF TIME

- Too many demands on my time
- Too many conflicting priorities
- Not enough time for me

THE ARCHETYPES

- Fast Tracker
- Pressure Cooker
- Relationship-Focused
- Making Ends Meet
- Managing on Her Own
- Fulfilled Empty Nesters

THE LADDER OF BENEFITS

- Technical
- Functional
- Emotional

THE FOUR R'S

- Recognize
- Research

- Respond
- Refine

THE WANTS

- Love and connection
- Fulfillment
- Work-life balance
- Money as a marker

CATEGORIES OF GREATEST OPPORTUNITY

- Financial services
- Healthcare
- Service
- Food at home
- Food away from home
- Travel
- Cars
- Consumer electronics
- Time savings
- Education for children and women

now I'm getting a great reaction to this, especially as the head of the agency. So I have to be sure I reflect the right choices for the juniors. Every woman in the industry wears the male pantsuit and it's time for the industry to change."

The Winners' Checklist

- Is *listening and responding* second nature at our company? Do we, in fact, have a profile—continually updated and refined—of what's happening in the marketplace?
- What are the *dissatisfactions* in the category? How do they rank, by importance to consumers? Which ones can we address most successfully? Which can we address fastest?
- How can we *define our market* as broadly as possible? What minute-by-minute time-savings solutions are needed or could be

developed? Are there emerging market segments that are under-served? What are the dissatisfactions and needs in each of them?

- How do women make the *purchase decisions* for this category? What do they want? What do they need? How do they buy? When do they buy? What is the life cycle of the product for the consumer?

- Is the *product design* appropriate for women? Is it pleasing to the eye? Does it accommodate women's needs in use? Is the design based on needs of the particular consumer segment? Will women respond to the ingredients and raw materials used?

- Does the *merchandising* communicate the special way that the product or service responds to women's specific needs for time savings, connection, love, and beauty?

- How does the product deliver advantages at three important *moments of truth*—purchase, consumption, and referral (or lack of referral)?

- Does the *sales force clearly understand* why the product or service is better for women and more responsive to their needs?

- Does the *marketing deliver fireworks imagery* in the marketplace? Does it speak the truth? Does it tell a story? Will it turn skeptics into believers? Or will it show up on YouTube as yet another example of clueless marketing?

- Do we think of the product or service as just a step in a never-ending *process of continuous improvement, experimentation,* and *learning*?

- Are we thinking about this opportunity as a source of major big, new business, rather than as a small, ancillary segment?

THE ONCE AND FUTURE FEMALE ECONOMY

The rise of women—as possessors of wealth, purchasers, family members, influencers, philanthropists, employees, and leaders—holds within it what may be the largest commercial opportunity we have ever seen or will see in our lifetime.

There are hundreds of billions of dollars to be captured. Categories to be revitalized and won. Brand reputations to be built and sustained. New products and services to be invented. Great endeavors to be unleashed.

Untold amounts of good to be done for the world, and for women in particular.

We believe women will help our world emerge from the current crisis. They bring the power of education, drive, and ambition. This book offers insight into commercial opportunities. It is also a call to action for companies to maximize the productivity of the female workforce by providing flexible work arrangements, childcare, mentoring, and modeling. Leaders of major companies have a chance to decide to prioritize the female economy, systematically size the near- and medium-term emerging market, deeply and fully understand current dissatisfactions, and change holistically, not incrementally.

We have three major messages: (1) This is an undeniable emerging market. (2) It offers companies a real chance to separate themselves from their competitors. (3) Attacking and succeeding in the female economy will require skill, nuance, engagement, and investment.

We have sought to explain what women want, not only in the abstract, but in the particular—in goods, services, brands, and companies.

We have laid out many principles and practices that can be followed more or less completely and more or less immediately.

We have shown that companies that can successfully serve women gain great benefits: breakout growth, loyalty, category leadership, share gain, a refined innovation capability, and the ability to create a virtuous cycle.

We have told stories of products, services, companies, and individual women—both celebrated and everyday—that illustrate what the female economy already is and what it is likely to become.

All that remains is for the reader to accept and grasp that this phenomenon is real, important, and sustainable.

Women should have access to goods and services that meet their specific needs. When they don't find these, they have an obligation to demand them. Women's engagement with the world—both as members of the workforce and as members of social institutions, including families—must not be defined in ways that limit their ability to fully contribute. When such a limitation happens, individuals, organizations, and societies must be changed.

A world in which women's needs and wants are more fully met will be a better one for us all.

We have a model for such a claim: the Minoan society of ancient Crete.

Archaeologists and historians believe that men and women lived and worked there as equals. They worshipped only goddesses, including a mother goddess of fertility, a mistress of the animals, a protectress of cities and of the household, the harvest, and the underworld. It is believed that inheritance was matrilineal. Some historians say that the society was prosperous at a level never before seen and had an equitable distribution of wealth among its people. The civilization made rapid advances in agriculture, trading, metal making, and the creation of durable goods. The people lived in peace for some 500 years.

Might the rise of women around the world in this century lead to another golden age of similarly remarkable accomplishment—a global society of great wealth, widespread equality, and long-lasting peace and prosperity for all?

Acknowledgments

Behind this book was a fabulous consulting team from The Boston Consulting Group (BCG). Core members included: Amanda Brimmer, Sarah Minkus, Mackenzie Mudgett, Carrie Perzanowski, Lori Scherwin, Susan Schriver, and Benoite Yver. Particular thanks go to Lori for leading the team through the home stretch, to Susan for masterminding the global survey, and to Carrie for her inspired management of the team during the first two phases of work. We had three interns hard at work on various elements of the book: Rebecca Anastos-Wallen, Brinda Budhraja, and Monique Saint-Louis. The team was extraordinary—providing insight, helping us to find and see the truth, and working beyond the call of duty.

At various times, other BCG consultants provided help. In particular, we would like to thank Mark Abraham, Ivan Bascle, Lucy Brady, Jill Corcoran, Francois Dalens, Peter Daw, Peter Dawe, Christine Dum, Mary Egan, Karin Fleschutz, Christina Fradelas, Thomas Gaissmaier, John Garabedian, Jeff Gell, Julie Gish, Marin Gjaja, Karen Gordon, Steve Gunby, Per Halius, Hubert Hsu, Rich Huchinson, Ellen Hunter, Sunil Kapagoda, Jill Kidd, Kermit King, Rich Lesser, Tom Lewis, Zhenya Lindgardt, Debbie Lovich, Tom Lutz, Joe Manget, Bjorn Matre, David Michael, Yves Morieux, Andrej Mueller, Ron Nicol, David Olsen, David Pecaut, Nneka Rimmer, Catherine Roche, Ann Schneider, Marty Silverstein, George Stalk, Roselinde Torres, Raj Varadarajan, John Wong, Karin Zimmermann, and many others.

Gaby Barrios and Emmanuel Huet were very helpful in the design and execution of the worldwide survey. We also thank Jeannine Everett for her help in survey design and execution. We had a great team helping in Japan, including Ryoko Fujii, Sawako Kazume, Ayako Kitano, Ai Nakayama, Kumiko Saikubo, Daisuke Shoka, Miki Tsusaka, and Koji Yamagata. In financial services we had advice from David Bronstein, Chris Fatherley, Arnd Gilde-meister, Alenka Grealish, Matt Stover, Steve Thogmartin, Andrea Walbaum, and Anna Zakrzewski.

We had invaluable feedback from our BCG partner Steering Commit-tee. Serving on this committee were: James Abraham (India), Hans-Paul Buerkner (Germany), Charmian Caines (United Kingdom), Patrick Ducasse (France), Cliff Grevler (Canada), Rune Jacobsen (Scandinavia), Monish Ku-mar (Financial Services), Carol Liao (China), Sharon Marcil (United States), Nicola Pianon (Italy), and Miki Tsusaka (Japan). Antonella Mei-Pochtler and Martina Rissman provided insights into the German market as well. Hans-Paul, the CEO of BCG, was incredibly supportive, providing feed-back and substantial investment and ensuring engagement by our partners around the world. Thanks also to BCG chairman and former CEOs John Clarkeson and Carl Stern.

We were lucky enough to interest Bill Matassoni in the book. His ad-vice and counsel helped us to see the full potential of this research on the power of recognizing women and market application. John Butman brought to the project an extraordinarily gifted development, research, writing, and editing team from The Butman Company, Inc., including Janine Lib-erty, Anna Weiss, Patricia Lyons, and Clara Silverstein.

We are very grateful to Hollis Heimbouch at HarperCollins for her engaged support on this project from its inception. Hollis brought energy and attention to this project. Her advice carried impact and value. Thanks, too, to Sarah Rainone, also at HarperCollins, for her astute and clear edito-rial suggestions. Thank you also to our agent, Todd Shuster, of Zachary ShusterHarmsworth, for his support and encouragement.

Particular thanks to Eric Gregoire for help in bringing our book to life in the market.

Special thanks also go to Kristin Claire, Michael's long-term executive assistant; Marge Branecki; and Amanda Vrany.

We also need to thank many others in BCG production for their help, including: Patricia Biesen, Cheryl Ciriello, Meredith Cologna, Rob Conrad, Darilyn Dinsmoor, Krista Donnelly, Tom Fallon, Dawn Francesconi, Eliza-beth Lamoglia, William Lee, Shon Little, Jill Quinlan, Chris Weiss, and Julie Zamolewicz. We need to thank David Cahill, Brian Falcione, and Charles Momneny for their help with the survey. We owe thanks to Marie

Martinez and Caitlan Werner. We also want to thank the BCG Knowledge Group, including Rudy Barajas, Robin Blumenthal, Cheryl Gaus, Alexandra Hafner, Minami Hoshino, Heidi Huang, Andrea Hurtado, Anne-Marie Moreau, Maria Pruess, Dot Smith, Dmitry Vukolov, and Karin Zimmermann. Thanks also to Bob Contino, Josh Copp, and Mark Rosenthal.

We had significant help in translations, including: Rashi Agarwal, Svetlana Basovsky, Johannes Becker, Marco Bernardi, Leo Chang, Haibin Chen, Jade Cheng, Mara De Monte, Andrew Dunn, Gustavo Furuta, Silvia Gussoni, Victor Mamou, Belen Monedero, Prasad Nair, Jorge Ontiveros, Violetta Ostafin, Isabelle Pinson, Hari Ramakrishnan, Armando Ribeiro, Beverly Sausner, Maxim Tarasevich, June Usuba, Koji Yamagata, and Selin Zalma.

We had help with distribution of our survey from our great BCG network with particular thanks to Ana Azuela, Sachpreet Chandhoke, Angela Guido, Catriona Larritt, and Florencia Solazzi. Our helpers in translating the thousands of inputs from women around the world included Branca Ballot, Marco Bernardi, Matt Birris, Guillaume Brian, Maria Castano, Johann Dong, Pauline Fan, Ramin Farhangi, Satoshi Fukui, Brian Landry-Wilson, Jara Lasuen, Vlada Lotkina, Christoph Méier, Adrian Monsalve, Carlos Palacios, Pedro Romón, Mills Schenck, Khaled Tawfik, Gerardo Trueba, and Carolin Vaas.

Special thanks to Christy Carlson, Harlan Chemers, Leon Dreimann, Scotty Edwards, Stephanie English, Jim Jewell, Jeff Mory, and Carol Whittemore for their contributions, encouragement, and advice.

Thank you to the thousands of women around the world who participated in our survey, and special thanks to the hundreds who agreed to meet and talk with us about their lives and needs.

Special acknowledgment goes to a variety of organizations for help in survey distribution, including Students in Free Enterprise (Lane Garnett and Bruce Nasby), iRelaunch (Carol Cohen and Vivian Rabin), and International Inner Wheel (Kamala Ramakrishnan). We were also helped at the following institutions: Club Tuck Women in Business, Harvard Women's Student Association, INSEAD Women in Business (Marguerite Fitzgerald), Kellogg Women in Business Association, Rotman School at the University of Toronto (Leigh Gauthier), Sloan Women in Management, Stanford Women in Business (Melike Abacioglu), University of Chicago Women in Business, and Wharton Women in Business.

Thanks to Kate's sister Liza for helping to frame the needs of working mothers. Thanks to Kate's mother and father for ideas and suggestions—and a lifetime of support.

Special thanks to Michael's wife, Gerry, for reviewing multiple drafts of the manuscript and helping him to see how challenging a question "What more do women want?" really is. Thanks to Michael's daughter Heather for helping us to see the needs of 20-somethings as a distinct and focused segment. And a big last thank-you to Michael's teenage son Charlie for continually providing his suggestions on core needs and market opportunities.

Notes

Chapter 1. The World's Most Demanding Consumers

1. Devon Pendleton, "The World's Billionaire Women," *Forbes*, April 15, 2008.
2. Tamar Lewin, "At Colleges, Women Are Leaving Men in the Dust," *New York Times*, July 9, 2006.
3. Ibid.
4. "2008 SAT Total Report," College Board, 2008.
5. "Physician Characteristics and Distribution in the U.S.," American Medical Association, 2008 edition and prior editions; "Faculty Gender Equity Indicators," American Association of University Professors (AAUP), 2006; "A Current Glance at Women in the Law," ABA Commission on Women in the Profession, 2007.
6. "1997 and 2007 Catalyst Census of Women Corporate Officers and Top Earners," U.S. Census Bureau.
7. "Key Facts about Women-Owned Businesses," Center for Women's Business Research, 2009, http://www.nfwbo.org/content/index.php?pid=10.
8. Neil Macfarquhar, "U.N. Study Finds More Women in Politics," *New York Times*, September 19, 2008.
9. Samantha Booth, "Curves Helped Us Turn Our Lives Around," *Daily Record*, January 21, 2008.

Chapter 2. The Archetypes and Life Stages

1. Marion Hume, "Not Your Mother's China," *Time*, February 18, 2008.
2. Michelle Conlin, "Work-Life Balance: How to Get a Life and Do Your Job," *BusinessWeek*, August 14, 2008.
3. Lilian Goh, Polly Hui, and Helen Wu, "No Hurry to Wed, Say Career Women," *South China Morning Post*, February 24, 2007.
4. Marci Alboher, "Starting Businesses as an Encore for Women," *New York Times*, July 8, 2008.
5. "India's Manual Scavengers," *Economist*, July 10, 2008.

6. "Pet Cover 'Fastest Growing Sector,'" *Channel 4 News* (UK), September 17, 2008, http://www.channel4.com/news/articles/business_money/pet+cover+fastest+growing+sector/2456802.

7. Belinda Smith, "It's a Dog's Life at Work," *Telegraph* (UK), September 16, 2008.

8. Olivia Barker, "Doggone It, That Pooch Has a Nice Pad: Pampered Pets Get Their Own Rooms, Closets, Even TVs," *USA Today*, August 24, 2007.

Chapter 3. Brands That Understand

1. Christina Lye, "Offshore: Westin Builds Brand Loyalty," *Edge Malaysia*, April 10, 2006.

2. Laura M. Holson, "Smartphones Now Ringing for Women," *New York Times*, June 10, 2008.

3. Katherine Zoepf, "Dammam Journal: Saudi Women Find an Unlikely Role Model: Oprah," *New York Times*, September 19, 2008.

4. Beth Belton, "Lafley on P&G's Gadget 'Evolution,'" *BusinessWeek*, January 28, 2005.

5. Kai Ryssdal, "Interview Transcript: Conversations from the Corner Office: Procter & Gamble CEO A. G. Lafley," *Marketplace*, May 19, 2008.

6. Belton, "Lafley on P&G's Gadget 'Evolution.'"

7. P&G annual report, 2008.

8. Leslie Wexner, interviewed by Michael Silverstein.

9. Linda [no last name given], "Gerber: Trusted Name in Baby Food and Baby Care, or Masters of Emotional Manipulation?" *Purple Is a Fruit (clubmom.com)*, April 18, 2007, http://purplefruit.clubmom.com/purple_is_a_fruit/2007/04/gerber_trusted_.html.

10. Sonia Reyes, "Positioning: No Time for Pregnant Pause as Gerber Delivers Drama," *Brandweek*, April 16, 2007.

11. "Nestlé Analyst Day Presentation," April 12, 2007.

12. Aili McConnon, "Gerber Is Following Kids to Preschool," *BusinessWeek*, August 18, 2008.

13. T. A. Badger, "One in Five 2-Year-Olds in U.S. Eats Fries Daily: Early Eating Habits Set Stage for Obesity," *Gazette* (Montreal, Quebec), October 26, 2003.

14. M. McPhee, "Gerber Graduates Microwavable Meals," *Epinions*, August 24, 2004, http://www.epinions.com/review/Gerber_Graduates_Microwavable_Meals/content_153053073028, and K. Minder, "Gerber Finger Foods Fruit Puffs—Dissolving Treats Please Moms," *Epinions*, July 20, 2008, http://www.epinions.com/review/Gerber_Finger_Foods_Fruit_Puffs/content_437905100420.

Chapter 4. Food: Answering the Daily Question "What's for Dinner?"

1. John Arlridge, "Peace, Love, and Profit—Meet the World's Richest Organic Grocer," *Guardian*, January 29, 2006, http://www.guardian.co.uk/lifeandstyle/2006/jan/29/foodanddrink.organics.

2. Tesco Web site, http://www.tesco.com/clubcard/clubcard.

3. Tesco Web site, http://www.tescocorporate.com/plc/about_us/strategy/international.
4. Carol Hymowitz, "Raising Women to Be Leaders," *ShortSchrift.blogspot*, March 21, 2007, http://shortschrift.blogspot.com/2007/03/sullivan-sisters.html.
5. Michelle Dammon Loyalka, "Amy's Kitchen: Entrée to Oregon," *BusinessWeek*, July 15, 2005, http://www.businessweek.com/print/smallbiz/content/jul2005/sb20050715_321045.htm.
6. "We Love: Rachel Berliner, Amy's Kitchen Cofounder," EveryWoman'sVoice.com, March 11, 2008, http://www.everywomansvoice.com/?q=node/383.

Chapter 5. Fitness: Still Looking for a Holistic Solution

1. Christine Cupaiuolo, "Study: Weight Not Necessarily an Indicator of Health," *Our Bodies Ourselves*, August 12, 2008, http://www.ourbodiesourblog.org/blog/2008/08/study-weight-not-necessarily-an-indicator-of-health.
2. Bally Total Fitness Franchise Web site, http://www.ballyfitness.com/franchising.aspx.
3. "Nationwide Health Concerns May Be Pumping U.S. Fitness Behavior," sportinggoodsbusiness.com, April 21, 2004.
4. Elaine McArdle, "Sweating with the Enemy," *Boston Globe Magazine*, June 19, 2005.
5. Samantha Booth, "Curves Helped Us Turn Our Lives Around," *Daily Record*, January 21, 2008.
6. Ibid.
7. Sally McLean, "I'm in Shape for My Little Black Dress," *Daily Record*, December 19, 2006.
8. Dana Borcea, "Ahead of the Curves," *National Post* (Canada), November 15, 2003.
9. "Curves Shapes Up for More Gyms," *Nikkei Weekly* (Japan), January 7, 2008.
10. "Curves and Rodale Launch CurvesComplete.com," *Drug Week*, November 30, 2007.
11. "Nintendo Wants Your Mom to Get Wii-Fit," *Financial Post*, May 16, 2008, http://www.canada.com/story_print.html?id=eef7323b-376b-41af-9b1d-cc05f0dcab91&sponsor=.
12. "Oprah Blames Weight Gain on Abusing Food," MSNBC Web site, January 5, 2009, http://www.msnbc.msn.com/id/28509617.

Chapter 6. Beauty: The Next Product Needs to Do It!

1. "In Search of Scientific Excellence: L'Oréal U.S.A. Announces Call for Applications for 2007 Fellowships for Women in Science Program," *CSR Wire*, August 14, 2006, http://www.csrwire.com/News/6116.html.
2. "Another Glowing Endorsement for Olay Regenerist Serum," *PRNewswire*, October 24, 2008, http://www.prnewswire.co.uk/cgi/news/release?id=210841.
3. Nordstrom Web site, http://shop.nordstrom.com/S/2997108?cm_cat=datafeed&cm_pla=skin%2Fbody_treatment:women:moisturizer&cm_ite=la_prairie_cellular_cream_platinum_rare:238752&cm_ven=Froogle&mr:trackingCode=253F9185-2D71-DD11-98CA-001422107090&mr:referralID=NA.
4. Takuya Hanada, Shiseido public relations department; Shiseido annual report, 2008.

5. Abby Ellin, "It's Botox for You, Dear Bridesmaids," *New York Times*, July 24, 2008.

6. Anne Bratskeir, "Oh, to Be Young Again: In a Society that Worships Youth, People Are Increasingly Willing to Spend Big Bucks to Maintain Theirs," *Newsday*, March 25, 2002.

7. Rhonda L. Rundle, "Keeping Up Appearances in a Downturn," *Wall Street Journal*, December 23, 2008, http://online.wsj.com/article/SB122999145997128503.html.

8. Ransdell Pierson, "Botox Maker Allergan Cuts Forecasts amid Downturn," ptproductsonline.com, October 29, 2008, http://www.ptproductsonline.com/reuters_article.asp?id=20081029inds025.html&frmTagFilePath=%252Fnews.asp.

9. Hollie Shaw, "Dove's Real Women Fly on Stage," *National Post* (Canada), May 8, 2008.

10. Jack Neff, " 'A Step Forward': In Dove Ads, Normal Is the New Beautiful," *Advertising Age*, September 27, 2004.

11. Jane Simms, "Real or Insincere?" *Marketing*, October 16, 2007, http://www.marketingmagazine.co.uk/news/745024/Real-insincere.

12. Alyssa Giacobbe, "Dispatch: Coming to a Sephora Near You," *Boston*, January 18, 2009.

Chapter 7. Apparel: Always Hunting, Never Satisfied

1. Valerie Hill, "I Shop, Therefore I Am," *Daily Post* (Liverpool), April 27, 2007.

2. "Halle Berry and Roberto Cavalli Celebrate His H&M Line!" *People Online*, October 27, 2007, http://stylenews.peoplestylewatch.com/2007/10/27/halle-berry-roberto-cavalli-celebrate-his-hm-line.

Chapter 8. Categories of Greatest Dissatisfaction: Financial Services and Healthcare

1. "Health Insurance Coverage of Women Ages 18 to 64, by State, 2006–2007," *Kaiser Family Foundation*, December 2008, http://www.kff.org/womenshealth/upload/1613_08.pdf.

2. Robert Pear, "Women Buying Health Policies Pay a Penalty," *New York Times*, October 30, 2008, http://www.nytimes.com/2008/10/30/us/30insure.html?pagewanted=print.

Chapter 9. The Low-Growth Economies: Europe and Japan

1. IKEA Web site, http://www.ikea-group.ikea.com/404.php.

2. Russell Shorto, "No Babies?" *New York Times*, June 29, 2008.

3. Miele Web site, http://www.miele.de/ae/domestic/company/2335_4859.htm.

4. Barilla annual report, 2008.

5. Inditex annual report, 2007.

6. Danielle Demetriou, "Where Children Take a Back Seat to Dogged Pursuits," *Globe and Mail* (Canada), July 24, 2008.

7. Veronica Chambers, *Kickboxing Geishas: How Modern Japanese Women Are Changing Their Nation*, New York: Free Press, 2007.

8. Demetriou, "Where Children Take a Back Seat to Dogged Pursuits."

9. Uniqlo Web site, http://www.uniqlo.com/us.

10. "Jobs for the Girls," *Economist*, May 1, 2008, http://www.economist.com/business/Printer Friendly.cfm?story_id=11294323.

11. Nicholas D. Kristof, "When Women Rule," *New York Times*, February 10, 2008.

12. Neil Macfarquhar, "U.N. Study Finds More Women in Politics," *New York Times*, September 19, 2008.

13. Daisy Sindelar, "World: Women in Government Still Rarity in Many Countries," *Radio Free Europe Radio Liberty*, March 8, 2007, http://www.rferl.org/articleprintview/1075134.html.

14. Roberto Ortiz de Zárate, "Women Rulers Currently in Office," Women World Leaders Web site, October 4, 2008, http://www.terra.es/personal2/monolith/00women5.htm.

15. Shorto, "No Babies?"

Chapter 10. The Optimistic Economies: BRIC, Mexico, and the Middle East

1. "Women and Poverty," *Women's Funding Network*, 2008, http://www.wfnet.org/the-network/groups/women-and-poverty.

2. Daisy Sindelar, "World: Women in Government Still Rarity in Many Countries," *Radio Free Europe Radio Liberty*, March 8, 2007, http://www.rferl.org/articleprintview/1075134.html.

3. Nicholas D. Kristof, "When Women Rule," *New York Times*, February 10, 2008.

4. Neil Macfarquhar, "U.N. Study Finds More Women in Politics," *New York Times*, September 19, 2008.

5. Elaine Iritani, "Fostering Good Will with Jobs," *Los Angeles Times*, July 31, 2005.

6. Mei Fong, "Li Ning on the Beijing Olympics," *Wall Street Journal*, August 25, 2008.

7. Larry McWilliams, interviewed by Michael Silverstein.

8. Natura annual report, 2008.

9. Robert Murphy, "H&M to Open Women-Only Store," *Women's Wear Daily*, May 23, 2008, http://www.wwd.com/beauty-industry-news/h-m-to-open-women-only-store-1556189/print/?navSection=people-companies&navId.

Chapter 11. Women Want More for the World

1. Nicole Johnson, "Women's Clout in Donating to Charities Grows," *St. Petersburg Times* (Florida), January 2, 2007.

2. Michelle Guido, "Fund for Women Has Awarded Millions to Groups in 165 Countries," *San Jose Mercury News*, November 16, 2003, http://www.accessmylibrary.com/coms2/summary_0286-9032048_ITM.

3. "Tribunal Hears How Bosnia's Serbs Used Rape as Weapon," *St. Petersburg Times* (Florida), July 3, 1996.

4. Tom Post, Alexandra Stiglmayer, Charles Lane, Joel Brand, Margaret Garrard, and Robin Sparkman, "A Pattern of Rape," *Newsweek*, January 4, 1993.

5. Kristina Shevory, "When Charity Begins in a Circle of Friends," *New York Times*, September 19, 2005.

6. Ron Barnett, "Giving Circles Mix Fun and Fundraising," *USA Today*, February 27, 2008.

Conclusion. Women Ascendant: A Future of Parity, Power, and Influence

1. Catherine Rampell, "As Layoffs Surge, Women May Pass Men in Job Force," *New York Times*, February 5, 2009.

2. Jessi Hempel, "In the Land of Women," *Fortune*, January 22, 2008.

3. Ilene R. Prusher, "The Birth of Hope," *Christian Science Monitor*, March 17, 2004.

4. DPA, "More Helpful Husband Tops Working Mothers' Wish List," *Earth Times*, August 5, 2008, http://www.earthtimes.org/articles/show/223466,more-helpful-husband-tops-working-mothers-wish-list.html.

5. Boris Groysberg, "How Star Women Build Portable Skills," *Harvard Business Review*, February 2008, http://www.harvardbusiness.org/hbsp/hbr/articles/article.jsp?articleID=R0802D&ml_action=get-article&print=true&ml_issueid=BR0802.

6. 10,000 Women Web site, http://www.10000women.org/press.html.

7. Caroline Simard, Andrea Davies Henderson, Shannon K. Gilmartin, Londa Schiebinger, and Telle Whitney, "Climbing the Technical Ladder: Obstacles and Solutions for Mid-Level Women in Technology," Anita Borg Institute for Women and Technology, 2008, http://anitaborg.org/files/Climbing_the_Technical_Ladder_Exec_Summary.pdf.

8. Elizabeth Olson, "Women Business Owners Seek Better Access to Federal Contracts," *New York Times*, October 2, 2008.

Index

Page numbers in *italics* refer to charts and tables.